LONGMAN CRITICAL READERS

General Editor:
STAN SMITH, Professor of English, University of Dundee

ANDREW MARVELL

Edited and Introduced by

THOMAS HEALY

LONGMAN

London and New York

Addison Wesley Longman Limited
Edinburgh Gate
Harlow
Essex CM20 2JE
United Kingdom
and Associated Companies throughout the world

Published in the United States of America
by Addison Wesley Longman Inc., New York

First published 1998

ISBN 0-582-21910-8 Cased
      0-582-21907-8 Paper

British Library Cataloguing-in-Publication Data

A catalogue record for this book is available from the British Library

Library of Congress Cataloging-in-Publication Data

Andrew Marvell / edited and introduced by Thomas Healy.
      p.   cm. — (Longman critical readers)
      Includes bibliographical references and index.
      ISBN 0-582-21910-8 (hardcover). — ISBN 0-582-21907-8 (pbk.)
      1. Marvell, Andrew, 1621-1678—Criticism and interpretation.
   I. Healy, Thomas, 1954-   . II. Series.
   PE3546.A866   1998
   821'.4—dc21   98-12921
                                                        CIP

Set by 35 in 9/11.5pt Palatino
Produced by Addison Wesley Longman Singapore (Pte) Ltd.,
Printed in Singapore

Contents

General Editors' Preface

The outlines of contemporary critical theory are now often taught as a standard feature of a degree in literary studies. The development of particular theories has seen a thorough transformation of literary criticism. For example, Marxist and Foucauldian theories have revolutionized Shakespeare studies, and 'deconstruction' has led to a complete reassessment of Romantic poetry. Feminist criticism has left scarcely any period of literature unaffected by its searching critiques. Teachers of literary studies can no longer fall back on a standardized, received, methodology.

Lecturers and teachers are now urgently looking for guidance in a rapidly changing critical environment. They need help in understanding the latest revisions in literary theory, and especially in grasping the practical effects of the new theories in the form of theoretically sensitized new readings. A number of volumes in the series anthologize important essays on particular theories. However, in order to grasp the full implications and possible uses of particular theories it is essential to see them put to work. This series provides substantial volumes of new readings, presented in an accessible form and with a significant amount of editorial guidance.

Each volume includes a substantial introduction which explores the theoretical issues and conflicts embodied in the essays selected and locates the areas of disagreement between positions. The pluralism of theories has to be put on the agenda of literary studies. We can no longer pretend that we all tacitly accept the same practices in literary studies. Neither is a *laissez-faire* attitude any longer tenable. Literature departments need to go beyond the mere toleration of theoretical differences: it is not enough merely to agree to differ; they need actually to 'stage' the differences openly. The volumes in this series all attempt to dramatize the differences, not necessarily with a view to resolving them but in order to foreground the choices presented by different theories or to argue for a particular route through the impasses the differences present.

The theory 'revolution' has had real effects. It has loosened the grip of traditional empiricist and romantic assumptions about language and literature. It is not always clear what is being proposed as the new agenda for literary studies, and indeed the very notion of 'literature' is questioned by the post-structuralist strain in theory. However, the uncertainties and obscurities of contemporary theories appear much less worrying when we see what the best critics have been able to do with them in practice. This series aims to disseminate the best of recent criticism and to show that it is possible to re-read the canonical texts of literature in new and challenging ways.

RAMAN SELDEN AND STAN SMITH

The Publishers and fellow Series Editor regret to record that Raman Selden died after a short illness in May 1991 at the age of fifty-three. Ray Selden was a fine scholar and a lovely man. All those he has worked with will remember him with much affection and respect.

Acknowledgements

The publishers are grateful to the following for permission to reproduce copyright material:

Cambridge University Press and the authors, for extracts from THE POET'S TIME: Politics and Religion in the Work of Andrew Marvell by Warren L. Chernaik, 'Marvell's Horatian Ode and the politics of genre' by David Norbrook in LITERATURE AND THE ENGLISH CIVIL WAR (eds) Thomas Healy and Jonathan Sawday, and the article 'Andrew Marvell, Oliver Cromwell and the Horation Ode' by Blair Worden in HISTORICAL JOURNAL 1984; Cornell University Press for extracts from 'The Garden State: Marvell's Poetics of Enclosure' by Jonathan Crewe in ENCLOSURE ACTS: SEXUALITY, PROPERTY, AND CULTURE IN EARLY MODERN ENGLAND ed. Richard Burt and John Michael Archer. Copyright © 1994 by Cornell University; the author, Professor Paul Hammond and the Editors of THE SEVENTEENTH CENTURY for the essay 'Marvell's Sexuality' © Paul Hammond 1996; International Thomson Publishing Services and the authors for extracts from THE TREMULOUS PRIVATE BODY by Francis Barker. pubd. Methuen & Co., 'Postmodernism and English Renaissance Texts' by Jonathan Goldberg in VOICE, TERMINAL, ECHO: Postmodernism and English Renaissance Texts pubd. Methuen & Co.; the author, Annabel Patterson for an extract from MARVELL AND THE CIVIC CROWN pubd. Princeton University Press. Copyright © 1978; Scolar Press and the author for 'Virgin and Whores: The Politics of Sexual Misconduct in the 1660's' by Steven Zwicker in THE POLITICAL IDENTITY OF ANDREW MARVELL edited by Conal Condren and A.D. Cousins, pubd. Scolar Press 1990; The University of Chicago Press and the author for an extract from THE POLITICS OF MIRTH: Jonson, Herrick, Milton and Marvell by Leah S. Marcus (Chicago & London, Chicago University Press, 1986).

I would like to thank Alan Stewart and Caterina Albano for bibliographical help, Birkbeck College for a grant to cover research assistance, and Stan Smith for encouraging this project. Margaret Healy has, as usual, been a support throughout.

In the case of some of the extracts where the original made reference to material outwith the present selection, I have added to or amended the text slightly in order to allow the reader to follow references more easily. Otherwise, I have not altered the selections. In all the essays, however, I have been forced to reduce the documentation in notes to save space. Readers keen to gather detailed references are advised to turn to the original publications for the full scholarly apparatus.

All references to Marvell's poetry are to *The Poems and Letters of Andrew Marvell*, third edition, ed. H.M. Margoliouth, revised Pierre Legouis with the collaboration of E.E. Duncan-Jones, 2 vols (Oxford: Clarendon Press, 1971). Abbreviated as *Poems and Letters*.

References to *The Rehearsal Transpros'd* are to *The Rehearsal Transpros'd and the Rehearsal Transpros'd, The Second Part*, ed. D.I.B. Smith (Oxford: Clarendon Press, 1971). Abbreviated as *Rehearsal Transpros'd*.

References to Milton's prose are to John Milton, *Complete Prose Works*, ed. D.M. Wolfe, *et al.*, 8 vols (New Haven and London: Yale University Press, 1953–82). Abbreviated as *CPW*.

Introduction

Writing in history

As with many early modern literary writers, critical perspectives of Andrew Marvell over the last twenty years have been transformed by re-establishing history as the crucial factor in understanding his work. The dominant strain of Marvell criticism has attempted to locate his views and sentiments within the closely delineated political and social environments of Civil War, Republican, Protectorate and Restoration England. It is notable that it is a historian, Blair Worden, who can be said to sum up the impetus behind a good deal of recent critical activity with his observation that 'Marvell's public poems are occasional poems, responsible to their occasions'.[1] In contrast with most earlier twentieth-century criticism where claims of topical specificity were frequently the basis of hostile comment about the stature of Marvell's poetry, notably his Restoration satires, Worden's remarks have been energetically espoused by recent critics who have demonstrated their responsibility to the poetry's occasions by attempting to negotiate them thoroughly.

Establishing the place of Marvell's writing in history has meant more than merely detailed accounts of the texts in their contexts. His imaginative writing has not been crudely witnessed as only a reflection on material circumstances; that, for example, by understanding the events surrounding Cromwell's return from Ireland to England in 1650, the 'meaning' of *An Horatian Ode* becomes clear. Equally, though, Marvell's work has not attracted New Historicist preoccupations with the circulation between past and present in the textuality of history; nor has it been the focus of arguments about containment and power derived from Michel Foucault, which have been so influential in considering Renaissance drama.[2] His writing, however, has been the focus for a good deal of theoretical thought about how texts operate in the cultural moments which produce them. As historiography increasingly recognises, there is a narrative to history, and the rhetorical, generic and

1

other narratological strategies employed in the shaping of fictions may also be seen operating in the shaping of historical experience.[3] The categories and techniques used in examining imaginative writing are perceived as of increasing importance for exploring all types of texts: journals, State records, even parish registers and account books. Marvell's attempts to shape history in poetry, to express aspects of the extraordinary social and political changes his England experienced in the mid-seventeenth century, and to register, too, the difficulties in knowing history, have prompted critical responses which recognise the need for carefully prepared conceptual models through which to explore a poetry at once both private and public, elusive and articulate, about the conditions of its time.

Marvell's poetry further challenges conventionally defined relations between literature and history because it is difficult to date a good deal of it with any precision. Virtually all Marvell's pre-Restoration verse was not published until after his death. Although it is possible to place many poems within topical debates and assume dates of composition, we have no way of knowing whether the versions we read contain later alterations; or, perhaps more crucially, whether these poems emerge from immediate responses to events or are the consequence of Marvell's looking back at a recent past. A poet who so carefully cultivates different poetic masks (his poems' narrators include, among others, young women, pastoral field-workers, and high-minded patriots) might also readily adopt historical personae who share neither the voice nor the moment of the poet. Throughout his poetry, Marvell adopts positions which insist that we can perceive history from many different outlooks – e.g. the touching naïveté of the nymph who cannot understand why the troopers have shot her fawn, the Horatian poet enjoining Cromwell to keep his sword erect – and refuses to allow us the easy security of characterising his position through a few reductive formulae which can be applied to each poem.

In her most recent study of Marvell, Annabel Patterson claims, 'the two most important facts about Andrew Marvell, biographically speaking, are that . . . he never married and that he spent almost two decades as a Member of Parliament for Hull'.[4] Actually, the most important aspect of what we know of Marvell's life seems to be the pains he undertook to keep his personal voice elusive. His extant correspondence, whether reports on Parliament to his Hull constituency or private letters, lack personal detail and refuse to state Marvell's own positions unequivocally: he never even reveals to his constituents how he voted in the Commons. His differing voices in the poems make it awkward to locate consistency in their views. What is interesting, though, is how Marvell's protean guises in poetry, his careful veiling of his stances in his correspondence, his usually ensuring that his prose

tracts were initially published anonymously, have not led recent critics
to conclusions about a character desiring disentanglement from public
life – the view widely adopted by the earlier twentieth century. The
Marvell who emerges from the criticism of the last two decades is of a
socially engaged figure working out a sophisticated and influential
political philosophy.

Castigating Tom May as a 'servil' wit and Mercenary Pen', Marvell
celebrates the true poet:

> When the Sword glitters ore the Judges head,
> And fear has Coward Churchmen silenced
> Then is the Poets time, 'tis then he drawes
> And single fights forsaken Vertues cause.

> ('Tom May's Death', ll. 62–65)

If we look to Marvell's own verse, or indeed his prose, as an instance of
the 'Poets time', any assumptions about fighting virtue's causes involving
uncompromising open confrontation with its opponents must be rapidly
given up. In a political environment where hostility and persecution
abound, and where writing is closely scrutinised by opponents, the singer
'of ancient Rights and better Times', who 'Seeks wretched good, arraigns
successful Crimes' needs to proceed obliquely. Real and assumed stances,
public and private positions, become issues criticism approaches with
an awareness that romanticised notions about a writer's integrity and
consistency of vision need to be carefully negotiated in the light of actual
social circumstances; and that contemporaries were likely attuned to
nuances in prose or poetry which largely escape current readers.

This recognition of the importance of both the hidden private life
and the carefully organised public life has helped shape the best Marvell
criticism over recent years. For example, Paul Hammond's interest in
public suggestive attacks upon Marvell's sexuality – in the concluding
essay of this volume – leads him to a reconsideration of sexuality in the
private lyrics, one which seeks to explore how Marvell's much prized
poetic ambiguity might be more carefully considered 'in the light of these
contemporary perceptions of Marvell's sexual ambiguity'. Hammond's
account is a forceful instance of how criticism has travelled a great
distance from T.S. Eliot's 1921 essay on Marvell – which rapidly
solidified as the foundation of most mid-century views. Eliot maintained:
'the really valuable part [of Marvell's verse] is probably a literary than
a personal quality . . . a quality of a civilization, or a traditional habit of
life.'[5] He goes on to proclaim that Marvell's 'best verse is the product
of European, that is to say Latin, culture'. For Eliot, Marvell is worth
reading when he can be depersonalised and depoliticised. During the
past twenty years, Marvell is undoubtedly felt to be at his best when

he is discovered negotiating a politics which arises from personal engagement.

Annihilating all that's made

Opponents of deconstructive theoretical positions have frequently attacked what they perceive as deconstruction's overtly formalist concerns. Deconstructive practices, they have argued, work to exclude history from texts by concentrating exclusively on the linguistic play, and the attendant deferral of meaning, which takes place within writing. Initially, it appears that an essay (included here) such as Jonathan Goldberg's 'Marvell's Nymph and the Echo of Voice', goes against the grain of much recent Marvell criticism when Goldberg begins his consideration of 'The Nymph complaining for the death of her Faun' asserting that: 'The poem defies referentiality. It is only, and entirely, self-referential.' This seems very close to Cleanth Brooks's New Critic's assertion in 1947, based on another Marvell poem, *An Horatian Ode*, that 'A poem has a life of its own . . . it provides in itself the only criterion by which what it says can be judged.'[6]

Jacques Derrida, deconstruction's foremost proponent, has always maintained, however, that deconstructive theory is not opposed to history. Rather its strategies for displaying aspects hidden, inconclusive or spectral within texts – the presences a text may apparently wish to conceal or refute – are precisely aimed at uncovering histories, but ones against the grain of dominant accounts. The return of the repressed in deconstruction allows apparently absent voices to be heard and this brings attention to histories which are as much about silences and absences as they are about articulate evidence. Goldberg, in claiming that Marvell's poem is 'only, and entirely, self-referential, "about" itself', also claims it is about 'what it represents in the world'. A recognition that an apparently narcissistic 'creative annihilation', which is the poem, is also linked to loss within an external world – whether it be private or public loss – helps to indicate how even an exposition of an apparently self-absorbed lyric does not isolate the piece from the world around it, but, as Marvell's poetry is always doing, helps to question the nature of the world, how it is known, imagined, written.

What is noticeable, therefore, about the vast majority of recent Marvell criticism is that, despite its various preoccupations with texts and history, studies tend to complement one another rather than adopt opposing perspectives. Although, for example, the essays of Blair Worden or Steven Zwicker – focused on Marvell and detailed political occurrences – critically seem to be pursuing very different goals than elucidating a poetic 'crisis of representation' which Jonathan Crewe's essay uses deconstructive strategies to present, nevertheless, as Crewe shows, Marvell's crisis of representation is also intimately caught up with his sense of the importance of 'politics' in affecting the whole fabric of the culture.

In contrast, you have only to scan the range of articles and books devoted to Shakespeare or Milton to realise the existence of a far wider diversity of critical perspectives, many wholly opposed to one another. Although little literary criticism these days tends to be rigorously wedded to a single theoretical model, it is noticeable how influential psychoanalytic theory has been with certain writers about Milton, whereas Marvell critics who deal with areas in which such theory might be expected to figure are scrupulous in maintaining a specific historical dimension which largely eschews psychoanalytic models – for instance Francis Barker's consideration of the body in 'To his Coy Mistress' or Paul Hammond on Marvell's sexuality. Curiously, too, despite Marvell's poetic representations of women, and especially younger girls, his work has generated little explicitly feminist criticism. Further, Goldberg's mid-1980s deconstructive reading of 'The Nymph complaining' is one of a very few recent attempts to focus predominantly linguistic oriented theoretical work on Marvell's texts.

As even a brief glance through the essays of this volume demonstrates, the central concern with history within recent Marvell criticism does not elicit work which is all of a piece. But until recently the history that surrounded Marvell was largely ignored by literary critics. Although, famously, in the early 1950s Cleanth Brooks and Douglas Bush clashed over whether historical understanding should play a part in interpreting *An Horatian Ode*, when the history of Marvell's world was evoked it was usually assumed to be something which could be acquired from a textbook-style survey of the mid-seventeenth century rather than a much contested area of debate among historians.[7] And in general, when history, and particularly the politics generated by that history, was acknowledged to be a crucial part of Marvell's poetry, critics did not respond favourably to it. Stated or unstated assumptions about good poetry and politics not properly mixing were characteristic of much twentieth-century criticism, so to acknowledge the centrality of politics for Marvell was to question the superiority of his verse. Partly as a result of this, generations of students grew up exposed to a handful of Marvell's shorter lyrics and thought of him as a 'Metaphysical', sharing more in common with Donne than with Milton, Dryden, or Rochester – let alone as a political theorist whose work can be argued to anticipate Locke. Few read the Restoration satires; the lengthy Civil War occasional poems, with the exception of the *Horatian Ode*, were also either ignored, or, in the case of *Upon Appleton House*, largely examined in the light of the various Renaissance intellectual ideas upon which the imagery was founded.

The Marxist impetus

The late 1970s witnessed a substantial shift in attitudes towards Marvell's work and this profound critical change is still being carried through. One of the principal features of this transformation has been the rediscovery of Marvell, with Milton, as promoters of a godly English Republic during the Civil War period of 1640–60. Christopher Hill was a decisive influence in helping to promote this re-thinking of both figures. The leading British Marxist historian of the seventeenth century since the early 1940s, Hill had long argued for witnessing the English Civil War as a social revolution, a class and economic struggle which challenged the establishment and, therefore, to be hailed as a positive event. As long ago as 1946, Hill had declared that 'if we study Marvell with a knowledge of the political background of his life we can discover in the great lyrics new complexities'.[8] Hill's outlook, however, was not particularly significant for literary critics until the 1960s and 1970s when Marxist-derived criticism, notably that of Raymond Williams, became widely influential. The publication in the 1970s of Hill's *The World Turned Upside Down, Milton and the English Revolution* and an edition of the selected writing of Gerrard Winstanley, however, had a decisive impact on literary scholars beginning to rethink seventeenth-century writing.[9] Hill's Milton book, for example, is a sustained attempt to show Milton as a hero of this era of transformation, a thinker influenced by radical social visionaries and not the poet of an elite rarefied literary culture. Hill also promoted the importance of Milton's prose work as central to an appreciation of his poetry. Like Milton, Marvell had worked as Latin Secretary to the Council of State during Cromwell's Protectorate. He had subsequently written one of the first pieces in praise of Milton's *Paradise Lost* and had defended Milton after the Restoration. The affinities between the two as the most eloquent defenders of 'the good old cause' which had prompted Parliament's rejection of the Stuart monarchy during the 1640s and 50s was given a new distinction under the influence of Hill's perspective that the class and ideological divisions which continued to affect Britain could be traced back to this period. For a generation of scholars with pronounced sympathies for a cultural materialist analysis of literature, and a favourable disposition towards literary writing which sought to challenge social orthodoxies, Milton and Marvell as poets of the English Revolution rather than the Great Rebellion offered a powerful incentive to re-assess their defence of Republic and Protectorate in a positive, dynamic light.

Poetry and prose

Interest in Marvell has never matched that accorded Milton, whose position as a defender of 'the good old cause' both during the Civil War and afterwards has been extensively examined. Indeed, Marvell's maturing politics during the Restoration is only now beginning to attract proper study. Where Milton's prose is readily and authoritatively available, there are no scholarly modern editions of much of Marvell's and it is only recently that students of Marvell have begun seriously to recognise the centrality of Marvell's prose tracts and pamphlets written during the Restoration, and only in the last five years that critical attention of the 'Restoration Marvell' has begun to vie with the 'Renaissance Marvell'.[10]

It is likely that this new attention focused on Marvell's evolving politics will continue. A major international conference on Marvell in July 1996 had almost as many papers devoted to considerations of the prose writing as were devoted to the poetry. Plans are underway to produce a major scholarly edition of *The Growth of Popery and Arbitrary Government* and other prose tracts. Marvell is re-emerging as a significant figure in the growth of Whig political thought. In the past, Marvell's continuance in Parliament after the Restoration has frequently been used to suggest he was of no settled political convictions, or that, all along, he had preferred the Royalist cause. But current work indicates Marvell is crucial for understanding how the republican ideals generated during the Civil War did not become merely the province of the dissenting margins – the intractable 'fit audience but few' – after 1660, but contributed centrally to the developing philosophy of Liberalism during the Enlightenment. More than Milton or Dryden, Marvell is emerging as the writer who challenges the artificial period division that so frequently separates English literature of the Restoration from that of the preceding decades of the seventeenth century. I have little doubt that the successor to this volume in, say, twenty years time will print a substantial number of essays devoted to Marvell's prose and that Marvell's importance as a political thinker will begin to rival his position as a poet.

That I have largely ignored the prose in the selection of work here is, in part, a recognition of a feature which besets much literary criticism today: that its concerns are increasingly focused on fellow specialists and not on undergraduate students. It must be confessed that, despite the substantial re-orienting of Marvell criticism towards the major occasional poems over the last twenty years, for the vast majority of undergraduate students, 'Marvell' largely remains *An Horatian Ode* and the same handful of short lyrics which formed the basis of his reputation 25, 50, almost 100 years ago. The reasons for this are various, but ultimately have a substantial amount to do with Marvell's relative place in most

English degree structures, particularly in comparison with Milton. Where it is quite common to find courses devoted to Milton, or where Milton figures very substantially, Marvell is often consigned to a few weeks' study in a wide survey of seventeenth-century or Renaissance literature. That a large number of students tend to devote a disproportionate amount of time on such courses to reading and writing about Marvell is a testament to his power to excite interest. But it is difficult for such students to negotiate Marvell's representation of history in the major occasional poems without falling back on rather reductive and formulaic presentations of that history and its varying political and social ideals. Particularly when we recall how much religion played a crucial part in both defining the period's politics and in the representation of social issues, the seventeenth century's apparently alien organisation of cultural categories can appear baffling and overwhelming for students attempting to read the major poems. And when the criticism they turn to only demonstrates that the positions are decidedly more involved than might be first imagined, their response is often to leave these complexities to the specialists! Of course, there are ways of negotiating some of these difficulties and innovative course structures which allow time to developing students' understanding of the issues the major poems involve. But it also true that for many students Marvell remains a writer of a number of 'metaphysical lyrics'; and they are largely content to accept Dr Johnson's smug formulation that what is distinctive about such poetry is its 'yoking together of heterogeneous images' rather than investing the considerable time necessary to grapple with why the seventeenth century did not see its structures of analogies heterogeneous in the ways later periods have tended to.

The true survey

My selection of critical essays has been predicated on the assumption that the readers of this volume are involved with Marvell's poetry. As indicated above, much recent criticism about Marvell produces complementary perspectives and my arrangement of essays is designed to take advantage of this. The ordering attempts to offer the reader who may have some familiarity with the poetry, but less with Marvell's culture, the opportunity to gain some sense of general positions as well as to read work focused on specific poems devoted to specific occasions.

Warren Chernaik's essay importantly points to the theological principles which underlie much of Marvell's secular concerns about 'government', whether of self or state. Chernaik's 1983 book, *The Poet's Time: Politics and Religion in the Work of Andrew Marvell*, from which the piece included here is extracted, was a groundbreaking study in its demonstration that the political and social issues which occupied

Marvell's Restoration prose help to clarify the apparent private utterance
of his lyrics. Chernaik shows Marvell's recurrent preoccupation with the
consequences of the Fall: the irony of human reason being able to explore
ideals of liberty and government only to be continuously confronted with
the human imperfection which is a consequence of sin. Chernaik's book
is one of a handful of studies which helped transform critical approaches
to Marvell by proposing a greater unity to his writing, confronting critical
views of the earlier part of the century which had tended to separate
lyric utterance from what was seen as Marvell's other less accomplished
writing.

Francis Barker's discussion of Marvell's most widely-known lyric, 'To
his Coy Mistress', considers the question of the body's possession by a
male author. For Barker the poem resists the sentimentalising 'persuasion
to love' of the *carpe diem* motif and instead shows Marvell employing
'the calm science of the bourgeois order' which is a fundamental part
of seventeenth-century discourses of the body. Barker notes how the
dismemberment of the body displays a male discourse and a female
silence. Absence, too, is what Jonathan Goldberg finds in his consideration
of 'The Nymph complaining for the death of her Faun', a 'solitary time'
in which an assertion of pastoral idyll only inscribes loss. For both Barker
and Goldberg, Marvell's assertion of poetic presence, of possession,
also reveals his characteristic 'doubleness', a voice aware of its own
dislocation and dispossession. Jonathan Crewe also explores what he
terms Marvell's 'metapoetic commentary on his own lyric enterprise',
a poetry of 'self-critical impulse', through a consideration of his use of
pastoral. Pastoral has long been a feature for which Marvell's poetry has
been justly celebrated. But, as Crewe demonstrates, what is noteworthy is
the fragility of the idealised enclosures Marvell erects, how his pastoral
provokes 'creative annihilation'.

As I indicated earlier, Barker's, Goldberg's and Crewe's recognition
of Marvell's self-critical exposure of poetic artifice does not lead to a
view that he believes there is nothing which can be said or known about
his times. Seemingly paradoxically, the poet's apparent self-absorption
readily leads to perspectives on his era which enable a public poetry.
Leah Marcus's discussion of Marvell's longest poem, *Upon Appleton
House*, shows how the poet rehearses a catalogue of features associated
with politically charged popular festive forms and with a Royalist-
oriented poetics of retreat precisely in order to show that there can be
no retreat. Crewe's and Marcus's contributions well illustrate one of
the strengths of the best Marvell criticism: the combination of careful
'close reading' of poetry (with an acute eye for Marvell's display of
generic manipulation and literary echo) matched with an awareness
of the political consequences for such manipulations within his
contemporary history.

Marcus's view of Marvell is much influenced by Bakhtin's theory of the carnivalesque, the 'upending' or inversion of serious culture through its parody. As she suggests, Marvell has a tendency to adopt a from-the-bottom-looking-up perspective in his later satires. But Marvell's employment of witty, grotesque parody is always aimed at reform. He does not wish to erect a series of disfiguring mirrors on his world merely to expose its fundamental absurdity. Marvell is not a postmodernist refusing a 'grand narrative' to history. It is the seriousness of his history, one he believed ordered and arranged, ultimately, according to a pattern decreed by Divine Providence, paired with his realisation of the pathos of a humanity destined to confront the consequences of imperfection (of self and of State) which motivates his display of the excesses and fallacies which confront his world.

As Blair Worden's and David Norbrook's essays on *An Horatian Ode upon Cromwell's Return from Ireland* show, Marvell's sense of 'doubleness', in this case the respective claims of Charles I and a republican Parliament to legitimacy of national rule in a much-divided Britain, does not lead to self-absorbed uncertainty. Norbrook, citing the work of Jerome McGann, articulates the central motivation of much recent Marvell criticism, arguing that 'all literary works . . . are inhabited by lost and invisibilised agencies. . . . One of the chief functions of criticism is to remember the works which have been torn and distorted by those losses.' In both essays, what is proposed is a republican celebration of Cromwell, Marvell's greeting of a moment in English culture which has been misread by later generations because, as Norbrook succinctly puts it, 'the cause was lost'.

Both these essays reveal a crucial feature which current historiography confronts, the absence of 'objective accounts' of what happened in mid-seventeenth-century Britain. How Marvell's age is presented rests with ideologically motivated organisations of knowledge. The very question of what to call the events of 1640–60 – the English Revolution, the Great Rebellion, the Interregnum, the Civil War or Civil Wars – exemplifies how a current 'naming' of these events, let alone Marvell's role in them, is still a highly charged arena between the political right and left.[11] Traditionally, literary criticism around Marvell has consciously or unconsciously aligned itself with Royalist positions. Herbert Grierson's proposal that 'The metaphysicals were all on the King's side . . . for they were on the side of the humanities; and the Puritan rebellion . . . was in itself and at the moment a fanatical upheaval' is an extreme articulation of this alignment, but its sentiments tended to have been more shared than opposed until recent times.[12] In detailing the moment of political urgency for the Republic in 1650 which *An Horatian Ode* addresses, Norbrook and Worden show how the revival of lost agencies helps advance our understanding of the relation of poetry and politics in the mid-seventeenth century, and afterward.

In an effort to recapture the lost agencies which surround Marvell's work, Annabel Patterson's consideration of Marvell's continuing praise of Cromwell in two of the great occasional poems, *The First Anniversary* and *A Poem on the Death of O.C.*, also focuses on the particularities of Marvell's employment of poetic traditions, of those traditions' contemporary deployments in seventeenth-century English culture, and of the cultural resonances surrounding Cromwell during the Protectorate. In one sense, Patterson's discussion should figure at the beginning of this collection. It was her 1978 study, *Marvell and the Civic Crown*, from which her contribution here is taken, which stimulated a great deal of the dynamic which has re-oriented Marvell criticism. One of Patterson's greatest achievements was to push Marvell criticism away from rather simplistic sweeping generalisations about poetry and politics. In her contribution to this collection she demonstrates how Marvell's use of encomium in celebration of Cromwell did not mean he was some wide-eyed sycophant or paid propagandist of the Protectorate regime. Marvell's admiration for Cromwell is not divorced from a poetry of shrewd analysis and scrupulous attention to meaning, a carefully judged attempt which tries to inaugurate a new poetry for a new phase of British political life. In doing so, Marvell was pursuing a high seriousness with his poetic role which readily parallels Milton's.

In 1978 William Empson observed how the last few generations had tried to distance the Restoration Marvell. But, Empson remarked, 'one cannot quite escape from the Satires by saying that they were written as a painful duty, obviously against the grain.'[13] Empson noticed a populist, jarring, note in Marvell's Restoration poetry which was linked to his earlier occasional poems, but he did not glean its stylistic function. Steven Zwicker, whose recent book *Lines of Authority* has helped clarify the relation between poetry and court politics in the period 1660–90, is historically alert to why this discordant note is present.[14] As Zwicker's brilliant analysis of *The Last Instructions to a Painter* in the essay included here shows, it is precisely the 'low-mindness' of the satire which helps carry its urgent argument about deformity in the body politic which is physically manifest in the sexual excesses of its court. Zwicker furthers Leah Marcus's observation about Marvell adopting perspectives 'from below', showing how he echoes the crudity of popular print culture to castigate sexual misconduct because of what it represents about a restored monarchy unable to provide for the nation the security or healthy abundance which was its promise. Like Swift, Marvell's satire is masterful in presenting the repellent in a manner which forces home its serious implications.

Zwicker notes how the concluding tone of *Last Instructions* recalls that of *An Horatian Ode*, and this refusal to separate the pre- and post-Restoration Marvell is an important feature of recent criticism. Traditionally, most of the shorter lyrics are felt to date from the 1630s and 40s, the period up to Marvell's employment by the Protectorate government and his subsequent career as an MP. The long poems to Fairfax and Cromwell are the product of the 1650s, and the satires on affairs of state date from after the Restoration. Beyond the fact that, obviously, occasional poems cannot be written before their occasions, there is, though, no real evidence for the dating of much of Marvell's poetic output. The vast majority of the poetry did not appear publicly until it was published in 1681, three years after Marvell's death, and, unlike Donne's, for example, this work does not appear to have widely circulated in manuscript. One of the oddities of a text such as *An Horatian Ode* is that, despite its public mode of address, there is no evidence which suggests Cromwell, or anyone else, read it during Marvell's lifetime. Marvell's ambiguity and 'doubleness' in expression, his adoption of personae in his texts, as well as his apparent concealment of work which has a public voice fosters a sense of enigma around him.

Paul Hammond's concluding essay of this collection attempts to negotiate some of the qualities of this enigma through an examination of Marvell's homosexual interests. Gender and identity increasingly are recognised to play a crucial factor in the forming of literary expression and Hammond's consideration of Marvell is part of a larger project seeking to understand how homosexual desire might be imagined in a period when the homoerotic could not inhabit a coherent textual space. Fashioning a poetic space for a language of sexual ambiguity is what Hammond sees as one of Marvell's particular achievements. What Hammond is not attempting is a reading of Marvell's poetry as 'homoerotic poems deliberately dressed up and passed off as something else', nor 'as if they were a patient's dreams where repressed desires break through'. His starting point is contemporary attacks on Marvell's sexual nature, the representation of him as impotent, an amphibian, a sodomite. This public representation of a private face, the merging of public and private which is also a feature of Marvell's poetry of criticism, becomes a critical tool which can be used by late-twentieth-century readers to tease out meaning from a poetry which is 'teaching us how to live ambiguities, and is thinking through the strangeness of self-understanding.'

Restoring Marvell to history in the criticism of the last twenty years has not explained away his poetry. An alertness both to political and literary nuance among Marvell's most impressive recent critics has not reduced his poetry's capacity to surprise and challenge. Certainly, the critical location of Marvell within English culture of the mid-seventeenth century has not curtailed his work's ability to generate meaning, or controversy. Interestingly, the Marvell which emerges out of this recent critical work often resembles the dominant views about Marvell during the first hundred years after his death. To grasp recent criticism about Marvell, it is worthwhile recalling his place in critical history.

A critical heritage

If the 1970s mark a watershed in the history of Marvell criticism, what took place before can be relatively easily characterised. Throughout the eighteenth and early nineteenth centuries Marvell had a reputation for political intrigue and as a defender of English liberty against an oppressive establishment. In contrast, from the mid-nineteenth century until the late twentieth, he was seen as the writer of a handful of lyrics whose qualities were among the highest in 'metaphysical poetry'. In her introduction to *Andrew Marvell: The Critical Heritage*, Elizabeth Story Donno neatly sums this up: 'In 1753 Andrew Marvell was styled the "poet laureate of the dissenters" otherwise known as "fanatics"; in 1901 he was styled the "laureate of grass and greenery" '.[15] These two aspects of Marvell were based on giving prominence to entirely different aspects of his work.

Marvell died suddenly in 1678 and, although the circumstances do not seem mysterious, it was suggested there was foul play because of the scandal caused by *An Account of the Growth of Popery and Arbitrary Government* which had been published anonymously the preceding year. A large reward had been offered for information regarding its author or printer, such was the Government's displeasure over this tract. Marvell escaped any direct reprisal, despite many correctly identifying him as the author from the work's appearance, but an aura of political intrigue had begun to surround him. The second edition of *An Account* published shortly after his death bore his name and for a number of years it was circulated that Marvell must have somehow been privy to the designs of the Popish Plot, because his tract seemed to predict it. The Tory journalist Sir Roger L'Estrange attacked Marvell in 1679 as the prophet of the growth of fanaticism: 'an *Enemy* to the *Monarchy* of *England* as to the *Ministers*: And it is no wonder, that the *Secretary* to a Common-wealth would write with the *Spirit* of a *Re-publican*.'[16] Thus, Marvell became witnessed as the defender of 'the good old cause', the hero of the emerging Whigs and the bane of the Conservatives, the opponent of Roman Catholicism, and a thorough patriot. Although his poems were published posthumously in 1681, they do not appear to have attracted particular attention. Throughout the eighteenth century it was his image as a defender of liberty rather than his qualities as a writer of verse which was celebrated. Even when his poetry was reprinted in new editions, the introductions promote Marvell's political stature not his poetic one. Thomas Cooke, the editor of the second edition of Marvell's 'collected verse', claimed his design 'is to draw a Pattern for all free-born *English-men* in the Life of a worthy Patriot'.[17] The next edition, that of Captain Edward Thompson in 1776, also emphasised Marvell's politics. The frontispiece has an engraving of Marvell and Milton greeting the rising of Liberty as a phoenix in America. In both editions, the expectation appears to be that readers will find the greatest interest in the Restoration satires. Both also print some (Cooke in 1726) or most (Thompson in 1776) of Marvell's letters to the Corporation of Hull reporting on events in Parliament, again bringing attention to Marvell's political role.

By the mid-nineteenth century all these aspects of Marvell were largely scorned. In 1892 A.C. Benson condemned Milton for introducing Marvell to public life, and to this 'we owe the loss of a great English poet'.[18] Marvell as a political figure and as a topical satiric poet had been replaced by the writer of a handful of choice lyrics. A two-volume edition of his poetry in the popular Muses' Library series in 1892 placed the lyrics in volume one and the satires in volume two, signalling this separation of roles. Reviews suggest few readers turned to the second volume. For instance, E.K. Chambers's characterisation of Marvell presents a figure who would have been unrecognisable to the eighteenth century:

> Marvell writes love poems, but he is not essentially a love poet. . . . His real passion – a most uncommon one in the seventeenth century – is for nature, exactly as we moderns mean nature, the great spiritual influence which deepens and widens life for us.[19]

A growing hostility to the public face of Marvell and to any attempt to place his work in history is further evidenced by a review in the *Times Literary Supplement* of Augustine Birrell's life of Marvell which appeared in the series *English Men of Letters* in 1905:

> Marvell wrote some poetry of unique charm and one ode of the highest distinction and dignity. . . . If there ever was a poet whose delicate graceful work could be appreciated classically by Mr. Birrell in a short characteristic essay, it is the poet of 'Appleton House', and the 'The Garden', the 'Coy Mistress' . . . yet here is a monograph . . . which has had to be eked out with . . . all the politics and intrigues of the Restoration – matters which have no bearing on Marvell's literature as we value it.[20]

Examining Birrell's life, this displeasure with the Restoration Marvell is all the more indicative of the change in critical temper, because, rather than an old-fashioned celebration of the patriotic Marvell, Birrell, too, is fixated on a socially disengaged poet:

In the whole compass of our poetry there is nothing quite like
Marvell's love of gardens and woods, of meads and rivers and birds.
It is a love not learnt from books, nor borrowed from brother-poets. It
is not indulged in to prove anything. It is all sheer enjoyment.[21]

Birrell, in fact, passes over the late seventeenth and the eighteenth
centuries' preference for the public satiric verse by 'feeling certain' that
'from 1681 onwards ingenious souls read Eyes and Tears, The Bermudas,
The Nymph Complaining for the Death of her Fawn, To his Coy Mistress,
Young Love, and The Garden with pure delight'.[22]

Elizabeth Story Donno has capably demonstrated that T.S. Eliot's
consideration of Marvell – the most influential single piece of criticism
on mid-twentieth-century perspectives – was hardly innovative. Rather,
he brought together existing opinions: 'one might call this the plagiarism
of received ideas'.[23] Eliot claimed the distinguishing features of
seventeenth-century poetry were wit and magniloquence. Wit is 'a tough
reasonableness beneath the slight lyric grace'; magniloquence, 'the
deliberate exploitation of the possibilities of magnificence in language'.[24]
Marvell possesses 'an educated mind, rich in generations of experience'
which 'finds for him the proper degree of seriousness for every subject
which he treats'.[25] Like much of Eliot's criticism, the Marvell essay is, in
one respect, a self-confessed failure. Eliot concedes he is unable to define
precisely what constitutes Marvell's lyric brilliance. But this is all part
of a rhetorical strategy. For Eliot, Marvell is part of a civilising process
which readers largely either instinctively recognise or proclaim their
barbarism by being in doubt about. His stated difficulty in characterising
Marvell's verse helps enforce Eliot's reflections upon the difficulties of
living in a tarnished age which has lost much of the appreciative
'educated' qualities of this earlier period.

For fifty years after Eliot's essay most literary criticism either
sought to expand upon its proposals or to answer its strictures. This
often produced very erudite considerations of the generic and rhetorical
qualities of Renaissance poetry, encouraged speculation on arcane
Renaissance philosophical ideas, generated some exciting work on
pastoral, and, generally, prompted sensitive readings of the lyrics.[26]
Eliot's 1921 article had been produced to mark the occasion of the
tercentenary of Marvell's birth. At the tercentenary of his death in
1978 two volumes of essays were produced, both well illustrating
mid-twentieth-century preoccupations.[27] Overwhelmingly they are
directed at the lyrical Marvell. Many of their contributions are valuable,
but titles such as 'Marvell's Metaphysical Wit', 'Reversals Transposed:
An Aspect of Marvell's Imagination', 'Andrew Marvell: the Aesthetics
of Inconclusiveness', 'The Meadow Sequence in *Upon Appleton House*:
Questions of Tone and Meaning' reveal their concentration on the

'interiority' of poetic utterance rather than Marvell's engagement with history.[28] One of the best of these 1978 tercentenary essays is Barbara Everett's 'The Shooting of the Bears: Poetry and Politics in Andrew Marvell'.[29] An ambitious reconsideration of Marvell and his reputation, Everett also illustrates one of Eliot's most persuasive suppositions for later criticism: a belief that Marvell reflected civilised verse in a decaying age.

> It is the depths of the mind, a world within and yet beyond the dying culture of his time, which becomes Marvell's subject: a green world always extending like an abyss within the formal enclosures of the age.[30]

Everett acknowledges the change in Marvell criticism which has begun in the 1970s and contrasts it to earlier decades:

> Marvell rose into prominence, in the 1920s and '30s, as the creator of an acutely private art; and to read his brilliant, individual poems was perhaps like inheriting, at the end of a throttling civilisation, a small landed estate to retreat to and live in freely. If taste is turning now . . . towards the occasional verse, then this probably says more about our own ever more publicly-oriented society . . . than it does about Marvell's poems.[31]

At the start of *An Horatian Ode*, Marvell contrasts two types of figures:

> The forward Youth that would appear
> Must now forsake his *Muses* dear,
>   Nor in the Shadows sing
>   His numbers languishing.
> 'Tis time to leave the Books in dust,
> And oyl th'unused Armours rust:

(ll. 1–6)

It can be said that for the first seventy-five years of this century literary criticism read these lines with pathos predominating; its sympathies inclined to regret the leaving of books and muses disproportionately. In contrast, during the last twenty years criticism has increasingly approached these lines as the positive proclamation of a new energetic cultural dynamic. 'Languishing' is something which many of Marvell's personae do, but it is not something the poet recommends. Far from witnessing Marvell at the end of a dying Renaissance, Marvell critics now celebrate him as one of the moulders of his age: a figure actively in and of his time rather than out of it. May this continue.

Notes

1. See WORDEN below p. 97.
2. See RICHARD WILSON and RICHARD DUTTON (eds), *New Historicism and Renaissance Drama*, Longman Critical Readers (London and New York: Longman, 1992) for a consideration of New Historicism.
3. A key influence here, though more widely embraced by literary scholars than historians, has been Hayden White. See WHITE's *The Content of the Form: Narrative Discourse and Historical Representation* (Baltimore and London: The Johns Hopkins University Press, 1987).
4. ANNABEL PATTERSON, *Andrew Marvell*, Writers and their Work (Plymouth: Northcote House, 1994), p. 12.
5. T.S. ELIOT, 'Andrew Marvell', *Selected Essays* (London: Faber and Faber, 1932), p. 251. Eliot's essay first appeared in the *Times Literary Supplement* in 1921.
6. CLEANTH BROOKS, 'Marvell's Horatian Ode', in John Carey (ed.), *Andrew Marvell*, Penguin Critical Anthologies (Harmondsworth: Penguin Books Ltd, 1969), pp. 179–80. Brooks's essays first appeared in *English Institute Essays* (1947), pp. 127–58.
7. BROOKS, *ibid.*, pp. 179–98; and 'A Note on the Limits of "History" and the Limits of "Criticism"', *Sewanee Review*, 61 (1953), pp. 129–35. DOUGLAS BUSH, 'Marvell's Horatian Ode', in Carey, *ibid.*, pp. 199–210. The article first appeared in the *Sewanee Review*, 60 (1952), pp. 363–76.
8. CHRISTOPHER HILL, 'Society and Andrew Marvell', *Modern Quarterly*, 4 (1946), p. 6.
9. CHRISTOPHER HILL, *The World Turned Upside Down: Radical Ideas during the English Revolution* (London: Maurice Temple Smith, 1972); *Milton and the English Revolution* (Faber and Faber, 1977); GERRARD WINSTANLEY, *The Law of Freedom and Other Writings*, ed. Christopher Hill (Harmondsworth: Penguin Books, 1973).
10. The exception is the excellent edition of *The Rehearsal Transpros'd and the Rehearsal Transpros'd, The Second Part*, ed. D.I.B. Smith (Oxford: Clarendon Press, 1971).
11. See ANNABEL PATTERSON, 'The Very Name of the Game: Theories of Order and Disorder' in Thomas Healy and Jonathan Sawday (eds), *Literature and the English Civil War* (Cambridge: Cambridge University Press, 1990), pp. 21–37.
12. SIR HERBERT GRIERSON, 'Introduction' to *Metaphysical Lyrics and Poems of the Seventeenth Century* (Oxford: Oxford University Press, 1921), p. xxix. The most considered attempt to show Marvell's Royalist sympathies is J.M. WALLACE, *Destiny his Choice: The Loyalism of Andrew Marvell* (Cambridge: Cambridge University Press, 1968) which argues Marvell's underlying preference for constitutional monarchy.
13. WILLIAM EMPSON, 'Natural Magic and Populism in Marvell's Poetry', in R.L. Brett (ed.), *Andrew Marvell: Essays on the Tercentenary of his Death* (Oxford University Press for the University of Hull, 1979), p. 36.
14. STEVEN N. ZWICKER, *Lines of Authority: Politics and English Literary Culture, 1649–1689* (Ithaca and London: Cornell University Press, 1993).
15. ELIZABETH STORY DONNO, *Andrew Marvell: The Critical Heritage* (London, Henley and Boston: Routledge & Kegan Paul, 1978), p. 1.
16. *Ibid.*, p. 75.
17. *Ibid.*, p. 109.

18. *Ibid.*, p. 249.
19. *Ibid.*, pp. 268–69.
20. *ibid.*, p. 308.
21. *Ibid.*, p. 306.
22. *Ibid.*, p. 305.
23. *Ibid.*, pp. 15–18.
24. Eliot, *op.cit.*, pp. 252–3.
25. *Ibid.*, p. 262.
26. See for example, R.L. COLIE, *'My Echoing Song': Marvell's Poetry of Criticism* (Princeton and London: Princeton University Press, 1970); D.C. ALLEN, *Image and Meaning: Metaphoric Traditions in Renaissance Poetry* (Baltimore and London: The Johns Hopkins University Press, 1960); H.E. TOLIVER, *Marvell's Ironic Vision* (New Haven and London: Yale University Press, 1965); D.M. FRIEDMAN, *Marvell's Pastoral Art* (London: Routledge & Kegan Paul, 1970).
27. *Andrew Marvell: Essays on the Tercentenary of his Death, op.cit.; Approaches to Marvell: The York Tercentenary Lectures*, ed. C.A. PATRIDES (London, Henley and Boston: Routledge & Kegan Paul, 1979).
28. All these essays are found in *Approaches to Marvell*, *ibid.*
29. BARBARA EVERETT, 'The Shooting of the Bears: Poetry and Politics in Andrew Marvell', *Andrew Marvell: Essays on the Tercentenary of his Death, op.cit.*, pp. 62–104.
30. *Ibid.*, p. 95.
31. *Ibid.*, p. 65.

1 The Poet's Time*

Warren L. Chernaik

This extract from Warren Chernaik's seminal study of Marvell focuses on ideas of Christian liberty. For Chernaik, to understand Marvell requires confronting the vexed question of human freedom within the context of a seventeenth-century Protestantism which emphasised the fallen nature of mankind as a result of Adam's original sin. This sense of loss informs all aspects of Marvell's consideration of human affairs, whether personal or public. But it does not bring about despair; rather a type of exhilaration: the possibility of educating ourselves so that we can confront and, to an extent, repair the consequences of our original transgression. Marvell is perceived as a passionate advocate of humanity's liberty, refusing to accept – as many during his era did – that the fate of each individual is predestined within the divine scheme of things. This leads Chernaik to view Marvell as a type of proto-Romantic, believing in the power of the imagination, notably developed in poetry, as means of human empowerment. Crucially, Chernaik's book sees Marvell's prose and poetry as addressing the same concerns, linked to philosophical, theological and political issues which are closely integrated.

Though the context in each case is secular, the terms in Marvell's evocations of the ideal government are openly or implicitly theological. In describing the British limited monarch as 'the onely Intelligent Ruler over a Rational People' (*Growth of Popery*, p. 4) and claiming of the British constitution that 'there is nothing that comes nearer in Government to

* Reprinted from Warren L. Chernaik, *The Poet's Time: Politics and Religion in the Work of Andrew Marvell* (Cambridge: Cambridge University Press, 1983), pp. 141–50.

the Divine Perfection' (p. 5), Marvell is suggesting that, though man's state is fallen, it may be possible to 'repair the ruins of our first parents'.[1] In the perspective of Marvell's Christian irony, man remains a rational being even in his fallen state, for all the proofs he constantly gives of his irrationality. Like Milton, Marvell reminds us of the 'Divine Perfection' man threw away at his first fall to warn us of the folly of throwing it away once again. The sad likelihood that man will make a desert out of a peaceful and flourishing landscape, where 'the whole Land at whatsoever season of the year does yield him a plentiful Harvest' (*Growth of Popery*, p. 4), that like Eve and Satan he will succumb to the temptation of greater power and dissatisfaction with what he has, does not negate a poet's responsibility to provide a 'warning voice' (*Paradise Lost*, IV, 1). In his satires and political writings, Marvell is a realist in recognizing the brutal cynicism with which men in power feed their insatiable wills and an idealist in urging alternative standards of conduct, in insisting that it is not yet too late.

Marvell's characteristic ironic tone reflects an awareness that, however much we may regret it, the world is fallen and that we must therefore chasten our expectations. The morality implicit in much of Marvell is that of the education of Adam and Eve in the last books of *Paradise Lost*: though we may be tempted to 'give ear to proud and curious Spirits' (*Rehearsal Transpros'd*, II, 231), to fall prey either to 'a vast opinion of [our] own sufficiency' (I, 15) or to despair, ultimately we must learn 'to be content with such bodies, and to inhabit such an Earth as it has pleased God to allot us' (II, 231). Underlying both the outward-looking, militant irony of Marvell's satires and the impersonal, detached, freely proliferating ironic wit which is Marvell's signature in his lyrics is a further form of irony turned inward, Christian wit. Man's lot, with the body and soul uneasily coexisting as irreconcilable and inseparable enemies, is itself ironic. His 'vain Head, and double Heart' ('A Dialogue between the Soul and Body', l. 10) assure both that his unresolved paradoxes will cause him pain and that he will be incapable of finding any solution or relief. Man, as Marvell sees him, is doomed to feel the anguish of parallel lines, wracked by a yearning to 'joyn', yet helplessly extending side by side into infinity ('The Definition of Love', l. 23).

Yet, as a final twist of irony, in man's weakness and frustration lies his strength. It is his consciousness, his capacity for feeling guilt, pain, and loss, his unique though sometimes unwelcome gift of retrospective awareness, the weight of conscience which he cannot, even if he wished to do so, 'atturn and indenture' over to others (*Short Historical Essay*, p. 21), that enables man to find a path to freedom. It is by the 'Opposition of the Stars' ('The Definition of Love', l. 32) that love is defined: 'Magnanimous Despair' (l. 5) enables the lovers of 'The Definition of Love' to attain a perfection denied ordinary lovers, whose 'Tinsel' (l. 8) joys soon fade.

The couple of 'The Definition of Love' have been initiated into experience, unlike the happy innocents 'with whom the Infant Love yet playes', described in stanza 1 of 'The Unfortunate Lover', who imagine themselves secure in a vegetative pastoral contentment, unaware of their inability 'to make impression upon Time' (l. 8). Gifted with consciousness, the post-lapsarian lovers of 'The Definition of Love' are able to defy the 'Tyrannick pow'r' (l. 16) of fate, which in separating them can only intensify their love. In 'The Unfortunate Lover', the pains and frustrations of love in the fallen realm are emphasized, rather than any possible transcendance, yet here too the lover gains a form of apotheosis in resisting the forces of envious fate, 'cuffing the Thunder' (l. 50) and dying in music. Here perhaps it is the confrontation of pain which gives man his identity.

Neither earthly tyrant nor outer necessity, Marvell argues, has the absolute power their partisans claim. A belief in an essential human freedom which no outward force can touch is central to Marvell's thought, as to Milton's. In his verse and prose satires, as in such poems as *An Horatian Ode*, 'The Definition of Love', 'To his Coy Mistress', and *Upon Appleton House*, Marvell consistently emphasizes the role of free choice in a providentially ordered universe. The conception of an iron necessity which rendered all human action futile and made all talk of moral choice superfluous, a necessity 'that was pre-eternal to all things, and exercised dominion not only over all humane things, but over *Jupiter* himself and the rest of the Deities and drove the great Iron nail thorough the Axel-tree of Nature', was antipathetic to him. The doctrine of a 'Universal Dictatorship of Necessity over God and Man', so attractive to predestinarians and apologists for earthly rulers ('I have some suspicion', he writes of Parker in *The Rehearsal Transpros'd*, 'that you would have men understand it of your self, and that you are that Necessity'), in Marvell's view robs the universe of any meaning and simply deifies power (II, p. 230). Marvell rejected Hobbist reason of state as he rejected Calvinist predestination: to him, man is a reasonable creature and therefore free. No form of outward necessity can negate man's responsibility to choose between right and wrong, to determine, with the aid of his conscience, 'Humane Reason guided by the Scripture' (II, p. 243), how to behave in his daily life. The soul is given an 'immortal Shield', and must 'learn' to bear its weight ('Resolved Soul', ll. 1–2). Neither truth nor morality, as Milton says in *Areopagitica*, can flourish in a climate of prescription, 'unexercis'd and unbreath'd' (*CPW*, II, 515); through exercise, through exposure to experience, the resolved soul learns to discriminate.

Like Milton, Marvell consistently sought to reconcile a belief in a divine providence (in Milton's definition, 'that by which God the father views and preserves all created things and governs them with supreme wisdom and holiness, according to the conditions of his decree') with a belief that man was a free agent responsible for his own acts.[2] In their emphasis on man's freedom, Marvell, Milton, and the Puritan libertarians directly or by implication challenged the orthodox Calvinist belief in predestination. Because their view of morality stressed the role of free choice and man's endowment of rationality in this way, rejecting any form of determinism as they rejected earthly authority, the libertarians frequently came under attack by guardians of Calvinist doctrinal purity. The last of Marvell's prose works, *Remarks upon a late Disingenuous Discourse* (1678), is a defence of the dissenting clergyman John Howe against attacks by more orthodox Calvinists for upholding the doctrine of free will against rigid predestination. Though the circumstances of the 1670s, when the Puritans had long been out of power and Calvinist theology was no longer dominant in England, differed greatly from the prevailing climate of opinion in the Commonwealth and Protectorate years, nevertheless Marvell's position in *Remarks* is closely akin to that of such libertarian radicals of the 1640s as John Goodwin and to Milton in *De Doctrina Christiana*, as well as in *Paradise Lost*. Like Milton, Marvell is careful to distinguish between God's prescience or omniscience and any form of necessitarianism, arguing that God's foreknowledge of events in no way implies a predestination that limits man's ability to choose freely among alternatives. In *Remarks*, Marvell repeatedly draws the distinction between 'a thing so plainly reveal'd in the Word of God as his Prescience is, and so agreeable to all rational apprehension, and a Notion so altogether unrevealed as this universal Predetermination yet appears, and so contrary if not to the whole scope and design of Divine Revelation, yet to all common understanding and genuine sense of right Reason' (pp. 76–7).[3] To the Calvinist doctrine of predestination, Marvell and the libertarians opposed the Lutheran doctrine of justification by faith: though they by no means make man's redemption depend on man alone, unaided by God's grace, they reject the view of man as the purely passive object of God's decrees. Sinners, in Milton's and Marvell's view, are responsible for their own sins: 'as to Evil', Marvell writes, citing biblical proof-texts, 'that also of St. James, is sufficient conviction, cap. I. v. 13, 14. *Let no man say, when he is tempted, I was tempted by God; God cannot be tempted with Evil, neither tempteth he any man:* But every man is tempted, when he is drawn aside by his own lusts and enticed.' To deny man the freedom to use his God-given reason to choose an appropriate course of action, Marvell argues, is to make God the author of sin:

> But how much doth *It* reflect upon God and that Religious sense
> which we ought to cherish of him . . . when it makes God to have
> determined Innocent *Adam*'s Will to the choice of eating the fruit that
> was forbidden him? . . . To *Illustrate* (as it pretends) so black a thing,

it parallels God's moving him to that Act rather than to another, *with a Writing-Master's directing his Scholars hand.* If the Cause be not to be defended upon better terms than so, what Christian but would rather wish he had never known Writing-Master, than to subscribe such an Opinion; and that God should make an innocent Creature in this manner to do a forbidden Act, for which so dreadful a vengeance was to insue upon him and his posterity? (*Remarks*, pp. 4–5, 125–6)

Such works as *The Rehearsal Transpros'd*, *The Growth of Popery*, and *Last Instructions*, like *Remarks*, are grounded in a conception of freedom and experience which can be described as libertarian or non-Calvinist Puritan. A similar view is implicit in many of Marvell's lyrics, which tend either to be aids to the embattled soul (Marvell at his most Miltonic, as in 'A Dialogue, between The Resolved Soul, and Created Pleasure') or, more often, reflections on, or definitions of, the human condition. Education into experience is his recurrent theme, and experience, as with Vaughan and the romantic poets, is normally defined in terms of loss. The central irony of human existence is man's fallen, alienated state in which he longs after a recovered wholeness 'beyond a Mortal's share' ('The Garden', l. 61). The realm of freedom and unchanging truth in Marvell's poems is often explicitly Christian: the unenlightened and puzzled mower and the weeping nymph, introduced to a reality of unrelieved pain so out of consonance with anything they had previously known, the imperious infant T. C. as yet protected from any such knowledge, the coy mistress who wishes to deny its existence, are distinguished from the converted shepherd in 'Clorinda and Damon' or the resolved soul, both of whom recognize that 'Where the Creator's skill is priz'd, / The rest is all but Earth disguis'd' ('Resolved Soul', ll. 35–6). Yet if Marvell's moral universe is Miltonic, there is a fundamental difference in attitude between the two poets. The acute pain of the nymph, her sense that the rules have changed, that a universe hitherto comprehensible has suddenly been deprived of harmony and meaning ('It cannot dye so. Heavens King / Keeps register of every thing', 'The Nymph complaining', ll. 13–14) has its Miltonic parallels, but no answer is even implied to the nymph's agonized questions. It is striking how often Marvell's poems are left unresolved: 'The Nymph complaining for the death of her Faun' is like a version of *Paradise Lost* ending with Book IX. Marvell's attitude toward the naïfs and infants who populate his poems is ambivalent: the hard freedom of truth is consistently shown to be morally preferable to enslavement to pleasing fictions, and yet in common with Vaughan, Blake, and Wordsworth Marvell sees the capacity of imaginative or mythopoeic sympathy, so much a prey to circumstances, so fragile when exposed to the harsh air of experience, as representing one of the few ways by which man can free himself from his surroundings. What children lose, the poet retains: the poetic imagination unites the gifts of innocence and experience. In somewhat similar terms, John Creaser has identified Marvell's wit with gaiety transfiguring dread, 'the mind's declaration of independence from the Fall' and its attendant train of fears and sorrows.[4] And yet for Marvell the realist, the mind's sovereignty over contingencies can never be complete. He keeps returning in his poems to the one inescapable fact which defines the human condition, the question which can never be answered:

> What luckless Apple did we tast,
> To make us Mortal, and Thee Wast?
>
> *(Upon Appleton House*, ll. 327–8)

The extended dialogue in Marvell between hope and despair, between the fervent belief that *'Paradice's only Map'* (*Upon Appleton House*, l. 768) lies open before us and the forlorn conviction that the world is 'not, what once it was', but a 'rude heap' (ll. 761–2), in which we are irreparably and irremediably cut off from the good for which we long, is the dialogue at the heart of seventeenth-century Puritanism. Both Marvell and Milton see, the situation of the blind and shorn Samson as representative, not least in his ultimate solitude. Without any certainty outside the inner court of conscience, man can never know with any certainty whether he has been saved. Marvell consistently emphasizes the exposed isolation of the man who seeks to follow the imperious demands of conscience, with its 'prickling leaf' which 'shrinks at ev'ry touch' (ll. 357–8): a temporary respite from the pains of existence is possible, but essentially for Marvell the man of conscience, restless and questioning, rejecting the voice of worldly authority in all its forms, rejecting even the consolation of a sense of solidarity with fellow believers, is left alone with his own unanswerable questions.

The firm conviction that God directs all things does not in itself make for serenity, since the ways of God are not only unfathomable but often incompatible with human ideas of justice, to say nothing of our preferences. Even those who dedicate themselves to the service of God, 'such as thou hast solemnly elected, / With gifts and graces eminently adorn'd / To some great work', Milton writes in *Samson Agonistes* (ll. 678–80), are often thrown down 'lower then thou didst exalt them high' (l. 689): 'Just and unjust, alike seem miserable, / For oft alike, both come to evil end' (ll. 703–4). In moments not of promised glory but 'on evil days though fall'n, and evil tongues; / In darkness, and with dangers compast round, / And solitude' (*Paradise Lost*, VII, ll. 26–8), the conviction that God provides for his servants is difficult indeed to sustain. It is tempting at such a time to succumb to despair, to see, as Marvell did in his later years, not a 'wish'd Conjuncture' of the destined moment and the chosen people, but the actual 'Conjuncture' of a tyrannous, 'absolutely powerful' king, a supine parliament ('we are all venal Cowards, except some few'), and a disease seemingly spreading from the court to infect the entire nation. 'In such a Conjuncture, dear *Will*,' he writes to his nephew William Popple in 1670, 'what Probability is there of my doing any Thing to the Purpose?' (*Poems and Letters*, II, pp. 315, 317).

When in *Last Instructions* Marvell compares England in its state of decline to the bound Samson, there is no suggestion of a possible regeneration, no sense that the dark ways of providence will suddenly be illumined, that suffering will turn by unforeseen ways into triumph. Instead, the lines suggest only ignominy, in evoking the former greatness and potential for good which have been laid waste by man's folly and venality. The possibility is broached that the 'wondrous gifts' of God will indeed be 'frustrate' (*Samson Agonistes*, l. 589), that God has averted his eyes from the English. In punishment for their iniquities, the English, reduced to spectators, are forced to watch the Dutch navy sail undisturbed into British waters and destroy or capture those British ships which once, 'Oaken Gyants of the ancient race, / . . . rul'd all Seas' (*Last Instructions*, ll. 577–8).

> The Seamen search her all, within, without:
> Viewing her strength, they yet their Conquest doubt.
> Then with rude shouts, secure, the Air they vex;
> With Gamesome Joy insulting on her Decks.
> Such the fear'd *Hebrew*, captive, blinded, shorn
> Was led about in sport, the publick scorn.
>
> (ll. 731–6)

The 'Black Day' (l. 737) of England's humiliation, so different from the 'blest Day' (*First Anniversary*, l. 155) for which Marvell had seen presages under the reign of Cromwell, is made more painful by the memory of past glories and blighted promise. The imagery of rampant disorder explicitly provides standards by which the state of England in 1667 may properly be judged, but the lines do not suggest any immediate solution, except insofar as shame may lead to a resolve to bring about change:

> Thee, the Year's monster, let thy Dam devour.
> And constant Time, to keep his course yet right,
> Fill up thy space with a redoubled Night.
> When aged *Thames* was bound with Fetters base,
> And *Medway* chast ravish'd before his Face . . .
> Now with vain grief their vainer hopes they rue,
> Themselves dishonour'd, and the *Gods* untrue.
>
> ('Last Instructions', ll. 740–52)

25

Pain and ignominy are often the human lot, and at times no response is possible other than sterile and fruitless mourning or the recognition that all joys, all hopes are transitory. Implicit in the laments for fallen England in *Upon Appleton House* and *Last Instructions*, as in those passages in *Paradise Lost*, x, where Adam mourns his own separation from the glory, happiness, and beauty he has known, is the conviction that the decrees of God are unalterable. To Marvell, as to Milton, wisdom begins with the acceptance of man's fallen state. "Tis pride that makes a Rebel': to inveigh against divine providence, Marvell says in a letter to Sir John Trott on the death of a son, is 'the over-weening of our selves and our own things' (*Poems and Letters*, ii, p. 312). One major lesson the Christian learns from experience is 'Humility': 'A Soul that knows not to presume / Is Heaven's and its own perfume' ('Resolved Soul', ll. 29–30). Only if we recognize our fallen condition and accept the limitations imposed by it, Marvell says, can we hope to transcend it.

Freedom then is possible, according to Marvell, only after we have come to learn that 'the world will not go the faster for our driving' (*Rehearsal Transpros'd*, i, 135). The recognition that we can never know 'where Heavens choice may light' (*First Anniversary*, l. 147), that men at all times labour in darkness, that even when we seek to serve God's cause our efforts are likely to end in utter defeat in a world in which injustice rules, need not lead to despair, but to a kind of exhilaration. Free from the distraction of false hopes, we can confront the truth openly, without recourse to comforting evasions:

> The Grave's a fine and private place,
> But none I think do there embrace.
>
> ('To his Coy Mistress', ll. 31–2)

'The poet's time' occurs when the cause of virtue appears most desperate, when outward fortune appears implacably hostile, when his weaker allies have fled in dismay. It is at that time, when the temptation is greatest to succumb to despair or to abase oneself at the altar of success, that the poet finds courage to endure in his recognition that virtue alone is free:

> Then is the Poets time, 'tis then he drawes,
> And single fights forsaken Vertues cause.
> He, when the wheel of Empire, whirleth back,
> And though the World's disjointed Axel crack,
> Sings still of ancient Rights and better Times,
> Seeks wretched good, arraigns successful Crimes.
>
> ('Tom May's Death', ll. 65–70)

Notes

1. JOHN MILTON, 'Of Education', *Complete Prose Works*, ed. D.M. Wolfe, *et al.* 8 vols (New Haven and London, 1953–82), II, pp. 366–7.
2. JOHN MILTON, *De Doctrina Christiana*, trans. John Carey, *ibid.*, VI, p. 326.
3. Cf. MILTON, *ibid.* 163–5; 182–3; *Paradise Lost*, III, ll. 111–25.
4. JOHN CREASER, 'Marvell's Effortless Superiority', *Essays in Criticism*, 20 (1970), p. 108.

2　Into the Vault*

Francis Barker

The essays from which Francis Barker's consideration of 'To his Coy Mistress' is drawn demonstrate how the seventeenth century witnessed 'a new set of connections between subject and discourse, subject and polity, and in doing so altered fundamentally the terms between which these mutually constitutive relations held.' Barker is interested in a political history of the body, which, engaging with the work of Michel Foucault, he perceives as closely linked to the rise of bourgeois order. He sees Marvell's poem as reflecting a transitional state: it demonstrates both the emerging clinical gaze of science and the Jacobean spectacle of cruelty which is a mark of a sovereign power enacting revenge. His piece well illustrates the desire of recent criticism to 'read against the grain' of previous literary categories – in this instance the modes associated with *carpe diem* or 'seize the moment', a persuasion to love common in Renaissance lyric verse – in order to register texts' involvements with complex cultural shifts.

If Rembrandt's painting *The Anatomy Lesson of Dr Tulp* is the site of a corporal struggle, so too, although with a different outcome, is that other great anatomy lesson of the period: Marvell's 'To his Coy Mistress'. Each designates a crucial parameter for the modern body, and just as the painting in one of its movements makes the body text, so also does the poem, even as it unmakes the body it textualizes.

Although the sharp pleasure of the poem corresponds to an effect of power in one of its more spectacular forms – the delight to be had from dismembering a woman's body – it is still widely read as the light and conventional lyric of the Renaissance libertine. There is no shortage of readings, permitted by the ineffable distance which has come

---

* Reprinted from Francis Barker, *The Tremulous Private Body: Essays on Subjection* (London and New York: Methuen, 1984), pp. 85–94.

to separate literature from all other discourses and all other instruments of domination and resistance, that seek to exhaust the meaning of the poem in the essentially sentimental remark that it summons up, once again, the ancient *carpe diem* motif, urging the beloved to amorous delight before the rush of time wastes love, youth and beauty alike. But this is a reading which stops short of registering what it is no longer so necessary not to see: that the poem is riddled by seventeenth-century discourse of the body. It is a truncation which has been, no doubt, the product of the hygienic attitude to the pleasures of the body of an age whose moral ideology was, officially at least, more consolidated than that of the poem's own historical time, a legacy of the very process of corporal transformation and reinscription in which the poem itself participates. Filtered through the post-Cartesian deployment of healthy discipline – and more locally through a certain propriety which can now be described in only the loosest of ways as 'Victorian', libertinage has come to signify aristocratic dalliance. But if so, then Marvell, who was not an aristocrat, was clearly not a libertine either: as de Sade reminds us, pleasure entails demanding effort. It is true, of course, that the poem devotes a third of its length, in that ornamented, richly surfaced verse which typifies so much Renaissance love poetry (although here it is taut and economical, its iconic quality as intellectual as it is sensual), to fabricating a luxuriant, semi-mythical world of courtly adoration among vast dimensions and slow temporalities. And this is the affective basis for the indulgent if mildly censorious reading to which the text is normally subjected. But the poem itself rejects that affect, for although the question of whether or not the idyll of burgeoning empires and sweet riches has yet begun to cloy in Marvell's hands remains moot, it is clearly a world that is not, but rather a poetic *topos*, condensed and lapidary, which the text quotes, with some triteness in the couplets, only for it to be swept at once aside. The more insistent temporality of what the poem encodes as the actual world, hastening on towards one consummation or another, soon breaks in on love's vegetative Golden Age and lays it to waste. For against the idyll and its affect, the poem is uncompromising in its sexual objectives, not to say its 'sexual politics': this is a poetry with operative purposes, designed to seduce. It has no romanticized disdain for tactics.

There might have been some comfort for the averted eye, or even for the kind of temperament which resists critical effects in literature, to read in the poem's transition from the gentle courtship of Love's fantasy empire to this new command of 'my Lust', with its vision of 'desarts' and 'ashes', a lament for a cultured and cultural fashion of loving. But there is no regret in the text. The poem cites a poetic ideology of courtship aestheticized and distantiates it, identifying on this side of the old kingdom a sexual urgency from which there is no respite, least of all a sublimatory one. Here, on this side of the nostalgic fantasy, the poem says, love is not sacramental, it does not offer to redeem the lovers from the world, nor is it – for them or in itself – transcendent. On the contrary the poem twists away in another affective direction altogether, seeking in a reality principle, not the old empire but the new republic. The text ends neither in a sentiment of languishing indolence nor in one of satiated lust (either of which the libertine is frequently said to enjoy) but on an emphasis which is decidedly more rigorous. Goods are to be got, ultimately, by effort, and pleasures (if they are to be had at all, which the poem's final gesture does not guarantee) must be *torn* from inhospitable circumstances by struggle and amid conflict. The internal *milieu* of the poem is eventually one of 'rough strife', which, if it is a sexual metaphor is also in the historical context a political one. As the poem tends towards the future it reaches after objectives which will have to be wrested from life and from time, from history itself. This is, as Christopher Hill argued some time ago, an anti-epicurean ethic, and one which could be well described as militant and 'puritan', in its combativeness and its commitment to labour, if not actually in its emphasis on urgent sex.

In order to excavate the exact mode of the – contested – pleasure and presence of the body of the beloved, the poem must be read against the grain of the love-lyric into which the corporal discourse is imbricated; to decipher beyond what the poem says *of* its themes of love, sex and virtue (and beyond the interpretative chatter engendered by them), the discursive operations, hidden only by a certain kind of obviousness, *in its saying* of them, a rigorous literalism, perhaps even a nominalism will have to be the essential heuristic tool. For the literal body is in fragments: it is inscribed in the letter of the text as an inventory of parts, each in turn selected, treated and set aside: 'Thine Eyes', 'thy Forehead', 'each Breast', 'every part', 'the rest'. Marvell's 'beloved' is distributed across the text in discrete pieces. The body is scattered and diverse, the sum of its parts, although the totalization is never made, is greater – in textual extensiveness and sexual charge – than the whole: for it has no integrity, but merely a principle of the disconnectedness of its parts which belongs wholly to the discourse that articulates it according to a serial or spatial dispersal. It is appropriated and uttered within a syntax more reminiscent of taxonomy than of the expectations of love poetry. Equally distant from amorous lyricism, what have been called the '*imagos* of the fragmented body' are identified by Lacan as the classic signs of what the discourse of psychoanalysis calls aggressivity: the torn flesh and the ruptured, separated organs, the shattered frame and the severed limbs insist in the speech, the fantasy and the dreams of the subject as the marks of an unrelieved violence as an inherent condition of its very subjectivity. These *imagos* haunt too the cultural text – in Lacan's example, the work of Bosch, where they are recomposed into new, fantastic, monstrous forms, and for us the spectacular cruelties of the Jacobean stage, and here, with a slightly different inflection, this 'love' poem. At this, other, level 'To his Coy Mistress' is the bearer of that discursive aggression which dissects the body it has made word; and doubly so because, like Rembrandt's *Anatomy Lesson*, the dynamics of its body are, historically speaking, complex, its status contested within the text. For Marvell's poem has not yet laid the spectacular Jacobean *imagos* to rest, although it is also evidence of the historical impetus towards allotting the body to a final obscurity. The struggle can be read in the modulation of the body through the text. The initial, and for the major part of the poem essential, condition of the body is still one of visibility. The text exhibits, and even in its brutal way – within the economy of violence the *imago* of the fragmented body discloses within the conventional lyricism – celebrates the body of the beloved in public view. The body is still recalcitrantly and defiantly on display, even if in a radically analysed form. It is still there to be seen, and is acknowledged openly as the object and site of desire. But in tune with an entire developing perception of the dangerous passionateness of the pre-disciplinary flesh, the text rounds on this first condition of the body of the woman, and having first torn it to pieces, not satisfied even by this act of violation, seeks to quell the restless anger of its own desire by consigning it to the darkness and silence of the 'marble Vault'. To still in death the Other of its own frustration.

The movement is, once more, from the spectacular corporeality of the Jacobean plenum to the corporeal extinction which can be found in Pepys, and which forms one moment of the modern body. But precisely because this is a transitional text, power over the body has not yet been wholly assimilated into its modern forms, the mode of sovereignty sought by *The Anatomy Lesson* in its depiction of the calm science of the bourgeois order. If Marvell's dismemberment owes something to the measured precisionism of the judicial torturer, as does Tulp's, nor have the incisions yet become wholly clinical. So that as that last cut which 'should show your Heart' offers to the enquiring gaze of the surgeons gathered round the table the chief of the vital organs, so it also displays that bloody pumping heart which was so often held aloft to one audience or another gathered at the foot of the public scaffold, dramatic or penal. If the progress of this fractured body through the text has science in it, if this text *is* a discursive surgery, the operation isn't only carried out in the name of a detached and scientific curiosity but belongs also to both of those other seventeenth-century theatres of cruelty. As we watch the cure become an autopsy, we are also spectators where the lover's caress turns into an act of Jacobean slaughter and where the king's wrath issues in corporal revenge. The discovery of the bleeding heart is the last act of both the tragedy of the blood and the terrible price of treason.

But if the text contests within itself the status of this body, its final tendency is towards the corporal situation of the modern body in its absent moment. It conceives for the vivid body a grave destination beyond sexuality and publicity. It cannot yet figure, as the Rembrandtian instance begins to, a new set of social and discursive relations which will reinscribe in healthy presence the new flesh, but must reduce the body utterly to a neutral dust: the least condition of the body, a sexlessness paradoxically counterpointed in the conceit of necrophiliac exploration, by the feeble sexuality of the worms, of death's sterile chastity. The devastating punishment of the woman's 'coyness' which, even as it woos her, the text exacts in the very *form* of its courtship, decodes into the order of spectacular blood revenge, but the final gesture of the text's rendering of the body is towards another regime. It is to deliver the body into permanent incarceration in 'a fine and *private* place'. We are beyond the pleasure principle.

It will perhaps be labouring the obvious – although in a historical moment marked by such epistemic effort issuing on to so much mystificatory percipience, the literal and the obvious begin to require the most careful excavation – to suggest that whereas the dominant tendency of *The Anatomy Lesson* is towards the present aspect of the modern body, the reason that Marvell's lyric so vigorously ascertains the absent moment, its utter expurgation, is because of the gender as well as the sex of the body distributed across its text. Certainly it is *as body* that the woman is present to the poem, in the form, of course, of that absence. For if a troubled, censored, sexed discourse is the characteristic of modern subjectivity, the woman, on the other hand, is without discourse. She does not speak, not even with an implied speech suggested by momentary pauses for response, or other hesitations, in the inexorable male voice which utters the poem. In a place which the poem addresses and labels 'Mistress', 'Lady' – woman – there is silence. The poem reticulates within itself and at its threshold a literary structure of speech and silence, an apparently full male discourse and an empty place, which it is necessary to encounter certainly as a power relation, and perhaps even the site of a political engagement.

When the voice designates the woman's silence as 'Coy' it is essentially as an incorporative gesture that it does so, the utterance gathering the woman into imputed complicity with its own discourse of love. There is a certain tantalized fascination, complementary to the aggressive fetishization of the parts of the body, with the reluctance of the woman who is cast at first as guiltless: at least in the seductions of the fantasy empire, 'This coyness Lady were no crime'. But there is also something minatory, a threat of the potential violence – underpinned by the literal violence of the *imago* – latent in this apparently gentle appellation of the woman's passive resistance. Behind the initial banter of the lover's discourse and its ingenious persuasiveness is the implacable rattle of

'Times winged Charriot hurrying near', in the path of which what the male *persona* soon perceives in the woman's 'coy' reluctance as an artful refusal of sexuality comes to look more like a stubborn and destructive wilfulness, and her silence the sullen denial of an encratic speech not of persuasion but command. After all, Time is bearing down, and with it the entire weight and fury of the patriarchal tradition which, in the real republic, however much its ideology may mark out chastity as a proper register of femininity, none the less exists to secure the subordination of women. There is here a doubled structure of coercion operating behind the back of an apparent freedom, a strategy characteristic not only of the modern regime of gender but of the normal functioning of bourgeois domination as a whole. That the male voice must persuade and cajole rather than simply compel implies a right of refusal, but behind this indulgent male tolerance is the rage of a Pepys against the irrationality and delinquence of women; and here, in Marvell's punitive and finally morbid dissection, the Law offers to extract a terrible price for the woman's transgression of its desire.

Conceivably only another ruse of that same law would make us try to sustain an anti-reading of the poem, and thus to attempt to turn it against its own sexual fixing. But an analytic distinction can be forged between the male utterance of the poem and the text 'itself' (although they are empirically coterminous), constructing the text as radically distantiatory of the poem, and allowing us to apprehend, in spite of and at odds with itself, the poem's strategic and dominatory functions at work. The text as underside of the poem figures, in the woman's silent resistance, a refusal to enter into dialogue with the male voice and thus a declination of interpellation by its terms-setting, power-laden utterance; a resistance which is quiet here because to respond is already to be ensnared, but which must be held instead as marking textually a mute limit of the penetrative capacity of the male voice; and silent because it must yet find its own proper discourse and fight out its essential campaigns elsewhere, on another terrain: it is the silence of Freud's Dora, who walked out. From this perspective, reading the poem from the side of what it is not, from a place which the poem determinately cannot see if what it does give speech to is to be said at all, the male voice can be understood as crying vaingloriously and even somewhat pathetically into a silence it doesn't notice. No actual 'woman' is listening, or, if listening, only negligently and with scorn. Unknown to itself, although marked in the text, the poem encounters an autonomy (albeit from the side of the poem a 'passive' one) of which it cannot conceive and certainly cannot give to discourse.

The gendered voice that *is*, however, given to subjectivity revolves alone, and completely within the speaking of its own 'dialectic'. But there it constructs not only the woman's spoken absence but also, *sotto voce*,

the only mode of her speechless presence it will admit. For however
the silence which occupies the woman's place is read, it can never signify
for the poem the existence of the human subject which is to be the key
organizing figure of bourgeois culture, of its meanings and its texts. The
woman is an objectified body at which speech is aimed, and which the
poem organizes for the historical purposes at work here, but whose being
is, so to speak, sub-discursive: dumb, reduced, corporeal matter. It is
against this object-body that, even then, the violence of the poem is
unleashed. But because of the historical ambivalence of the body in this
compromised text, the gendered reduction cannot be total: enough
residual difference stemming from the older order – and illustrating,
methodologically, the *only* present value of the past: parallax – remains
in its visibility to prevent this gesture being wholly victorious. The poem
is after all a call for the consummation of the pleasures of the body:
sex is its publicly avowed objective even if violence is its formal desire.
The poem cannot tolerate the dangerous excess of the body it traduces,
but just as so many Jacobean texts disintegrate under the twin drive
to represent and destroy women, so this poem cannot wholly banish
it either, and assign its dangers utterly to confinement. That, at least,
remains minatory. Instead, as we have noted, the poem arcs away
towards an *ideological* result which, while it has traces of the body in
it – 'thy skin', through which, in textual mockery of the subjectivity
denied the woman systematically by everything that has preceded it,
'thy willing Soul' sweats, at 'every pore' – none the less acts as an
evasive bypassing of the discursive conflict which is thus historically
– although not poetically – left in suspense; and effects, with a shift of
grammatical number, a metaphysical fusion of the lover and the beloved,
a mysterious solidarity which can then issue triumphalistically on to the
ethical militancy of the last lines.

The success of the poem is in never having to face the text in history,
so that beginning in the address of more or less polite courtship, it can
end in protestant activism. It may turn out that the lover is the puritan's
familiar. If so, a thing they will have in common is that each is variously
committed, in a mirror-relation suited to the absence–presence thematics
of an unhistorical culture, to a campaign for the measure of the body and
its passions.

3 Marvell's Nymph and the Echo of Voice*

JONATHAN GOLDBERG

Jonathan Goldberg is one of the few critics who has championed deconstructive practices in examining Renaissance texts. Here, adopting Derrida's consideration of language as a signifier which refuses to be circumscribed by its ostensible signified, Goldberg considers how Marvell's lyric 'A Nymph complaining for the death of her Faun' deals with loss and creativity. Part of deconstruction's insistence on the instability of language, that it is always something in addition to the non-linguistic object it represents, has been for idealistic ends. Language's refusal to be contained by material reality, by dominant ideologies, or even by formal grammatical rules is celebrated as the means by which a creative dynamic is enabled, through which the new may be released. Deconstruction proposes that without linguistic instability we would be doomed to constant repetition of what already exists. In a *tour de force* of analysis which ranges across issues of genre, allegory, myth (that of Echo and Narcissus from Ovid) and psychoanalysis (notably Lacan's understanding of Freud), Goldberg shows how the poetic voice becomes the object of Marvell's poem. Endlessly repeating a loss in verse, the poetic voice disables itself from actually confronting this loss or of possessing anything – this linguistic attempt is perceived as deceitful. Yet, as Goldberg claims, this engagement with repetition becomes the means by which Marvell allows us to hear the echo of his own voice, enabling creative assertion. In most respects Goldberg's essay counters the impetus behind recent interpretations of Marvell in its lack of concern with locating the text in history. Indeed, its assertion that the poem 'is only, and entirely self-referential, "about itself"' almost recalls the formalism of New Criticism. But in the essay's opening question, 'What is to be made of loss?', Goldberg immediately raises issues not simply about Marvell's poem

---

* Reprinted from JONATHAN GOLDBERG, *Voice Terminal Echo: Postmodernism and English Renaissance Texts* (London and New York: Methuen 1986), pp. 14–32.

but about the processes by which the self (and its loss) may be spoken: the relation between signifier and signified which is at the heart of deconstruction.

What is to be made of loss? Perhaps this is every poet's question; certainly it is Andrew Marvell's. Whether considering politics, amatory experience, or the way that the mind works, Marvell joins creative energy to annihilative loss. His poems are replete with emblematic moments of creative annihilation: Cromwell and the severed head; Appleton House and the ruined abbey; the mower and his scythe. If every creative act in Marvell entails 'annihilating all that's made', we are probably safe in assuming that these emblematic moments are also deeply self-referential images for poetic activity, that it is not only the lover in 'To his Coy Mistress' who hears his 'ecchoing Song' in a vaulted burial chamber, not to his ears alone that soundings come as from across an abyss. In no text can the relationship of poetry to such an emblematic moment be more clearly demonstrated than in 'The Nymph complaining for the death of her Faun'. It is a poem whose plot entirely comprises that moment of creative annihilation and, as will be suggested in the pages that follow, it is a text that offers Marvell's most elaborated version of the meaning of that moment for his poetry and for himself as poet. The poem has long baffled criticism; in the interpretation offered here, an explanation for the difficulty of the poem may be found. The poem defies referentiality. It is only, and entirely, self-referential, 'about' itself, about how the text comes to be, how it relates to antecedent texts, what it represents in the world.

Here I need to acknowledge my debt to the brilliant introductory pages in Geoffrey Hartman's essay on 'The Nymph complaining'.[1] Like him, I wish to respect the terms of the poem, to regard the nymph as a nymph, 'a mythic being in a privileged relation to the wood-world of the poem, the world of fawns and nature' (p. 175), and yet to see 'a conspiracy between nymph and poet' (p. 176). And his understanding of the poem as 'an apotheosis of the diminutive powers of poetry' (p. 179) informs my own. I want to extend the implication of his provocative remarks, to answer his question, why allegorize, in the terms he suggests, by showing that the text is about its own deeply problematized voice, a voice called the nymph's only in the title of the poem. It is not precisely a human voice that we hear in the poem, nor is it a human object lamented in this elegiac occasion for speech. These transformations define the annihilative ground for the voice in the poem. That voice traverses, I will suggest, four modes of organizing speech: antithesis (ll. 1–24), repetition (ll. 25–34), allegory (ll. 55–92), and epigraph (ll. 93–122). Disjunctively, four modes that epitomize the major Renaissance genres available for handling loss – sonnet, lyric stanza, Spenserian epic, and epigram – are reviewed and reduced, and the possibility of reassembling a 'vision of lost and original unity' (p. 191), which Hartman sees as Marvell's aim, is finally relinquished.

Limitation upon limitation; a reduced speaker, on the margins of human speech, addresses the question of loss in a language marked by the constriction of all the modes of discourse available. Yet, all is not lost. In the excessive wake of these shrunken possibilities, Marvell allows us to hear the echo of voice that is his own.

Antithesis: 'There is not such another'

Who is speaking here, in the opening twenty-four lines of the poem? A voice, inconsolable, brought up short from an idyllic union, made to comprehend an event excluded from all prior modes of knowledge, all previous experience; a voice that names a bond with a stricken fawn and recoils from his irremediable wound. Yet, is this the entire content of this voice? Is this all it says? And how does it speak about this event? The voice here can see only one way to say what it has lost, can only frame discourse in the stark antitheses of shattered continuity, by noting an entrance hitherto unknown and unprepared for.

> The wanton Troopers riding by
> Have shot my Faun and it will dye.

> (ll. 1–2)

Yet, we know, reading on, that there has been a preparation, that the fawn's death is not the first loss that it initially appears to be.

Something is not being said.

Not only is the past suppressed as this voice starts speaking, not only is the history of the figures involved implicitly denied; this voice speaks as if it were discovering loss for the first time, but it speaks in terms that have been provided for it, that come before it. There is not only a story before this story, the story of Sylvio which the text reserves to tell after, there is a language before this entrance into language, the language of (Petrarchan) antithesis. Or, more starkly, there is before this voice speaks, language (in its binary structure) *as* antithesis. The voice here summons up antitheses, trying to control the situation of loss: wanton/innocent; good/ill; forget/register; justice/guilt; life/death. But the situation of loss is already, beforehand, written in antitheses: losing and having are an indivisible pair. The voice speaking here is caught in a priority that undoes the myth of priority that it presents. The voice says, here is first loss; but it says too, here is second loss, and not only by suppressing the story of Sylvio. It says it by entering language. The secondary of speech signifies that it is the falsity of the notion of first speech that is being seen through – revealed and enabling utterance – the falsity, then, that the poet knows when he speaks. 'It appears, strange as it may seem, that "signifier of the signifier" no longer defines accidental doubling and fallen secondary.'[2] Rather, as Derrida's sentence suggests, it defines an origin robbed of priority, robbed of its single status: original secondary.

Who speaks here? She is called a nymph, a creature both natural and divine, and she embodies the notion of divine presence in nature. Of what loss does she speak? Of a fawn, the embodiment of animality on the verge of humanity (fawn/faun). They are two marginal figures, two figures of marginality, representing encroachments and extensions, and yet exclusions from some central norm, the category of the merely natural, or the entirely human. Into this categorical void, the 'wanton Troopers' come. Excluded from and antithetical to the pastoral idyll of nymph and fawn, they have no place – no place, that is, except the one that the categories of more and less than human have made for them. They are the human, a necessary middle. The schema of antithesis that would deny them a place creates their place.

Nymph and fawn define one pair of antitheses; each of them is related (through further antitheses) to the troopers. The fawn's relationship to the troopers is simultaneously glancing and absolute, casual (they are simply 'passing by') and causal ('and it will dye' (l. 2)). Totality of union has been replaced with its opposite, total loss and abandonment; the idyllic union of fawn and nymph replaced by the shattering union of fawn and troopers. And for this disruption of pastoral pathos – a situation in which thoughts produce acts, in which union is intimate and total, in which categories are crossed and joined (a relationship signalled in the affective 'thee' (l. 4), the proprietary 'my' (l. 2), and in the absolute knowledge that stands behind 'thou neer didst alive/Them any harm' (ll. 4–5)) – for this disruption, explanation founders. All that remains is a voice caught in total opposition, irremediable, inexplicable antithesis. Antithesis, then, *as* explanation.

Antithetical oppositions define the multiple relations of fawn, nymph, and troopers. If not a causal principle of explanation, it nonetheless carries its own inevitability, one traced in an opening series of negations: 'un-', 'cannot', 'neer', 'nor', 'never', 'nor . . . nor':

> Ungentle men! They cannot thrive
> To kill thee. Thou neer didst alive
> Them any harm: alas nor cou'd
> Thy death yet do them any good.
> I'me sure I never wisht them ill;
> Nor do I for all this; nor will.

(ll. 3–8)

The lack of explanation, the generation of exclusionary negations, carries the force of necessity, the necessity of antithesis. Thus exclusionary negation, which barred the troopers from the pastoral idyll, defines their place: it is a discursive site. It is where the voice speaks in this opening section of the poem. The entrance into speech establishes and naturalizes antitheses; antitheses multiply within antitheses (fawn and nymph vs. fawn and troopers; fawn vs. troopers; nymph vs. troopers). What emerges from these multiple antitheses, as boundaries blur and centers shift, are identifications. Echo enters.

If the troopers are a necessary middle that embodies the antithetical identification of exclusion and inclusion, they go beyond this center to occupy an even more startling place, a more unsettling center. Excessive, 'wanton', they are beyond the category of the human, and in much the same way as the nymph and fawn are. The troopers have a central place in the idyll as 'ungentle men', as men, that is, who are not men but animalistic. The prefix 'un-' that triggers the sequence of negations negates the category that should include the troopers, the human race (*gens*), and creates as central a category of excess. The center is excessive by being a double center, affirming and denying the category of the human. Moreover, as transgressors of the boundary of the pastoral idyll, the troopers trespass those exclusionary limits in precisely the antithetical form of the one upon whom they have encroached, the fawn. Antithesis approaches identification. The idyll had involved, in the figures of fawn and nymph, the exclusion of the human; their marginality, at once excessive and privative, put antithesis at the center. As 'ungentle', the troopers occupy the fawn's position. That double center of fawn and troopers implies yet another antithesis to complete the pattern – and to undo the idyll. For if the idyll represented the antithetical union of fawn and nymph, the replacement of the fawn by the troopers might imply as well the antithetical opposition of fawn and nymph, the nymph now joined to the troopers.

Within the idyll, one sign of this is the alternate naming of the fawn in terms both of identification and opposition, inclusion and exclusion, excess and privation. The fawn is named 'thee' (a human designation) and 'it' (as an animal). Telling the story of the idyll, the voice speaks within the wound inflicted by the opposing, antithetical, 'ungentle' troopers; the account is generated from this principle of nomination, the wound gives the voice words. The fawn, in short, cannot be named without the troopers. The wound is the center, the place of meeting, the place of echo and voice. The empty space between categories is the exclusion necessary for union with the fawn. Pastoral pathos is founded, one might argue, on the wound of privation. This line of thought suggests the unthinkable, a complicity between the nymph and troopers, and not only in the alternate naming of the fawn. It is there in 'I'me sure I never wisht them ill' (l. 7); the troopers have been in mind before their violation of the idyll. The totalization of the idyll cannot exclude what it claims to exclude. Hence, in a final exclusionary gesture, the nymph prays *for* the troopers:

> But, if my simple Pray'rs may yet
> Prevail with Heaven to forget
> Thy murder, I will Joyn my Tears
> Rather then fail.

(ll. 9–12)

The prayer to forget is the hope of re-membering the fawn, of reconstituting the fawn through forgiveness, through the admission of destruction in the pastoral union. The voice in prayer re-enacts the casually murderous entrance of the troopers into the poem – pays the price of entering into language.

Into what language? As already suggested, it is an old story renewed here, the story of the lover who laments an absent or a denying or a denied beloved, in one way or another a beloved who is removed – improbably chaste, impossibly married, or thoroughly wanton. Or dead. Eros drives the lover to want what cannot be had. The lover cannot comprehend what he wants; if he does, he sees that he wants to want, sees, that is, that Eros and the beloved are complicitous in his frustrating desire. Wyatt sounds this note first in the English Renaissance: 'She that me lerneth to love and suffre', domesticating the Petrarchan tropes as traps, the prison of antitheses: I want/I love; I burn/I freeze; I am sick/I am well; I am wounded/I am whole. What is a sonnet if not a momentary monument built on denial and refusal, on antitheses that cannot be overcome, perhaps self-contained and isolated as a unit, yet continually replicating unfulfilled desire. The 'pretty roomes' of the sonnet, as Donne saw, are sepulchral. The form memorializes loss. Its wit, the epigrammatic twist by which it arrives at closure, more often than not involves the recognition that antithetical negations constitute the speaker's situation, locate the lover's voice.

The story in brief: the broken heart, language in the place of the lost object.

This voice has been lodged in the annihilative creativity of antithetical identification, generated by negations. Now it turns to a final antithesis and seeks a restorative reversal in the law of '*Deodands*':

> Ev'n Beasts must be with justice slain;
> Else Men are made their *Deodands*.

(ll. 16–17)

Deodands refer to animals which were sacrificed to the church or to the state for causing the death of men. The word names a law that would, if

it were reversible, compensate for loss in a principle of return. It
might fill the void. The learned word throws the voice into question.
Can it encompass this word and with it effect the antithetical reversal
of 'ungentle', crossing the human/animal boundary in the opposite
direction? No; all that will stand in the place of loss – in the void – is
the word itself, it alone the substitute for the lost object. The falsity of the
human system of justice and valuation, in the law of *deodands*, lies in the
notion of compensation, in the very idea that something can stand in
place of something else and thereby redeem what has been lost, either
as a replacement or as a sacrifice. Like all lovers, this voice can only say,
my heart is wounded and can find absolute closure only in accepting that
'there is not such another' (l. 23).

The voice plays across the languages that enter it, the legalism of
deodands, the petrarchanism of the wounded heart. Once again, then, it
is located in antithesis; and once more it gestures towards identification.
A final identification: union in blood:

> Though they should wash their guilty hands
> In this warm life-blood, which doth part
> From thine, and wound me to the Heart,
> Yet could they not be clean: their Stain
> Is dy'd in such a Purple Grain.

(ll. 18–22)

All the participants meet in blood as it parts, wounds, and stains.
Nymph, fawn, and troopers – all are constituted, made, placed, through
this encompassing loss, joined in the parting, sustained in the antitheses.
No law can move them into each other's place, no literalistic substitution
is possible precisely because in their irremediable relationships to each
other, they define the structure of loss and of frustrated desire. In desire
antitheses meet, never to be overcome. The final words of the first section
of the poem isolate the participants in the situation, trap them forever in
their positions: irredeemable troopers, irrecoverable fawn, inconsolable
nymph. These are their positions in the text; they are literary positions,
tropes. Each one an occupant of the wound, no one can compensate for
it. No one, that is, can constitute the presence of being-for-oneself that
would obliterate the void that constitutes identity and identification.

The fawn is the nexus of all antithetical relations, the place where
the nymph's desire and the 'wanton Troopers'' bullets meet. The fawn
names a site of loss. But the name also bears, in its etymology, a further
complication. *Fawn* derives from *foetus*, offspring. The fawn is the created
word, the object made in loss. Its createdness – its secondary as
embodied antithesis (human/animal) and as the locus of annihilation
and creation – is its origin. 'There is not such another': as a beginning
situation (as the beginning of the voice of this text), the fawn is the place

41

of antithesis and negation. A beginning that is not. The fawn is a beginning, then, of an order of words that arises in separation and ends in the heart's privation, that begins in the casual encounter with the 'wanton Troopers' and ends when discourse has apparently exhausted the possibilities of standing in the place of loss: 'There is not such another in/The World, to offer for their Sin' (ll. 23–24). This plot of beginning and ending is folded in the antitheses that shape the voice in the opening section of the poem. What is narrated is a story of loss from the beginning.

Whose voice is this? Where is this voice? In the situation of a poet, voice inside of voice, located and dislocated in the generation of antitheses, in the offspring that precedes the voice and is itself preceded. This is the situation of voice in this text – a hall of mirrors reflecting back to what comes before the possibility of having a voice. Voice in the text standing for the poet. Standing disowned.

Before this poem began, the voice says, there was silence. A lie. Within the timescheme of the poem there is a before that comes after. Outside the text (is there an outside the text?), there are the texts that come before this one, the text we have called the sonnet, enshrining centuries of lovers in their antithetical complaints, lovers lamenting losing as having, having their words for loss instead of the beloved. Within this text, the word for loss is the (always already, from the beginning) lost object, the fawn. The fawn is what the voice made, made into speech. The fawn is, thus, what made the voice. A word, a pun, the original word that is two, animal and human, fawn and faun. The word that does violence. The h[e]art.

Repetition: 'solitary time'

Disjunction, and the voice begins again, from the beginning. Has it heard itself? Now it hears, it says; it hears an echo. Here is the story, it says, I will tell it exactly as it happened; without duplicity, I will tell the story of duplicity.

> Unconstant *Sylvio*, when yet
> I had not found him counterfeit,
> One morning (I remember well)
> Ty'd in this silver Chain and Bell,
> Gave it to me: nay and I know
> What he said then; I'me sure I do.

(ll. 25–30)

The voice insists, it says, that these are the words; insisting, it says it again. Hear that voice, it repeats, that is the voice of duplicity, punster

Sylvio, heartbreaker, bestower of the fawn, giver of language. Hear him,
it says; he speaks double; I hear that, but I speak single. Say it again.
Hear me, the voice insists . . . 'I remember well . . . I'me sure I do.' I do
not speak like that. Like him. That is not my voice. I admit echo, the
voice says: call it Sylvio, not me.

> Said He, look how your Huntsman here
> Hath taught a Faun to hunt his *Dear*.

(ll. 31–32)

I say, Sylvio 'Left me his Faun, but took his Heart' (l. 36). I repeat, I do
not echo. I repeat.

Who is Sylvio, what is he? Counterfeit, 'when yet/I had not found
him counterfeit' (ll. 25–26), a first instance of prior duplicity, the 'wanton
Troopers' again, at first – 'unconstant' (l. 25) echoes 'ungentle' (l. 3).
Sylvio is the original violator of the pastoral idyll; he represents first loss.
And more. What's in a name? Translate Sylvio: woodborn huntsman,
a name already written in Ovid, in Spenser, a declension of *silva*, tree;
Silvae, an anthology of poems. Virgil's Silvia, the girl whose pet Ascanius
kills, counterfeited, a transformation already written when Guarini
turned Tasso's chaste Silvia into his Silvio.

'Unconstant *Sylvio*' (l. 25), original pastoral duplicity, the tree become
text, cross-category in and beyond nature. 'Unconstant *Sylvio*': so the
voice begins again. Telling for the second time the beginning story,
and immediately language is double, duplicitous, and doubled again,
in Sylvio's gift of the fawn/h[e]art/deer/dear. Who is Sylvio? Who, if
not the original provider of the pastoral idyll, bestower of the fawn as
mediating gift, giver of the word: 'his Gifts might be/Perhaps as false or
more than he' (ll. 49–50). He provides the gift as go-between, the broken
h[e]art of Sylvio and the nymph. At first the fawn is (once again) the
vehicle of relationship, where the puns meet: 'look how your Huntsman
here/Hath taught a Faun to hunt his *Dear*' (ll. 31–32). Here, then, is the
etiology of the word in the first story which we are only hearing now
(as the repetition of the story heard first, the story of how the h[e]art
came to be wounded), etiology as explanation now: the wound
inevitable, already, at first. In the beginning was the word – as repetition,
substitution, doubling.

And the voice now locates the pastoral idyll ('mine idle Life' (l. 40)) not
as original, but as substitution, not as priority, but as a second instance.
Twice over: by telling this beginning second, and within the story it tells.

> Thenceforth I set my self to play
> My solitary time away,
> With this: and very well content,
> Could so mine idle Life have spent.

(ll. 37–40)

The voice that heard the counterfeit echo in Sylvio now echoes itself. Does it hear itself, hear that it counterfeits the exchange of words and gift with Sylvio when it re-counts the pastoral idyll, and recasts it as a game? Can it hear that it does with the fawn what Sylvio taught, manipulating the word as a projection of the heart?

Hear these echoes: the fawn is 'light/Of foot, and heart' (ll. 41–42). 'Light' and therefore 'unconstant'? 'It seem'd to bless/Its self in me' (ll. 43–44). Merely *seemed*, a counterfeit? Bless . . . wound? Who is playing with whom? ('And did invite,/Me to its game' (ll. 42–43)). The hart the hunter? Playing time away, spending life, playing for keeps, or to lose? What is the economy of this game? How many times can the heart be broken?

The voice answers, once, in this 'solitary time' (l. 38). 'O I cannot be/Unkind t'a Beast that loveth me' (ll. 45–46). The voice affirms the 'solitary time' and the singularity of what was once, by repeating. 'Unkind' the echo of 'ungentle', 'unconstant'. Trying to undo repetition (Sylvio's gift), to deny denial ('*Sylvio* soon had me beguil'd' (l. 33)) and to locate a time without loss, the voice repeats itself, loses itself in the voice of echo it admits it hears (in another, not in itself). Beguiled itself, it offers the empty idyll as content. Attempting to escape duplicity, the voice is inscribed in duplicity. The pastoral idyll is a dream of priority shaded by secondarity. It comes second, after loss. It reinscribes loss. It cannot avoid repetition.

For the voice establishes its singularity and purity, its inviolateness, by being violated. It repeats insistently: 'I remember well . . . I know/What he said . . . I'me sure I do./Said He. . . .' Doubletalk, the language of Sylvio. Insisting on its innocence, the voice echoes the duplicitous voice it would disown; its 'own' voice a declension of the words of Sylvio. *He* says, 'Hath taught a Faun to hunt his *Dear*' (l. 32). *I* say, 'Left me his Faun, but took his Heart' (l. 36).

The story of the idyll is a repetitious refrain. 'So short a time' (l. 52) recalls 'one morning' (l. 27). 'I am sure' (l. 51) echoes 'I'me sure' (l. 30). 'Espie' (l. 52) glances at Sylvio's 'look' (l. 31). Repetition echoes and suspends identification; it allows the voice to go on. Commenting on 'the declaration of love (a banal, *already written* sequence, if ever there was one)', Roland Barthes characterizes repetition as 'very precisely, the fact that there is no reason to stop.'[3] The voice repeats its declaration, and denies it does so. Denial is inscribed in the repetition, spacing it, saving it from the collapse into tautology. But not, therefore, undoing repetition, not, thereby, cutting off the idyll from the duplicities of Sylvio. The 'solitary time' is inscribed within the circle of repetitions, inscribed as repetition. The space of the disjunction can be seen in the movement from 'I know' (l. 29) to 'I do not know' (l. 47):

> I know
> What he said then; I'me sure I do.

> I do not know
> Whether it too might have done so
> As *Sylvio* did.
>
> (ll. 29–30, 47–49)

The voice that knows Sylvio's echo does not know its own, does not know what it tells in its idyllic recounting. Attempting to make the idyll immune against the incursions of repetition (the voice of Sylvio), it affirms the difference only by repeating. Difference is thereby deferred in repetition. Or, in brief, the declaration:

> Thy Love was far more better then
> The love of false and cruel men.
>
> (ll. 53–54)

Whose love (loving the fawn, loving men, the fawn's loving, Sylvio's)? 'Thy Love' echoes 'the love'.

What is this 'play' of echoing voices, of acknowledged and unacknowledged repetition if not the stanzaic mode of lyric poetry? For example: the sonnet sequence, piling sonnet upon sonnet so that they become stanzas in a long poem, a hundred new positions of denial and frustration re-occupying the single stance until, perhaps, frustration can be acclimatized, until the disowned voice becomes fully naturalized in the inexorableness of repetition. Or, to take another example, it is the voice of Sidney's Astrophil in song, singing Stella's words, 'No, no, no, no, my Deare, let be,' singing, that is, the beloved's words so that they become his, denying himself doubly by denying denial and thus, in echo, finding a way out of frustration, making a final exit. Let be: cease and continue. Or, the refrain in Wyatt's lute song, ending itself in the echo of the beloved's refusal: 'I have done.' The lyric stanza, another echo chamber, founded in repetition and the continual reshuffling and repositioning of words, so that the lover takes as his own the words that disown him; the lover has voice in other words. To end each stanza by echoing again – in the refrain of repetition – is also to begin again. Refrain: repeat and be stopped. That is the idyll.

The voice here has begun again by telling second the story of what came first, and by installing in the center of this story of duplicity the idyll of 'solitary time'. The center, however, is not immune to what circles around it. The fawn/h[e]art/dear/deer is at the center: repetition circles through that center, penetrates the idyll, violates its solitary state. Knowing repetition, the voice attempts to undo repetition. And repeats. So, the poet of refrain stops repeating by repeating, finally playing out all the positions of the word, all the meanings it might have. Or so it seems. Is the word exhausted, does the voice arrive at a terminal, in the refrain? Or, rather, is not the refrain inevitably endless? 'When thou hast done, thou hast not done. . . .'

What voice is here? The voice that hears double and repeats those doubling words, the voice that hears its double words as a solitary tale. One voice, or two? Sylvio, who gave this voice words when he gave the h[e]art, gave words instead of his heart *and* gave his heart in the h[e]art; and so giving, wounded his dear. To make this story solitary and univocal, the voice that speaks it echoes the voice of Sylvio. Seeking its own, speaking itself, the voice finds echo.

What voice? One or two?

If Echo, then Narcissus.

Allegory: 'to fill:/ . . . to fold'

Let me tell you a story.

Once there was a nymph who could not speak herself. Denied her own voice, she could only speak when another did, and then could only repeat the words she heard.

And she fell in love with someone who could not know himself.

When he spoke, she spoke. 'Is anyone here?' he said; 'Here,' she said; he thought it was his voice he heard, but when he saw her, and saw he was deceived, he fled, until he found a form he could love, a mirror of perfection, on which he fed his eyes (he couldn't hear the words he saw the image say), until, replete and empty ('Plenty makes me poor,' he cried), he died, and with him the image died as well.

And she, then, lost her form, and became a stone, a hollow.

Her name, Echo; his, Narcissus.[4]

Deep within itself, denying time, denying history, denying echo, the voice says: let me tell you a story, about the garden, my garden, without Sylvio, without the troopers. This is my story, the whole story, full, replete. Do not expect to understand. I hear my voice, but you cannot. I know my story, but you cannot.

> I have a Garden of my own,
> But so with Roses over grown,
> And Lillies, that you would it guess
> To be a little Wilderness.

(ll. 71–74)

Voice of denial. Voice of pleasure. Voice of death.

Disjunction. Once again, a new section of the text (ll. 55–92) announces itself with a 'first': 'With sweetest milk, and sugar, first/I it at mine own fingers nurst' (ll. 55–56). The voice begins again, back in the garden again, as if that framed moment of solitude were not circled round in sylvan duplicities. But, before, it had been enclosed in the eddying circles of repetition, in the voice of echo. Now, the story is to be told as a story, a sequence, one thing after another. But not the whole story, just the story of the idyll in the garden, filling 'solitary time' to meet the requirements of 'first' and last.

What voice is this? One that would preserve itself – have its *own* – in that prior time, identifying itself as itself only in the garden with the fawn. Denying the whole story, it makes a part whole; denying the repetitions in the whole story (to tell that, it had not narrated a story, but had spoken as if repeating a refrain), the voice returns to the garden to elaborate the game that raises the question again, who is playing with whom? What can one's own be? The game is hide and seek: "Twould stay, and run again, and stay' (l. 68), a familiar game – of repetition, denial and negation – immortalized by Freud ('*Fort! Da!*') since it holds out the possibility of a beyond . . . beyond the pleasure principle.[5] The voice preserves itself by entering into the game. Playing with the object it becomes the object with which it plays. To preserve itself, voice objectifies itself in its identification with the object of play. The game is one of substitution, making a replacement object serve when the real object is gone – and becoming that object, having *it* as one's own. The one who plays the game and the one who is absent meet in the substitute object. In Freud, it is an indifferent object, a spool of thread thrown and retrieved, a mere thing. And in 'The Nymph complaining'? How can the voice preserve itself, its purity, and avoid the contaminating eddies of repetition in which it would cease to own itself? How? By objectifying. No fawn in this section of the poem, no h[e]art; those words do not enter the voice here; it will not enter that perilous territory, overcharged and echoing. No, the voice says 'it'. Over and again – twenty-six times – the voice says 'it'. The singular 'it' caught in iterability.

Banish Sylvio, banish troopers, banish the heart. And what remains? Voice itself, present to itself, and the memory of the fullness in the garden, remembered totality, consummate union, one with 'it' and with itself. Such is the story. A Ficinian dream?

> What . . . does the intellect seek if not to transform all things into itself by depicting all things in the intellect according to the nature of the intellect? And what does the will strive to do if not to transform itself into all things by enjoying all things according to the nature of each? The former strives to bring it about that the universe . . . should become intellect; the latter, that the will should become the universe.[6]

To make mind present to itself, to fill the mind and the universe as mirrors of each other, what must be done? Speak of 'it'. Merge into the object. Speak of one's own.

Speak of 'it' and of nothing else. Deny every analogy that would locate 'it' anywhere but in the garden. Preserve that place from the perils of echo. Preserve it from all intrusion, even from someone who might hear this voice speaking. Own it all by disowning everything.

So, first, the voice begins in excess, with a superlative that marks the superabundance and fullness of this exclusive preserve. Begins 'with sweetest milk, and sugar, first' (l. 55), a story of a growing perfection that has nothing to do with processes of natural growth or ordinary time or space. The voice goes beyond 'sweetest' in an extraordinary declension, to 'more . . . sweet', 'so sweet': 'It wax'd more white and sweet than they./It had so sweet a Breath!' (ll. 58–59). Outstripping all comparisons, whether they mark difference ('For it was nimbler much than Hindes;/And trod, as on the four Winds' (ll. 69–70)), or similarity ('It like a bank of Lillies laid' (l. 82)), whether it rests or moves. It joins with this 'it' to go beyond compare:

> And oft
> I blusht to see its foot more soft,
> And white, (shall I say then my hand?)
> NAY any Ladies of the Land.

> (ll. 59–62)

'Shall I say then': the voice hears itself speaking, apprehends the excess in its question, and goes beyond it in its capital denial, joining itself to what it sees to make it voice an object beyond compare, to make its voice that object. Comparisons fill the voice – 'more', 'much', 'so', 'as', 'like' – only to disable comparison, only to say: 'It is a wond'rous thing' (l. 63).

It: place of meeting for voice and object, wondrous fusion, oneness. Joined in one breath. Speaking, and blushing, the voice rushes to a transcendent whiteness, moving with 'it' like the wind on 'little silver feet' (l. 64), generating, as it speaks, a garden of blushing roses and 'flaxen Lillies' (l. 81), generating 'it' as 'Lillies without, Roses within' (l. 92). Mirrors upon mirrors. Voice is the generation of breath: 'It had so sweet a Breath!' (l. 59). Breath and blush and a white hand release 'it', join with 'it' in the return of breath to breath, white on white, red to red. It returns 'to print those Roses on my Lip' (l. 86); to lie on 'whitest sheets' (l. 90). Through the garden, it runs and returns, a circuit: what the white hand generates moves on swift feet. What game is this? What story of return?

The story begins, 'first', nursed by hand, and it closes with a 'print' (l. 86) and a white sheet, moving all the while on *feet* (ll. 60, 64) as white as the hand that fed it. Between the lips, uttering, kissing, there is the story itself, of voice becoming object, returning to itself in the image of voice. The image: where 'it' moves, that place beyond comparison, made in comparison, the garden of lilies and roses, the mirror of voice and object. That place of transcendent mediation, 'you' would 'guess/To be a little Wilderness' (ll. 73–74). You would misread the image and not see that it lies beyond compare. You would misread the voice as image. See the text.

The voice speaks of 'it' as a garden that 'you' would not see as it does, and it speaks, too, of an object that can't be seen; '[I] could not, till it self would rise,/Find it, although before mine Eyes' (ll. 79–80). Voice: it can't be seen. Such is the story of the voice coming into its own, what it makes as its own. 'I it at mine own fingers nurst' (l. 56). 'I have a Garden of my own' (l. 71). Its own into its own; on the breath (conspiracy?); in the mirror. The voice disappears into 'it' and emerges as the *image of voice*, invisible as the print of voice – as the printed page. Voice extends to 'it' and extends it, letting it come and go. Sylvio's 'silver Chain' (l. 28) has become the 'silver feet' (l. 64). The full voice (full of 'it'), empties into 'it' (by feeding 'it', releasing 'it'), letting 'it' come into its own – the mirroring garden of red and white. It is filled with roses, folded in lilies. Filled and folded, 'it' folds back upon itself. Folds and fills the unseen and unheard. What 'you' cannot see. The incorporate garden, the garden of the mind, the image of voice; 'you' cannot look in the mirror that returns the voice. Here it is: repletion (the feeding) of emptiness and loss; dissolution/incorporation. Into it, the one body, the word without echo. It is not the h[e]art.

You cannot see it. Here it is: this is a voice of multiple denials, refusing analogies for the incomparable 'it', denying Echo to preserve voice. To preserve it – and to deny that what is preserved is, precisely, what is denied: echo. Voice, but only in 'it', in the mirror. Sustained and filled in this fold. In denial lies its pleasure: 'all its chief delight was still/On Roses thus its self to fill' (ll. 87–88). Voice is emptied into 'it', and fills and empties itself in 'its self'. Replete and full in the satisfaction of loss and emptiness, the pleasures of denial. For in its play, the object that mirrors voice – the object that *is* voice – refuses union, keeps its distance, fades in the mirror, imperceptible to voice, imperceptible as voice. Become the image of voice, acting out the voice, it plays with itself. Its own with its own, folded.

Here it is: the story of denial. No mention of Sylvio, the troopers, the fawn. Here it is: stringing out a story.

What voice is this? Voice of Narcissus. Voice full of itself, denying Echo, setting itself up in a mirror, moving towards and away from an object that it is, an object that is the image of its voice – and as insubstantial. Echo, the image of Narcissus.

Voice of pleasure, narcissistic gratification, luring, leading on, teasing, tantalizing, playing – and denying. Fullness of pleasure coupled with emptiness of satisfaction. The satisfaction (empty/full) of having one's own, the return of a kiss, the mirror of red and white in the garden, that place of reflection of a mind toying with itself. The full voice, Narcissus says: 'plenty makes me poor.' The empty voice, Echo says: 'I am present.' The voice is full of 'it'; call it Echo. There is only one voice in this text, the echo of voice.

What voice echoes in the dissolve into 'it'? Iteration, dissolving the object, defusing fusion and oneness and one's own, filling (emptying) presence with a fold. The text echoes a voice of presence to oneself, or of nature full of voice. Ovid . . . and Chaucer are *dissolved* in this text. 'Whan Zephirus eek with his swete breath/Inspired hath in every holt and heeth'; 'it had so sweet a Breath' (l. 59) 'and trod, as on the four Winds' (l. 70). Breath, air, voice conspire against inspiration. Dissolve Petrarch's L[']aura; voice, landscape, beloved object, word-made-flesh. Or flesh-made-word? Such are the voices remembered, dismembering this voice. The voice of Spenserian allegory.

Allegory is a mode making use of endless and inadequate analogies; allegories speak in a voice that keeps comparing in order to move beyond compare, in a voice of continuous metaphor that becomes 'darke conceit' in its very elucidation. In its etymology, allegory (*allos-agoreuein*) means a speaking beside the point, cryptic, private utterance, voice 'present' to itself, not out in the open. Allegory, the voice of the veil (recall the *Fort! Da!*). And, in allegory, the figures ('characters') are parts for wholes. Recall Spenser's story of Amoret and *her* bleeding heart, which is also the story of Amoret *as* her bleeding heart, Amoret distanced, objectified, separated from her heart. When her heart is restored – when the circuit of return is 'complete' – when she gets back her own, Amoret is then 'perfect hole' (*Faerie Queene* III. xii. 38. 9), whole and hole. The wound remains – the wound in perfection (completion) – and closure is denied. And in allegory, narrative is woven in an endless replay. Like 'flaxen lillies' (flaxen from *plectere*, to braid). Allegory a full (and empty), plaited tale. Episode upon episode (mirror upon mirror), each time the same (iteration), yet in the very sameness (wound and w[h]ole) difference, perplexing. You would mistake a garden for a wilderness. You are strung along, caught in an endless replay. You can't quite find it. You are promised an end, left 'to another place . . . to be perfected' (*Faerie Queene* IV. xii. 35. 9). That beyond proves to be a before, 'deepe within the mynd' (*Faerie Queene* VI, proem 5. 8), Spenser says, 'another place' where ending is beginning. Allegory drives towards Eden ever lost, endlessly deferred. As Paul de Man puts it: 'Allegory designates primarily a distance in relation to its own origin, and, renouncing the nostalgia and the desire to coincide, it establishes its language in the void of this temporal difference.'[7] The void – full, empty, and folded. The end of allegory is a 'first' without end. Such is the dream of the voice in this section of 'The Nymph complaining', the idyll in the garden of repletion, eternal spring ('all the Spring time of the year' (l. 75)), an Eden with trips, not falls, an Eden of the mind where desire is fulfilled, time stops, everything folds. The lure of allegory is a beyond . . . beyond the pleasure principle.

And so, we must ask again, what voice? Must ask what is suppressed to tell this story of full time, of replete voice, luxuriant garden. And must answer: the fold is empty. Fullness is folded around emptiness. This whole (this union, this oneness of one's own) is a hole. Death has been denied in this idyll. Death is this voice, as it is the basis for all (its) Edenic longings, responsible for the voice of pleasure, for the voice of play. Allegory is the voice of death.

The ludic transformations of eros and loss into hide and seek mean to render loss and absence unthreatening, to control loss by dissolving it into the object that can be manipulated to give pleasure, into an 'it', solid, stable, and completely indifferent. A spool of thread; 'it' on a chain. Such merging does not dissolve loss, however; it embodies it and enacts it as the location of pleasure. All pleasure. Voice dissolved/made into 'it': lost object, a reduced and displaced substitute object. Like all objects. The object that disappears and reappears in (through) the veil. Or the mirror of representation. Or the screen of memory. Or presence. Or being. This voice feeds itself with a story, pressing lip against lip, folding within a garden that mirrors the voice, folding subject and object to indistinction, filling with roses, fading with lilies. The garden offers an image of the play of mind and universe, contained and containing. L'histoire d'O?

Merging means loss. Beyond the visionary certainties (the certainties of vision), loss is registered. Blindness supports vision: 'Yet could not, till it self would rise,/Find it, although before mine Eyes' (ll. 79–80). It can't be seen. Its very whiteness is a blank. Folded in lilies, that blankness is annihilative. It lies in 'the flaxen Lillies shade' (l. 81). It lies 'where it should lye' (l. 78), dissolving the incorporate solidity of the 'it' in iteration, folding upon itself. There is no 'it self' except as it sacrifices itself:

> Among the beds of Lillyes, I
> Have sought it oft, where it should lye,
> Yet could not, till it self would rise,
> Find it, although before mine Eyes.

(ll. 77–80)

To feed the voice that generates it, it returns generation, replays it. It pays in blood. Such is the 'challenge' of 'the Race' (l. 66). The union, the kiss, the return of breath for breath, is a union in blood, embodying loss:

51

> Upon the Roses it would feed,
> Until its Lips ev'n seem'd to bleed:
> And then to me 'twould boldly trip,
> And print those Roses on my Lip.

(ll. 83–86)

Those blushing roses give this voice its voice.

Filled by loss, folded in a winding cloth, this story of 'first' dissolves into last:

> But all its chief delight was still
> On Roses thus its self to fill:
> And its pure virgin Limbs to fold
> In whitest sheets of Lillies cold.

(ll. 87–90)

A winding cloth, blank sheets. A page? A sepulchre? A bed? Or the coldness of a monument, sepulchre of Echo, her virgin limbs become stone, embodied/disembodied, the object at last. Still delights, unmoving. 'Had it liv'd long' (l. 91), the voice continues, the metamorphosis would have been complete, the dissolve perfected. 'Had it liv'd long', it would not have lived at all; folded in lilies, filled with roses, it would have lived to embody its death. 'Had it liv'd long': at last the voice admits iteration, repeating itself (see l. 47). Admits what has been denied. It ends – voice ends – as echo. The dream of Narcissus ends. Story-telling ends in its beginning.

As narration, allegory embodies death, a realm that the mind represents to itself as a space in which the human dilemmas of time and otherness are overcome because they are finally beside the point. Spenserian allegory, which is always seeking beginnings and never finding them, driving ever 'deepe within the mynd', is laid to rest by this voice. The 'it' is the memorialized other, eternalized as object, located in an Eden of the mind and as a plaything in a ritualized and endless sequence that plays to avoid loss, that would avoid loss by playing with it, and which therefore keeps itself from losing only by never having at all. This is the game of hide and seek. The voice here is finally so beside the point that it says what it would deny precisely because it has founded itself on denial. Inevitably, it is already inscribed in the voice of echo. And in speaking so beside the point of desire to avoid loss by holding on to the 'solitary time' and making it the entire story, the voice inscribes pure loss, inevitable loss, as its desire. The troopers' bullets, the duplicities of Sylvio, *are* this voice; 'it' is the death of the fawn. 'Had it liv'd long . . .'; with these words, the voice comes to itself. Comes, that is, to the end of itself, to the end of the dream of one's own. The object, sustained in the echo of iteration, is relinquished. The possibility of the inimitable 'it' is laid to rest and, with it, the possibility of the sustained and sustaining voice. Its fullness folds upon itself.

Time now to end; time for the poem of ending to become itself, for voice and all its echoes to be undone, filled and emptied. Time for the poem to give up its voice and to be what it is – text, the blank print. Time for the most severe reductions yet. Time to end itself as itself, in its own implacable, miniaturized monumentality.

(Read under erasure: itself, its, its own, is.)

Notes

1. GEOFFREY HARTMAN, ' "The Nymph Complaining for the Death of Her Faun": A Brief Allegory', in *Beyond Formalism* (New Haven: Yale University Press, 1970), pp. 173–92.
2. JACQUES DERRIDA, *Of Grammatology*, trans. Gayatri Chakravorty Spivak (Baltimore: Johns Hopkins University Press, 1974, 1976), p. 7.
3. ROLAND BARTHES, *S/Z*, trans. Richard Miller (New York: Hill and Wang, 1974), pp. 176–7.
4. See OVID, *Metamorphoses*, 3:339–510.
5. SIGMUND FREUD, *Beyond the Pleasure Principle*, trans. James Strachey (New York: W.W. Norton, 1961), ch. 2, pp. 8–9.
6. MARSILIO FICINO, 'Five Questions Concerning the Mind', trans. Josephine L. Burroughs in *The Renaissance Philosophy of Man*, ed. E. Cassirer, P.O. Kristeller, and J.H. Randall (Chicago: University of Chicago Press, 1948), pp. 200–1.
7. PAUL DE MAN, 'The Rhetoric of Temporality', in *Interpretation: Theory and Practice*, ed. Charles S. Singleton (Baltimore: Johns Hopkins Press, 1969), p. 191.

4 The Garden State: Marvell's Poetics of Enclosure*

JONATHAN CREWE

During the late Middle Ages, English land owners increasingly appropriated fields either cultivated by their tenants or traditionally maintained as common land open to all, and hedged them so that sheep could graze. While developing the national economy through the wool trade, this practice displaced the poor's access to land and was bitterly resented by the landless. For Jonathan Crewe, this practice meant that pastoral verse, in which the land is celebrated as beneficent and abundant for all, could only be sustained through irony or with an increasing sense of contradicting reality. Concerned with Marvell's extensive use of pastoral, Crewe examines his 'garden states' in a variety of poems, seeing the relation of the garden to the wider state of England as problematic. As with Jonathan Goldberg's preceding essay, Crewe is indebted to deconstructive practice and is also alert to Marvell's 'metapoetic' commentary on his own poetic utterance. But Crewe's use of deconstruction is to emphasise its potential for engagement with history and politics. Recalling that Derrida claims deconstruction is not ahistorical formalism but is fundamentally designed to deconstruct the formal enclosures language erects, Crewe proposes that Marvell's use of pastoral is organised to demonstrate its insufficiency in an increasingly turbulent world. The poet actually seeks to demonstrate the imperfections of the garden ideals his narrators try to create, aware that their pursuits of pastoral innocence may actually help despoil the world.

In 1970 Rosalie Colie published a book subtitled 'Andrew Marvell's Poetry of Criticism'.[1] She may thus have been the first to draw attention

---

* Reprinted from Richard Burt and John Michael Archer (eds), *Enclosure Acts: Sexuality, Property and Culture in Early Modern England* (Ithaca and London: Cornell University Press, 1994), pp. 270–89.

to the strongly critical and self-critical impulse in Marvell's lyric poetry.
One way this impulse manifests itself is in a certain epigrammatic
abstraction, impersonality, and crystallizing lucidity in Marvell's writing.
Another is the tendency of Marvell's poems to keep on rigorously
staging the formal impasses of Renaissance pastoral. Still another is
Marvell's production of a sustained metapoetic commentary on his own
lyric enterprise and its poetic antecedents. It is partly to this impulse that
I owe the term 'garden state' in the title of this essay. The phrase comes
from the lyric titled 'The Garden', and it is embedded, as many will
recall, in a wittily misogynistic stanza:

> Such was that happy Garden – state,
> While Man there walk'd without a Mate:
> After a Place so pure, and sweet,
> What other Help could yet be meet!
> But 'twas beyond a Mortal's share
> To wander solitary there:
> Two Paradises 'twere in one
> To live in Paradise alone.

> (ll. 57–65)

The phrase 'garden state' captures the tendency of Renaissance pastoral
to originate itself in a lost paradise, often specifically Eden, but then
insofar as that paradise *is* Eden, to originate itself misogynistically as
well, since to recall Eden is also to recall Eve's role in its loss. The phrase
performs more than this act of allusive recall, however. In it a problematic
relationship between a pastoral and a historico-political condition remains
unresolved. The phrase can imply a unified or total condition of pastoral
well-being (*otium*) from which the political is virtually excluded, or it can
be taken to project a merger of two still antithetical realms: garden and
state. It can implicitly oppose the *garden* state as a scene of cultivation
to the political state as one of disruptive ambition, violence, and waste;
and it can also posit a virtually ecological reconstruction of the political
state which desirably approximates the condition of the enclosed,
cultivated garden (*hortus conclusus*). These are traditional pastoral concerns
which lend themselves to a certain formal abstraction, yet the peculiar
conjunctions and dislocations of Marvell's poems are additionally those
of a neoclassical pastoral tradition understood to be in historic crisis,
and thus thrown back in confusion on many of its own most basic
assumptions and resources. Among the well-recognized precipitating
factors are the advent of the Civil War and popular revolt, the deposition
of Charles I and Cromwell's rise to power, the ongoing construction
during the seventeenth century of the early modern political state, and
the vexed political economy of land enclosure.

55

It can of course be argued that this 'timeless' poetic tradition is always in historical crisis, and can never be otherwise since it embodies a poetic formalism continuously at odds with historical actuality. This possibility is represented, for example, by the invasive figure of Time in Spenser's Gardens of Adonis or in Shakespeare's pastoral sonnets to the Young Man. Yet this abstract personification of time is also an over-simplification. For Renaissance poets, the specificity of historical crisis and the self-revising capacities of pastoral are at issue at least from Virgil onward. So is the political encoding of pastoral and the interplay in it between formal and historico-political inscription. For Marvell all these issues are unavoidable, and his poetry of criticism presents an informing commentary on them even in its failures to master them. I accordingly take my cue from Marvell in considering the fortunes of the garden state in his pastoral poems.

Despite my doing so, and despite my emphasis on the historical moment rather than the 'always and already', a continuing indebtedness to deconstruction will be apparent throughout this discussion, which accordingly cannot represent itself as an exercise in purely historical poetics. My purpose is not to claim Marvell as a deconstructionist before the letter or to assimilate him, as Jonathan Goldberg has done, to what is now sometimes called the postmodern Renaissance [see the preceding essay]. I am making a connection between Marvell's critical poetics and deconstruction partly because, in deconstruction as in Marvell's poems, the question of enclosure poses complex, general problems of formal and historico-political inscription. This complexity is sometimes belied by deconstructive polemics, as well as antideconstructive ones. Derrida, for example, responds thus to activist critics at both ends of the political spectrum, for whom deconstruction is just another ahistorical formalism: 'It is in the interest of one side and the other to represent deconstruction as a turning inward and an enclosure by the limits of language, whereas in fact deconstruction begins . . . by deconstructing this very enclosure.'[2]

This programmatic statement and others like it leave unanswered innumerable questions about the nature of linguistic enclosure – a phrase that already connects such enclosure to pastoral – as well as about the political implications of deconstructing it. No consensus exists about what necessarily follows, politically or otherwise, from the undoing of enclosure in which deconstruction begins. Rather than apply deconstruction as a codified method to Marvell's texts, then, I hope to generate a certain interplay between Marvell's critical poetics and the language of deconstruction.

The stanza I have quoted from 'The Garden' provides a good starting point. As well as being familiar, the stanza is one in which both the conventionality and the disconcerting peculiarity of Marvellian pastoral have previously been recognized. The conventionality has hardly seemed to need explanation, given Renaissance assumptions about the constitutiveness of convention, genre, and formal imitation in poetic composition. The peculiarity, by contrast, *has* seemed to call for explanation. This fantasy of the lost paradise as a condition of self-sufficient male solitude has often been read as that of an egregiously narcissistic, misogynistic male speaker. In this reading the virtual pathology of a consistent if self-betraying persona is often taken to be at issue. If we extend and shift the terms of this rhetorical reading somewhat, it can further suggest that a widespread cultural fantasy of the supposedly autonomous, originary masculine subject is being exposed in the poem. In other words, the speaker is less egregious and more betrayingly typical than might at first be supposed. In the stanza's revision of Genesis, paradise is the single state of man, while woman is constructed not as man's desired complement but as the belated supernumerary, added on by subtraction from the perfect man.

An overdetermined reading of this cultural fantasy would necessarily take account of its connection to the historical eclipse of monarchy in Marvell's time. Insofar as the masculine subject is increasingly cast in the mold of sovereign absolutism from the Jacobean period onward, the dethroning of Charles I entails imaginative and identificatory as well as political loss. A need both to mourn and to recoup this loss is revealed in 'The Garden'; in the wake of political monarchy the only masculine absolutism may well be the displaced, solitary absolutism of the imaginary garden state.

In these readings pastoral retirement is heavily invested with cultural and political meanings, but deep pastoral disturbance is not yet fully evident. What remains to be noticed is the conscious whimsicality of the stanza, in which Marvell attempts the self-distancing and mastering irony celebrated by the New Criticism. The correlative absence of any master narrative or true originary moment also calls for attention in a poem marked by abrupt shifts rather than by any consistency of narrative, dramatic persona, or pastoral locale. The speaker's Edenic fantasy does not even begin the poem, but seems like a belated and defensive response to more troubling fantasies of pastoral origin.

In 'The Garden' the initial movement of worldly relinquishment is also one of return to Ovidian pastoral-poetic origins. Pan and Syrinx are recalled in a conventional mode of Renaissance pastoral, and the return to these pastoral origins as a form of poetic renewal is linked to an equally conventional dialectic of worldly relinquishment and pastoral recompense. Yet to recall these Ovidian origins is to locate the pastoral source in a mythicized state of nature rather than in the cultivated setting of the garden. It is also to reconnect pastoral to a betrayingly violent origin. These disturbing implications are possibly heightened for Marvell by the Spenserian allegory in *The Shepheardes Calender*, in which Pan and

Syrinx are identified with Henry VIII and Anne Boleyn. Not only does pastoral tend to become a decorous mask for political brutality in this allegory, but, as Louis Montrose has argued, the outcome of thwarted male desire is not masculine poetic triumph as usual but the practically virgin birth of Elizabeth I as the disconcerting and displacing sovereign figure of the woman.[3]

In attempting to deallegorize this narrative and simultaneously purge it of violence, Marvell makes a pure love of trees into the original pastoral motive. The inflammatory violence of sexual desire is displaced onto human lovers, who wantonly carve their names on the bark. Implicitly, sexual desire is foreign to the first pastoral world, and is in effect overwritten on it. Yet an impasse is evident here insofar as the overwriting seems to be the only possible writing. Trees do not constitute a legible pastoral text; such a text can seemingly be produced only by defacing them. The discontinuity between pastoral motive and inscription seems unbridgeable in this Ovidian context, while the pure love of trees remains an eccentric reaction formation that might enable 'arborophilia' to be listed among the sophisticated perversions.

After this failed Ovidian opening, the return to origins and the dialectic of relinquishment and recompense are restaged in a series of garden settings in which, in keeping with a poem such as 'Bermudas,' Old and New World elements as well as wild and cultivated ones merge. The enabling condition of the garden fantasy is now a certain categorical breakdown, through which binary impasses are circumvented.

> What wond'rous Life is this I lead!
> Ripe Apples drop about my head;
> The Luscious Clusters of the Vine
> Upon my Mouth do crush their Wine:
> The Nectaren, and curious Peach,
> Into my hands themselves do reach;
> Stumbling on Melons, as I pass,
> Insnar'd with Flow'rs, I fall on Grass.

(ll. 33–40)

This moment of full bodily replenishment is succeeded, dialectically as it might now seem, by one of ecstatic bodily divestment:

> Casting the Bodies Vest aside,
> My Soul into the boughs does glide:
> There like a Bird it sits, and sings
> Then whets, and combs its silver Wings.

(ll. 51–54)

The paradise of oral gratification in the 'wondrous life' stanza implies a limitless abundance, yet, although the speaker's 'fall' may successfully be divorced from any negative biblical implication, it entails his own 'passivization' and a corresponding transfer of agency to the virtually force-feeding landscape, of which his body becomes the object. Insofar as a fantasy of 'original' maternal bounty informs this stanza, that condition of *otium* can seemingly be recovered only in a mode of suffocating excess, and vegetative incorporation.

The dialectical shift to the next stanza is accordingly an escape from the body through which masculine agency can be reclaimed and a different economy of gratification can be posited, namely, that of the omnipotent mind 'Annihilating all that's made / To a green Thought in a green Shade' (ll. 47–48). In this pleasurable moment of decreation, in which the mind displays its ultimate power (or aspiration) to reduce everything to its own 'coloration', all excess, including poetic excess, is to be reduced to zero, thereby restoring perfect equilibrium (green = green). Now, it is through a strong economy of radical impoverishment and imaginative negation that pastoral *otium* is to be reclaimed, and specifically to be reclaimed as an effect of masculine intellectual agency. Yet this movement in the poem is self-negating. Not only is the liberated masculine soul an exotic figure of 'feminine' narcissism – the bird of paradise that 'whets and combs its silver wings' – but the zero-economy of decreation is tantamount to one of death, with the pastoral subject reduced to a thought-possessed 'shade'.

Under whatever aspect the garden state as man's estate is reconceived in the poem, it turns out to have consequences at least as disagreeable as gratifying, while the poem's dialectic produces no moment of sublation. The powerfully self-centering if discontinuous 'I' of the poem (an 'I' whose sole continuity is evidently that of its self-centering desire) is finally dethroned when the speaker finds himself wandering in someone else's formal garden, not one of his own imagining. The garden text (or *florilegium*) is not the poet's but the anonymous gardener's; it is one of microcosmic imitation and limitation, not of creative freedom:

> How well the skilful Gardener drew
> Of flow'rs and herbs this Dial new,
> Where from above the milder Sun
> Does through a fragrant Zodiack run;
> And, as it works, th' industrious bee
> Computes its time as well as we.

> (ll. 65–70)

The dethroning of the speaker in this poem is connected to his failure to situate himself centrally in a coherent, timeless discourse of pastoral. Thus, insofar as 'The Garden' bids to be the definitive Marvell garden poem as well as the one in which the poetic imagination is most fully licensed to create 'far other worlds and other seas', this anticlimactic outcome, as well as the poem's belated attempt at ironic mastery, constitutes an imperfect paradigm – all the more so in that the poem is written in the *propria persona* of the pastoral poet. The numerous Marvellian pastorals scripted for such alternative, diminished, or impaired personae as the nymph complaining or the Mower can be read in the light of this failed *propria persona* attempt.

It is the nymph complaining who, perhaps more successfully than any represented masculine speaker, becomes the self-constituting inhabitant of her garden state, capable of delivering the punch line 'I have a garden of my own' (l. 71). Her evident capacity to succeed where the masculine garden subject has failed, and to succeed *him* as the Adamic garden subject, makes her at once a displacing and identificatory figure for the male garden poet. She constitutes 'her' garden state as one of continuing impenetrability by disabling the mastering and penetrating gaze of the viewer:

> I have a Garden of my own
> But so with Roses overgrown,
> And Lilies, that you would it guess
> To be a little Wilderness.

(ll. 71–74)

What is an enclosed garden to the feminine 'I' of the poem is an alien wilderness to the eye of the objectified beholder ('you'), who can only look on from the outside. This impenetrable enclosure is the secret garden into which access is possible only on the nymph's terms; to inhabit it is to inhabit her language – space only, and to become fully identified with her position.

This is the poem Jonathan Goldberg has plausibly identified as the canonical Marvell garden poem, in which the entire rhetorical repertoire of Renaissance pastoral is rehearsed. If so, one might add, it is a radically displaced and highly defensive version of pastoral in extremis. 'Nymph' is a pastoral signifier of the feminine which situates this figure indeterminably on a threshold between the human and the nonhuman, nature and culture. The position of the nymph is thus virtually uninhabitable. At the same time, 'nymph' is the signifier of an intense but virtually unpossessible female sexuality. Marvell's projection of pastoral innocence as the condition of the nymph thus entails a simultaneous denial of her sexuality and a desire to release or possess it. Moreover, since desire *for* the nymph as other is entailed in this pastoral configuration, the innocence of pastoral is tainted not just with a certain knowingness but with what an age more given to naming perversions might have called 'nympholepsy'.[4] Not only can the pastoral project not purify itself, but it becomes implicated in an exploitative sexual politics of masculine impotence. As we shall see, this rule applies to Marvell's represented tutorial relation to Maria Fairfax in *Upon Appleton House*.

Before turning to *Upon Appleton House*, in which these contradictory lyric scenarios are elaborated, let us briefly consider some further attempts by Marvell to envisage a good economy of the garden state. Ideally, this should mean a good general economy, the political, material, and psychic aspects of which positively coincide; yet any such condition seems unrepresentable in the lyrics. In them, the relation between material, political, and psychic formations generally seems negative, contradictory, or noncoincident. So much is already apparent in one of Marvell's early pastoral lyrics, 'Thyrsis and Dorinda'. In this poem Marvell can be said to repeat a widespread Elizabethan critique of Theocritan pastoral, that is to say, of the idyllic pastoral mode representing the lives of shepherds and shepherdesses. Under the historical pressures of land enclosure, the lethal antipastoral consequences of which were already represented in Thomas More's *Utopia*, pastoral idyll could be sustained only with an increasing sense of irony or contradiction. In Marvell's poem the pastoral privation and discontent of the shepherd and shepherdess are virtual givens. The shepherd world is one not of idyllic pastoral but of lack, inequality, and labor, and it is from within that world that idyllic pastoral is projected by the speakers into an Elysian afterlife. The shepherdess, who is already a Marvellian woman in the making, says:

> Oh sweet! oh sweet! How I my future state
> By silent thinking Antidate:
> I prithee let us spend our time to come
> In talking of *Elysium*.

> (ll. 27–30)

The shepherd obliges by doing just that, producing an Elysian fantasy: Shepheards there bear equal sway, / And every Nimph's a Queen of May (ll. 37–38). The pastoral idyll is no longer coextensive with the poem but has become embedded in it, while, of necessity, the pastoral personae become do-it-yourself pastoral poets. In the historical present of the poem, pastoral idyll is explicitly a pleasurable verbal artifice, a form of sweet talk (*dulce*) that seems mainly compensatory and wish fulfilling.

A significant difference does, however, emerge between the two speakers. Whereas the shepherd Thyrsis seems content to settle for deferred gratification and the endless elaboration of Elysian fantasy, the shepherdess wishes to inhabit that anticipated future in the present. She hopes that through the power of 'silent thinking' her 'future state' can be anticipated, in the sense not of being foreseen but of being fully possessed ahead of time. She also hopes that 'talking of Elysium' will be fully equivalent to inhabiting a 'time to come' that does not unambiguously refer to an afterlife. What the shepherdess demands, in effect, is strong pastoral, in which powers of mind and language can constitute an immediate political reality. The shepherd can produce only weak pastoral of deferral and wish fulfilment. Insisting on realization, the shepherdess ups the ante: 'I'm sick, I'm sick, and fain would dye, / Convince me now that this is true / By bidding with mee, all adieu' (ll. 40–42).

What follows this demand for verification is tantamount to a suicide pact. The shepherd consents, not because he believes in the veracity of his own fictions, but because he cannot bear to be parted from the shepherdess. She, despite having found pastoral artifice wanting, remains sufficiently captivated by it to make it subject to suicidal validation. Yet her wish to make pastoral come true seems to have been superinduced on a prior wish to die, and when the voices of the two speakers unite in the last choral stanza, their common language is one of pastoral melancholia. Elysian prospects have given way to a final retrospect on the world of pastoral *negotium* the shepherds are about to leave:

> Then let us give *Corillo* charge o'th Sheep,
> And thou and I'll pick poppies, and them steep
> In wine, and drink on't even till we weep,
> So shall we smoothly pass away in sleep.

(ll. 45–48)

It is not without radical irony that Marvell concludes this shepherd poem with melancholia and suicide. Yet what complicates the outcome is that a surprisingly exotic remedy for pastoral discontents is to be found in the Theocritan landscape. Not only are poppies grown, but the pastoral innocents have evidently stumbled on the recipe for laudanum: opium dissolved in alcohol. I hesitate to say that Marvell here anticipates the Romantic displacement of pastoral idyll into the exotic realm of the opium eater, but the surprising turn taken by the poem is nevertheless prophetic.

In later Marvellian poems pastoral renovation comes to depend, however problematically, on exotic, hypernatural forms of abundance indistinguishable from artifice, or on hyperinflationary economies. New World superabundance in 'Bermudas', with its 'priceless' apples and naturally occurring 'golden lamps', deconstructs the nature–culture oppositions of traditional European pastoral, and the speculative hyperinflation of Dutch tulipomania in 'The Mower against Gardens' figures an economy of radical disequilibrium rather than natural equilibrium. These are troublingly excessive, alien forms of renewal to which Marvell stages a deeply implicated resistance through the figure of the Mower.

In 'The Mower against Gardens', the Mower identifies ostensibly unnatural economies as bad ones, and proves to be no mean critic of their 'perversion' of natural kind. Yet the condition of the Mower's critique is that of being simply *against* gardens, a position in which he is at once a displaced and oppositional figure. From his vantage point the story of gardens gets retold from the beginning as one of bad masculine origin. Excessive male desire as primordial 'luxury' (the archaic English term for 'lechery') transforms the world into an international bazaar of 'luxury' objects, including human ones:

> Luxurious Man, to bring his Vice in use,
> Did after him the World seduce:
> And from the fields the Flow'rs and Plants allure,
> Where Nature was most plain and pure.

(ll. 1–4)

The history of gardens accordingly becomes one of endless uprooting and transplantation, in which the breakdown of natural categories or 'kinds' allows artificial hybrids such as fancy tulips to be produced for the luxury market. By implication the prolific language of pastoral is subject to the same rootless, debilitating artifice, constitutively so inasmuch as its figures are by definition removed from literal or natural meanings, and its flowers are always artificial. The implication of pastoral poets in this long history of denaturalization can hardly be denied, given the Renaissance understanding of figurative language as an uprooting and displacement of natural language. Yet the situation approaches crisis when the natural grounding of *all* identities and distinctions seems about to be eroded. When this happens in the poem, the English pastoral poet is threatened with imminent metamorphosis into a luxurious exotic. The 'Marvel of Peru', an exotic New World import otherwise known as *Jalapa mirabilis*, finds its way into the poem's flower catalogue (l. 18); it represents the new version of himself by which the domestic English Marvell is at once seduced and threatened.

An alternative scene of divine presence, cultivation, and innocent gratification must therefore be constructed. This the Mower proceeds to do by placing himself as well as the authentic scene of cultivation not just against but outside the garden. The true scene of cultivation is now paradoxically an outside inhabited by a decentered figure, not a richly cultivated inside opposed to a wilderness without. The divinely sanctioned community the Mower claims to inhabit as well as the abundant agricultural economy he claims to represent is definitively post-Theocritan; it is also represented as self-sustaining, despite the politics of pastoral enclosure:

> What, though the piping Shepherd stock
> The plains with an unnum'ered Flock,

> This Sithe of mine discovers wide
> More ground than all his Sheep do hide.
> With this the golden fleece I shear
> Of all these closes every year.

(ll. 49–54)

For the Mower, the meadow evidently sustains a golden-age economy in which the mythical wealth of antiquity materializes in a nonalienated and deallegorized form as golden harvest. It is for this productive rather than consuming economy that the Mower wants to take credit, identifying his own shearing of the meadows with their power of renewal. Yet the meadow is a curious open-closed, outside-inside space which can be conceived only in terms of a rather sophisticated topology. It is increasingly difficult to locate or conceptualize, and the encroachment of sheep runs is defeated only by the creation of this new kind of virtual space. It is not surprising that the 'grounds' of his critique – the meadows on which he takes his stand – become an 'abyss' in 'Upon Appleton House'. Moreover, his identification of productivity with mowing – that is to say, with cutting down rather than propagating – entails a complicated, resentful gender politics of female displacement and emulation, represented in his fantasy relations with the shepherdess Juliana. (One apparent outcome of these relations of emulous productive rivalry is the 'accident' in which Damon the Mower accomplishes his own downfall by cutting his foot with his scythe. His aggressive yet self-mutilating impulse seems thereby gratified.)

The limited and contradictory economies represented in the poems discussed so far are typically articulated by solitary, eccentric speakers. No general economy of the garden state or subject is adumbrated. If these economies can be dialectically subsumed in any general economy, perhaps it is the revolutionary one identified by Goldberg as that of 'creative annihilation'. It is only in terms of this posited general economy that a number of dispersed moments in Marvell's writings come together: that of the poetic mind in 'The Garden' 'Annihilating all that's made / To a green Thought in a green Shade' (ll. 7–8); of Cromwell, who 'ruin[ed] the great Work of Time / And cast the Kingdome old / Into another Mold' (*Horatian Ode*, ll. 34–36); of the decapitation of Charles I, in which the English 'state', like the Roman in a comparable moment, 'foresaw its happy Fate' (l. 72); of the destruction of the fawn in which the nymph's monumental complaint originates. This dialectical mode is a revolutionary one that may seem to incorporate and supersede the more static or nostalgic modes of traditional pastoral while rupturing its forms of containment. The Cromwell of the *Horatian Ode*, for example, who explodes out of his garden 'plot' and into political history is the dynamic alter ego of the pastoral dreamer who can only *reverse* creation by

'Annihilating all that's made'. Yet Cromwell as historical man of destiny is to end up diminished and haunted in the *Horatian Ode* by 'the spirits of the shady night', including his own dead, who have not fully succumbed to his revolutionary dynamism. In *Upon Appleton House* he may further be identified with the deathdealing mower who 'commands the field' (l. 418) after the retirement of General Fairfax. Thus the critically abstracted dynamic of creative annihilation seems no less prone to historical reversal and debilitating oxymoron than the poetic discourse from which it is abstracted.

With these preliminaries in mind, I now turn to *Upon Appleton House* as a poem in which Marvell's pastoral poetics are recentered on the great estate. It is true that the poem is often assigned to the so-called country-house genre, founded in English by Jonson's *To Penshurst*, and many of the considerations that apply to Jonson's poem are pertinent to Marvell's as well. Yet it is the landed estate rather than the house that constitutes the unit of representation in the poem, and the critical tendency just to assimilate Marvell's poem to Jonson's oversimplifies both poems as well as the relationship between them. This relationship is one of radical disjunction, and the notoriously strange or 'marvellous' effects of *Upon Appleton House* are ones of pastoral displacement and decomposition. In Marvell's poem, stress and even breakdown are strongly marked; enclosure spectacularly fails; and powers of masterly poetic composition are overwhelmed. The nation as garden state, to which an expanded pastoral-poetic vocation might correspond, has apparently succumbed to its own internal violence:

> O Thou, that dear and happy Isle
> The Garden of the World ere while. . . .
> What luckless Apple did we tast,
> To make us Mortal, and thee Wast?

(ll. 321–22, 327–28)

When enclosure is figured later in the poem, it is no longer that of the garden but of the bull ring in Madrid, as if enclosure produces violence instead of excluding it.

The country-house passage at the beginning of the poem, parallel to the one at the beginning of *To Penshurst*, sets up the English country house as a model of feudal stability, organic growth and succession, domesticity, and resistance to invasion, including aesthetic invasion:

> Within this sober Frame expect
> Work of no Forrain *Architect*,
> That unto Caves the Quarries drew,
> And Forrests did to Pastures hew.

(ll. 1–4)

As in *Penshurst*, again, the poem opens with a series of negations, yet here the negations generate no 'positive' sense of bounty. As the parallel with Penshurst is extended, forms of natural or domestic enclosure, as well as more abstract powers of geometric circumscription, come under pressure. 'Birds contrive an equal Nest; / [And] low-roof'd Tortoises do dwell, / In cases fit of Tortoise-shell' (ll. 12–14). The General Fairfax of the poem, however, master of Appleton House, is a troublingly restless and oversized figure at whose coming 'the Laden House does sweat / And scarce endures the *Master* great' (ll. 49–50). Although the modest architecture of the country house embodies ideal ratios which draw from the speaker the assertion that 'these *holy Mathematicks* can / In ev'ry Figure equal Man' (ll. 47–48), this assumption is radically undermined rather than confirmed as the poem unfolds.

In all these respects, *Upon Appleton House* seems disjunctively connected to Johson's *Penshurst*, and the disjunction becomes even more marked through the conspicuous absence of a *magna mater*, with whom both the magical bountifulness of the estate *and* efficient domestic management are associated in *To Penshurst*. The matrilocal construction of the Penshurst estate in the Jonson poem is the implied condition of its magical bounty, while the domestic confinement of the housewife enables this bounty to be economized and appropriated for a larger political order of sovereignty and patronage, in which poet and king exchange their gifts. In 'Appleton House', however, an oppressive inequality and disconnection seemingly defines the relationship between patron and poet. The place of the poet has to be renegotiated. In fact, the possibility of pastoral and poetic *displacement* is figured by the fate of the nuns who once occupied Appleton House as a convent.

Readers of Marvell will recall that the Appleton House referred to in the poem was originally a Cistercian priory called Nun Appleton, which came into the possession of the Fairfax family at the time of the dissolution of the monasteries. Shortly before the dissolution, the heiress Isabel Thwaites, betrothed to William Fairfax of Steeton, had been confined to the monastery by her guardian, the prioress. Fairfax obtained an order for her release, and then seized her from the convent by force. In Marvell's poem this story is retold, but a speech in which the nun tries to persuade the heiress of the attractions of convent life is also quoted at length. The nun's scheme is thwarted when the great Fairfax ancestor breaks into the convent, virtually abducts the heiress for marriage, and founds the heroic Fairfax dynasty. In this moment of founding violence, Providence supposedly announces itself in the triumph of a strongly masculinized, dynastic, nationalistic Protestantism. The nuns are said to dissolve like false enchanters, with no further place in the ongoing historical narrative, while the term 'nun' is deleted from *Nun Appleton House*. Attempting to situate himself in this providential script, the narrator delivers a belated rebuke to the nuns who attempted to resist this Fairfax invasion: 'Ill-counsell'd Women, do you know, / Whom you resist, or what you do?' (ll. 239–40). In terms of the providential script, the convent represents not only the false value of a cloistral chastity which would be famously denounced again in Milton's *Areopagitica*, but also the scandal of an antiprocreative (thus implicitly lesbian) women's community.

Despite the speaker's editorial intervention, Marvell's identification with the historically displaced figure of the prioress is apparent in the (uncensored) speech she addresses to the heiress. In that speech the nun produces a counterscenario to that of dynastic marriage, procreative self-immolation, and feminine disempowerment:

> Each Night among us to your side
> Appoint a fresh and Virgin Bride;
> Whom if *our Lord* at midnight find,
> Yet Neither should be left behind.

> (ll. 185–88)

Chastity is here identified not with abstinence but with immunity to masculine violation. Deconstructing many of the constitutive oppositions of pastoral, including those between nature and art, *dulce* and *utile*, economy and luxury, the nun reconstitutes the cloistral interior as an enclosed 'feminine' garden state:

> For such indeed are all our Arts,
> Still handling Nature's finest Parts.
> Flowers dress the Altars; for the Clothes,
> The Sea borne Amber we compose;
> Balms for the griev'd we draw; and Pasts
> We mold, as Baits for curious tastes.

> (ll. 177–82)

The convent as a scene of epicurean innocence incorporates a good deal of Marvell's pastoral itinerary, while the exclusionary discourse of the prioress makes her a political avatar of the nymph complaining. In our own terms, this poem within the poem might be identified as a site of continuing resistance to the dominant sexual ideology, or, better still, as a deliciously subversive closet poem embedded in the obligatory recital of Fairfax succession. Yet in the context of 'Appleton House' it figures the exclusion of the pastoral poet from history and his reduction to a state of 'feminine' inconsequence. The lesbian nun as poet – conversely the poet as lesbian nun – is a powerful figure only in her self-enclosing text, the historical displacement of which in the poem leaves it exposed to prurient Protestant interpretation. In this context the language of the nun, however innocently uttered, will be heard not just as 'subtle' but as a language of endlessly titillating and betraying double entendre. The would-be chaste text of the prioress is no more immune than that of the nymph to the historical violence of interpretation.

Yet if on the one hand his relation to Fairfax as patron threatens the poet with displacement and historical 'disappearance', on the other it allows him to interpellate himself in a dynastic and providential history of the Fairfax family. This interpellation logically excludes the poet from being the producer of the Fairfax narrative, but not from being an editorial commentator empowered to reconstitute historical hindsight as providential foresight. This is a strong position, ideologically speaking, but one embarrassingly undermined, as is the poem's providentialism, the premature retirement of Fairfax. As one who seemed providentially scripted to restore the English garden state after a mere violent interlude, and to project English power abroad, Fairfax has stepped out of his part and abandoned the field to the 'mower'. Instead of carrying history forward, he appears to have turned it adrift. The English garden state shrinks to the proportions of his own fortified garden, while on the boundless meadows outside history transpires in ways that seem to defy all powers of pastoral enclosure. In this scene figures proliferate uncontrollably without natural grounding since the meadow is now an 'abyss' where strange mutations of pastoral personae also occur. The mowers, numerous enough to congregate in 'camps', are indeterminably laborers or soldiers who 'command the field'. Despite her Theocritan name, Thestylis, onetime shepherdess, has become a 'bloody' figure (l. 401) on the Appleton meadows. She is evidently a figure of the woman turned militant, if not revolutionary, and is thus no longer playing her subjected part. Even more disconcertingly, Thestylis has acquired a voice of her own in which she talks back to her author, not just to a scripted pastoral interlocutor. She does so when he tries to take control of the meadow scene by reconstructing it as one of Mosaic deliverance and hence of providential meaning. 'He called us Israelites!' (l. 406), she cries in a celebrated outburst, and then dismantles the forced correspondences through which he tries 'to make his saying true' (l. 407).

The insubordinate speech of Thestylis is a crucial marker of the poet's loss of control over gendered pastoral representation in a correlative space of formal enclosure. The counterpart to this powerlessness is the speaker's shift into a spectatorial position from which an increasingly alienated and theatricalized landscape comes into view. More precisely, following the undoing of the pastoral author and the displacement of the omniscient editor, a series of world-historical scenes produced by 'engines strange' passes over the stage: Alexander's army; Memphis and the pyramids; the Roman camps. History dissolves into spectacle, and the multiplication of scenes implies a loss of interpretative as well as authorial control.

It is partly in response to this world turned strange that the speaker flees to the woodland as a virtual refugee. In an attempt to reclaim poetic

agency and pastoral identity, he must attempt to displace not just the
world but a poetic language turned strange:

> Let others tell the *Paradox*,
> How Eels now bellow in the Ox;
> How Horses at their Tails do kick,
> Turn'd as they hang to Leeches quick;
> How Boats can over Bridges sail;
> And Fishes do the Stables scale.

(ll. 473–78)

These outlandish paradoxes threaten all discursive 'reason'. The world
'scale', for example, has evidently shifted in this context from being a
noun that properly names the epidermal covering of a fish to being an
active verb that improperly enables the fish to get out of its element and
climb up stables, where horses belong. Moreover, in a wild parody of
country-house architecture, 'scale' reduces the stables to the proportions
of the upstart fish. Everything in language and (hence) in the natural
world appears to be out of place or functioning improperly. This fluidity
and categorical instability of language might be expected to empower the
poet-user above all, yet the empowerment is void insofar as language
itself appears to have acquired an uncontrollable agency by which the
putative 'user' is victimized. The hyper-poetic is no poetic at all.

Recovering self-possession and transferring this unmanageable
language to unspecified 'others' necessitates not only a withdrawal and
repositioning of the poetic self but another return to primitive lyric
origins, now construed as the birdsong imitated by the pastoral poet:

> The *Nightingale* does here make choice
> To sing the Tryals of her voice.
> Low Shrubs she sits in, and adorns,
> With Musick high the squatted Thorns.

(ll. 513–16)

The belatedly rediscovered lyric vocation of the failing garden-state poet
is a fugitive one, and the voice of the nightingale is also that of Philomel,
the feminine persona in a now avowedly violated and speechless guise.
This reoriginating song of the nightingale is also one of darkness, pathos,
and continuing pain, not lyric immunity. In short, the lyric vocation
can be renewed only as one of loss, wounding, and incapacity, and for
the male poet only in a mode of self-consciously bizarre ('antick')
eccentricity. It is a vocation that entails a high risk of civil discomfort,
and still higher risk of (re)investing 'nature' with its 'original' power of
suffocating enclosure and vegetative entrapment:

Andrew Marvell

> The Oak-Leaves me embroyder all,
> Between which Caterpillars crawl:
> The Ivy, with familiar trails,
> Me licks, and clasps, and curls, and hales.
> Under this *antick cope* I move
> Like some great *Prelate of the Grove*.

(ll. 587–92)

The 'I' who moves under what one reader has called his poetic 'carapace' looks less like nature's high priest than a parodic realization of the emblematic tortoise of the poem's early stanzas.

What is ultimately threatened in the poem seems to be a radical decomposition of the garden state and a general crisis of representation, both pastoral and historical. It is under these extreme conditions that the poem is problematically recentered on the figure of Maria Fairfax, the heiress of Appleton as nymph uncomplaining. This recentering is circumstantial insofar as Maria Fairfax was the heir to the Appleton estate in the absence of a Fairfax son, and it also seems like one more repetition of the Marvellian attempt to recenter the garden-state poem on the figure of the nymph. Yet here the attempt seems at last, more historically consequential than it does in any previous poems I have considered. The displacement of Fairfax in the poem by his daughter and the continuation of the family line here raises the radical possibility of a counterideological and counterdynastic lineage of the garden state as well as of its dynastic continuation through the daughter. In keeping with this double possibility, the figure of the virgin-nymph, which is also one of withheld sexuality and maternity, is sustaining and threatening to patriarchal inscription. She is sustaining inasmuch as she is overcoded in the poem – one might say hysterically so – with providential, apocalyptic, and redemptive meanings that cannot otherwise be supported or made to cohere. The implication of nearly all pertinent critical commentary is that the Appleton House nymph is being made the bearer of patriarchal meanings incapable of being sustained by the figure of the patriarch. She is thus doing double duty as the feminine 'other' *and* as the key placeholder in patriarchal representation. In this double guise she is, however, a difficult, contradictory figure. It is within her power as virgin to thwart as well as excite masculine desire, thus rendering Nature 'benumb' and 'viscous'; it is also within her power to manifest a sexuality intense enough to incinerate the pastoral landscape, leaving it 'wholly vitrified' (l. 688). This figure of the nymph is not a feminist one but an apocalyptic one of the feminine in patriarchal representation. She prefigures the end of history as patriarchal narrative, but also figures a repressed 'other' history awaiting its annunciation. Such is the true history of the garden state, still unwritten, and still to be written.

Notes

1. Rosalie Colie, *'My Ecchoing Song': Andrew Marvell's Poetry of Criticism* (Princeton: Princeton University Press, 1970).
2. Jacques Derrida, 'But, Beyond . . . (Open Letter to Anne McClintock and Rob Nixon)', in *Race, Writing, and Difference*, ed. Henry Louis Gates (Chicago: University of Chicago Press, 1986), p. 367.
3. Louis Adrian Montrose, ' "Eliza, Queene of the Shepheardes" and the Pastoral of Power', *English Literary History* 10 (1980), 153–82.
4. On 'nympholepsy' in Marvell's poems, see William Kerrigan, 'Marvell and Nymphets', *Greyfriar* 27 (1986), 3–21.

5 Pastimes with a Court*

Leah S. Marcus

During the mid-seventeenth century 'traditional' country activities such as morris dancing became highly politicised. Promoted by the Court in an attempt to emphasise a community of mirth and the continuity of 'olde England', such pastimes were opposed by Puritans as ungodly. As Leah Marcus shows, Marvell's *Upon Appleton House* is filled with the imagery of such activities, but it is a merry England now overrun by violence. Marcus's consideration of the poem is an attempt to reclaim its historicity. As she points out, for Marvell's contemporaries the poem's imagery would recall the course of the Civil War, and she demonstrates how politically charged Marvell's language is. But, as she also recognises, the political hieroglyphs Marvell offers us are not immediately clear. This was an era where both Royalist and Parliamentarians not only developed distinctive poetics, but also perfected the art of parody to undermine the opposing side. For the modern critic, locating what is parodic and what sincere can be an awkward endeavour. Marcus sees Marvell as attracted to old ideals but aware of their limitations and, thus, it is difficult to establish precisely what his poetic stance is. This essay is characteristic of the main direction of recent Marvell criticism in its recognition of how many of the poems reflect a culture destabilised by civil conflict – a world turned upside down.

Marvell's *Upon Appleton House. To my Lord Fairfax* is a perilous poem, not only in the playful snares it sets for its hapless readers, but in its preoccupation with images of destruction. It could credibly be described as a series of broken enclosures and pastimes overrun by violence. The

* Reprinted from Leah S. Marcus, *The Politics of Mirth: Jonson, Herrick, Milton, Marvell, and the Defense of Old Holiday Pastimes* (Chicago and London: Chicago University Press, 1986), pp. 240–63.

mock-heroic assault of the founder of Nun Appleton 'levels' the decadent cloister of the nuns; the harvest festival in the meadows turns bloody military triumph; even the garden, traditional *locus* of peace and repose, is modeled after a fortress and subtly invaded by the imagery of war. Nor do the woods offer a satisfactory refuge. Marvell enters Nun Appleton's 'sacred grove' to escape the anarchy in the meadows but reads disruption even in the symbolic language of the trees. The noble oak, monarch of the forest, falls to the assault of worms and woodpeckers; the poet, although managing to preserve himself within the woods against the 'darts' of passion, must plead for ensnarement by thorns and brambles, a less menacing replication of the assault he has escaped.

As readers have often noted, *Upon Appleton House* is also full of masquing imagery, a language of artistic transformation that jostles uneasily against the rituals of violence. The movement from meadows to woods suggests the transition from antimasque to main masque in Stuart court entertainments: the scenes in the meadows, moving tableaux of disorder, change as though by 'Engines strange' controlled by the wondrous machinery of an Inigo Jones. Then in the woods the poet enacts his own Hermetic 'mask' in deliberate imitation of the political Hermeticism of masques from the court of Charles. But Marvell's is a masque that undoes masquing. Entertainments at court had created a fusion between Caroline ideals and actual social conditions, a model for social betterment that displayed the transcendent mind of the king as the surest pattern for national renewal. Marvell's masque offers a series of 'unmetaphorings' which tease the actual out of the ideal by reversing vehicle and tenor. In Marvell's masque of the meadows and the woods, the realm of high ideals is repeatedly engulfed by history. Like the court masques and Cavalier poems which it imitates, *Upon Appleton House* is deeply immersed in the political climate of its time, a comment upon 'present occasions' by its very identification of its own artistic *modus operandi* as akin to the devices of a masque. But if his commendatory poem to Lovelace is any guide, Marvell was less than comfortable with Cavalier strategies for self-insulation. While Lovelace memorialized the forms of court entertainment in his poetry by crystallizing them in a protected space, *Upon Appleton House* violates Royalist images of enclosure. The Cavalier paradise cannot escape the 'fallen' world of political conflict but must bow to its reforging energies to emerge something other, quite new.

Of course *Upon Appleton House* is also a country house poem and like other members of the genre in its tendency to impose the imagery of the court upon a rural landscape. But it is a country house poem that, rather than establishing a paradigm for proper 'Contentment in the Country', praises rural retreat only in the process of undoing it as an ideal for perpetual imitation. The retirement of Lord Fairfax, commander in chief of the Parliamentary forces, was a profoundly ambiguous act. Through his retreat to the country, he could theoretically be seen as having conformed to time-honored Stuart policy. He 'got him to the country' to 'till' conscience and renounce the corruption associated with a center of political authority. But as a general, he had struggled against the king; his disavowal of the cause of the regicides did not make him a Cavalier. On his estate, the supposedly antithetical realms of 'innocent' country retirement and 'corrupt' action at the nation's center keep collapsing into each other. The old Stuart valorization of country life becomes increasingly comic as it is stripped of the ideals of peace and collective social renewal to which it had traditionally been bound. Country pastimes do not fare particularly well at Nun Appleton. They are either assimilated to a troubling vision of mayhem, as in the harvest 'festival' of the mowers who have triumphed over grass and nestlings, or they are diminished into triviality, as in the poet's own lolling by the river bank, an image of 'Affection for the Country' to be reformed into something tauter and finer by the influence of Fairfax's daughter Maria.

As Raymond Williams has pointed out, many of the estates celebrated in seventeenth-century country house poems, beginning with Jonson's *To Penshurst*, were in fact carved out through economic exploitation.[1] Marvell begins his poem by assuring his readers that Fairfax's is none of those. It was built without the mining and deforestation so dear to the hearts of seventeenth-century projectors 'That unto Caves the Quarries drew / And Forrests did to Pastures hew' (ll. 3–4). Instead, the estate originated in a lawful despoiling of a corrupt enclosure, the medieval convent into which Thwaites had been seduced by the scheming nuns. The image of the ruined cloister is reminiscent of the ruined British sanctuary lamented by Giordano Bruno and depicted in the opening tableau of *Coelum Britannicum*, but in Marvell's poem, there is no nostalgia for the effaced institution. The violation of the convent of '*Suttle Nunns*' is a salutary act of proto-Protestant iconoclasm – a new beginning founded upon the destruction of the old. "Twas no *Religious House* till now' (l. 280). Like the typical seventeenth-century country house, Nun Appleton is commended for its hospitality: its 'Stately *Frontispice of Poor*' and 'Daily new *Furniture of Friends*' (ll. 65, 68). But it is significant that the beneficiaries of the estate's generosity are depicted as though detachable from the house itself: a frontispiece and movable furniture rather than some inextricable part of the structure. Nun Appleton is no timeless replication of the feudal order. Its virtues are founded upon a clean break with the past.

Of course most Anglicans would have agreed with Marvell's portrayal of the hidden corruptions of monasticism. The cloister was not a 'thing indifferent' to be preserved on account of its 'long continuance' but a positive evil prohibited by Scripture. It is questionable, though, whether good Laudian Anglicans would have been comfortable with Marvell's subtle shaping of the rhetoric of the nuns to mimic the politicized Stuart version of the ideal of Christian liberty. The nuns' language of liberty-in-confinement calls to mind the familiar Cavalier praise of enclosure as the only space for freedom. They have their 'Liberty' within the walls, hedged about by bars that 'inclose' them off from men. It is not the nuns but the rest of the world who live confined, prisoners in the 'Den' of the larger world outside:

> 'Within this holy leisure we
> 'Live innocently as you see.
> 'These Walls restrain the World without,
> 'But hedge our Liberty about.
> 'These Bars inclose that wider Den
> 'Of those wild Creatures, called Men.
> 'The Cloyster outward shuts its Gates,
> 'And, from us, locks on them the Grates.

(ll. 97–104)

A 'suttle' argument indeed that reverses freedom and confinement, but not more subtle, perhaps, than the Royalist mode of argumentation it parodies – a sweetening over of coercion with the claim that real pleasure is to be found only through obedience to the authority of sacred enclosure.

Within the 'freedom' of their protected space, the nuns enjoy a paradise of combined ritualism and sensuality – a mingling of the 'insense of incessant Pray'r' and the 'Holy-water' of pleasant tears shed amidst cushioned opulence. Marvell is of course poking fun at a particularly florid strain of Roman Catholic spirituality. But, again, as in the Mower's attack upon gardens, his verse seems to hit closer to home, to parody that hothouse of combined ritualism and eroticism, the Cavalier libertine enclosure. We are back in the shadows of Comus's palace again, in a ritualized environment where life and art are interwoven to deaden the spirit rather than affording the innocent 'Liberty' that is claimed. And, as in earlier versions of the confrontation, the enemy of free mirth is the law. Lord Fairfax's ancestor first checks his instinct to rescue Thwaites by violence because he 'reverenceth ... the Laws' even as he respects 'Religion'; he comes himself from a family with eminence in the courts: 'For Justice still that Courage led; / First from a Judge, then Souldier bred' (ll. 231–32). But law and due 'license' are on his side. 'The *Court* him grants the lawful Form; Which licens'd either Peace or Force, / To hinder the unjust Divorce' (ll. 234–35). We will recall the juggling with paradoxical notions of 'law' and 'liberty' in Jonson's *Bartholomew Fair*. At Nun Appleton the other side wins – the law overrides a privileging of ritual space. It would be easy to make too much of Marvell's game with seventeenth-century political commonplace, particularly given the fleeting levity of the narrative in which it is imbedded. But the familiar issues are nevertheless engaged and resurface sporadically for the rest of the poem. Marvell borrowed his nonchalant way with politically charged language from the Cavaliers themselves, taking on their ease of manner, their seeming casualness with matters of great importance, but constructing an alternate vision of the relation of pleasure to virtue.

Having considered the origin and progress of the estate, Marvell appears prepared to abandon history for topography. Like Lovelace's Aramantha he surveys in turn a garden, a meadow, and a wood, finding that events from the nation's recent past keep intruding upon the landscape. He wanders about, reading political lessons in the natural hieroglyphs he encounters. But in each case, the inscribed message is significantly different from that read by Lovelace's heroine. Instead of reimmersing him in a welcome system of continuities, Marvell's reading of the Book of Nature cancels out primordial images of peace, unity, authority. In her garden Aramantha had found vestiges of May Day ritual. There are trace elements of that in Marvell's portrait of Maria: 'for She/Seems with the Flow'rs a Flow'r to be', apparently at one, in proper May Day fashion, with the green world about her. But the garden's dominant metaphoric system is military: if Maria is like the flowers, she will turn out to be more warrior than gentle goddess of spring.

Marvell's account of Fairfax's garden wittily parodies the standard elements of maying poetry: the natural worship of the rising sun, the falling of sacramental dew from the heavens, the irenic appeal to an ideal of community. In the garden at Nun Appleton, however, the flowers are exemplars of military preparedness. They awaken not to do obeisance to the sun as some Apollonian source of mirth and holiday fertility but to ready themselves for battle. Their sun is only a standard-bearer; they come to attention out of respect for its morning display of the company 'Colours'. Their morning music is not the traditional matins sung by choirs of birds, but an insistent reveille hummed out by bees. The flowers, like proper May Day flowers, are adorned with morning dew. But they find the dew corrosive, not sacramental. It inhibits their firepower. They scour it out industriously before filling their flasks with fresh 'powder':

> When in the *East* the Morning Ray
> Hangs out the Colours of the Day,
> The Bee through these known Allies hums,
> Beating the *Dian* with its *Drumms*.
> Then Flow'rs their drowsie Eylids raise,
> Their Silken Ensigns each displays,
> And dries its Pan yet dank with Dew,
> And fills its Flask with Odours new.

(ll. 289–96)

Of course all of this bristling militarism is accounted for in terms that seem to cancel out its menace. The garden was laid out by Lord Fairfax himself as a playful reminder of his life before retirement and is only *apparently* a fort; within it, war is not genuine combat but only a metaphor or simile. Yet, in *Upon Appleton House* metaphors have a way of undoing themselves. Before Marvell leaves the garden, its essential nature becomes problematic: is war only gardening or is gardening actually war?

As he strolls about examining the structure of the garden, Marvell begins to read messages there, to meditate on the vaster garden of England 'wasted' by a militarism that Fairfax's garden only imitates. Little by little, as he continues his reflections, war and the garden trade places in the metaphoric scheme of things:

> Unhappy! shall we never more
> That sweet *Militia* restore,
> When Gardens only had their Towrs,
> And all the Garrisons were Flowrs,
> Where Roses only Arms might bear,
> And Men did rosie Garlands wear?
> Tulips, in several Colours barr'd,
> Were then the *Switzers* of our *Guard*.
>
> The *Gardiner* had the *Souldiers* place,
> And his more gentle Forts did trace.
> The Nursery of all things green
> Was then the only *Magazeen*.
> The *Winter Quarters* were the Stoves,
> Where he the tender Plants removes.
> But War all this doth overgrow:
> We Ord'nance Plant and Powder sow.

> (ll. 329–44)

The very terms of Marvell's comparison suggest that war is intrinsic to the green world rather than antithetical to it. Even the primeval Britain he envisions – the 'Garden of the World' – was inscribed with the imagery of battle. What happens in the course of this witty passage is that the imagery engulfs its referents. Once, perhaps, militarism was only a trope. But now, in the present, it has become the reality and gardening its vehicle: 'We Ord'nance Plant and Powder sow.' War has 'overgrown' the garden like some rapid and pernicious weed. Marvell deconstructs the metaphoric system of the garden, and having done so, he can no longer perceive its militarism as purely metaphoric. The poet's expression of regret for Fairfax's retirement is laden with ambiguity in that the general's talents for 'cultivation' are inextricable from his militarism. He might have brought renewed fertility to the national garden: 'have made our Gardens spring / Fresh as his own and flourishing' (ll. 347–48), but he would have done so with the same arts, the same 'Pow'r' he had used in his waging of war. And having arrived at that perception, Marvell begins to observe that Fairfax's garden is no absolute retreat from the abandoned national wasteland of the Civil Wars. Instead of basking peaceably within a protected space, the flowers keep up the recent conflict by mimicking the political alignment of Fairfax himself, their 'Battery' aimed against Cawood Castle, proud seat of prelacy, as the general had earlier positioned vast armies against the king and Church hierarchy. By the end of Marvell's seemingly casual visit, history has invaded the garden.

What happens in the meadows is even more complex, a series of seriocomic 'revolutions' that have teased and maddened readers for over half a century. There has been considerable resistance lately to political reading of the 'masque of the meadows', and that has had the salutary effect of broadening our sense of the poem's variety and universality. But I should like to focus once again on the specific – on the contemporary 'lessons' Marvell embedded in his landscape of upheaval. There can be no question that, for his contemporaries, Marvell's succession of images would have called to mind the course of the Civil Wars, from an initial overturn of traditional hierarchy through increasing degrees of social leveling and disorder. In Interregnum poetry open spaces like the common fields tended to be associated with imagery of vulnerability and violence. The meadows at Nun Appleton are similarly open and assailable, a place where traditional festival motifs are played out under the mutable summer sun but also undermined from within by the instability of their emblematic status. Part of the essence of the Stuart antimasque had been its containment within a larger vision of order emanating from the mind of the king. The 'pageant' of the fields at Nun Appleton is like a series of antimasques in that it offers successive tableaux of disorder. But there is no certainty of containment: the figural representations of disorder repeatedly overflow the boundaries of the frame in which they have been placed. Art keeps crashing into life.

Marvell's description of the fields is designed to produce disorientation, or more literally, agoraphobia – an uneasiness with open space based upon an inability to predict its limits. He makes use of familiar motifs of festival disorder and inversion but without a clearly implied social context that would make the inversion comprehensible. In the usual poetry of mirth, it is possible to distinguish between the festival and the everyday, between a stable underlying hierarchy and the temporary festival forms that mimic and invert it. In Marvell's antimasque of the meadows, 'normal' hierarchy cannot be distinguished from its up-ended imitation; holiday topsy-turvydom becomes irreversible in that it is not followed by a predictable renewal of the everyday but instead shatters

the insulating structure in which it is placed. To observe this process,
let us consider the grasshopper, in Marvell's poem as in Lovelace's
Lucasta, a fragile monarch of the meadows:

> And now to the Abbyss I pass
> Of that unfathomable Grass,
> Where Men like Grashoppers appear,
> But Grashoppers are Gyants there:
> They, in there squeking Laugh, contemn
> Us as we walk more low then them:
> And, from the Precipices tall
> Of the green spir's, to us do call.

(ll. 369–76)

At first glance, this intriguing passage seems to mark out the traditional
holiday motif of *deposuit potentes*: the 'Abbyss' of the 'unfathomable
Grass' is a space marked off from the everyday in which normal
hierarchy is inverted. Grasshoppers and men trade places. Given the
standard meaning of the grasshopper in Stuart court iconography,
however, the passage can be read in just the opposite way. The
grasshopper was associated with Stuart 'Affection for the Country', as
in Lovelace's 'The Grasse-hopper'. *Upon Appleton House* appears to be
drawing upon the same courtly anacreontic tradition of the grasshopper
as *basileus*, proprietor of the meadows. But Marvell's image is more
radically equivocal: are these squeaking, contemptuous overlords the
embodiment of a traditional hierarchy or are they rather 'lords of
misrule' presiding over its inversion?

Perhaps they are both simultaneously. One way of sorting out the
passage would be to read it as social criticism, an indictment of the
traditional structure of society as itself a form of misrule in which
authority is determined by accidents of social and economic position.
It is the temporary luxuriance of the grass that gives the grasshoppers
their advantage. They tower over shrinking men despite their ludicrous
smallness because they are placed at the top. In Lovelace's 'Aramantha'
the meadows harbored images of magnanimous self-sacrifice – the
'natural' bovine largesse of an aristocratic caste threatened with
destruction from outside; but in Marvell, the laws of hospitality are
turned topsy-turvy by the 'landlords' themselves. The poet places himself
among the disadvantaged. He is one of those who 'walk more low' than
the grasshoppers. The passage is curiously reminiscent of Ben Jonson's
earlier complaints against arrogant landlords who withhold hospitality
or twist it into a means for asserting their class superiority, except that
Marvell offers no immediate counterexample to reaffirm the traditional
values. The effect is disorienting. In the abyss of the grass, there is
seemingly no place for the old laws of hospitality. The grasshopper is the

first of many political hieroglyphs offered for reading in the meadows
of Nun Appleton, a sign inscribed in proper Cavalier fashion upon a
rural landscape. But in Marvell's poem, reading the hieroglyphs is a very
chancy business. They are only partially legible because they have been
shaken out of a predictable context.

The grasshopper passage also contains fleeting suggestions of
ecclesiastical criticism. The green 'spires' that shelter the insects are
reminiscent of the heights of Cawood Castle or of a Laudian cathedral;
like the Laudian party as seen by its critics, the spires alienate the upper
levels of a hierarchy from the lower rather than bringing the two together.
Again, Marvell omits the clear context that would allow us to interpret
the inversion with confidence. Are the grasshoppers meant to suggest the
ecclesiastical authorities themselves or are they rather a tribe of ephemeral
holiday substitutes like boy bishops at a Feast of Fools – appearing in the
place of authority to squeak out the message of its temporary overthrow?
It would be easy to overplay the political specificity of Marvell's imagery
(and no doubt, I already have). What is most significant about the
passage from our point of view is that it creates a rift between the top
of the hierarchy and the bottom. The Stuart appeal to mirth had been
intended to renew a sense of community between the highest and
lowest elements of society. But in the meadows, what flows down from
the top is not benevolence but contempt. Fertility and nurturance do
not spread outward from a pinnacle at the center but up from the base
of the hierarchy. Men dive through the treacherous meadows, hazard
themselves in a 'sea' where only the highest seem safe, and miraculously
emerge with 'Flow'rs' from the bottom.

The second 'act' of the meadows, which perhaps we can christen the
'Antimasque of Mowers', puts men once again on top. The grass, before
a perch for authority, has become its 'precipice' and the Mowers, who
would earlier have been contemned by the grasshoppers, now become
the masters. Like Israelites escaped from an Egyptian bondage, they
easily divide the meadow-sea which earlier had seemed to engulf all that
was merely human:

> No Scene that turns with Engines strange
> Does oftner then these Meadows change.
> For when the Sun the Grass hath vext,
> The tawny Mowers enter next;
> Who seem like *Israelites* to be,
> Walking on foot through a green Sea.

> (ll. 345–90)

Suddenly the meadows became amenable to human cultivation, no
longer threatening in their vastness. The contemptuous, towering
grasshoppers are silent, out of sight. But that does not mean that the

landscape is redeemed from its potential for discord. As in the garden at
Nun Appleton, so in its fields, cultivation is inseparable from conflict.

Are Marvell's strange mowers, part Hebraic part Virgilian, to be taken
as farmers or military conquerers? A more pressing question – how is
their victory over the hay related to the earlier militarism of the garden?
One vital difference is in the degree of containment. The militarism of the
garden was highly disciplined, kept within boundaries determined by the
political alignment of General Fairfax himself. In the fields, it is much
less discriminating, an efficient engine of destruction that 'massacres' all
it encounters. The lowly escape no more than the high. When one of the
mowers inadvertently kills the fledgling rail, he hates himself for doing
so. But in yet another holiday overturn, his compassion is overriden by
the rapacity of 'bloody *Thestylis*' and the rest of the pillaging women. The
harvest turns into a disorderly 'rough music' or riot with the traditional
'unruly woman' at the top. The mowing episode, like the Mower poems,
contains unmistakable echoes from Virgil's Second Eclogue, a lament for
something that is lost or unvalued. We will remember the eloquent
political use Milton made of a passage from the Eclogue on the title
page of *Comus*. But the women have no such sentiment. For Thestylis,
the violence of the meadows is to be reveled in as a sign of divine
intervention. She proclaims the slaughtered rail a gift from heaven,
trusses it up, and prepares to feast upon it:

> But bloody *Thestylis*, that waites
> To bring the mowing Camp their Cates,
> Greedy as Kites has trust it up,
> And forthwith means on it to sup:
> When on another quick She lights,
> And cryes, he call'd us *Israelites*;
> But now, to make his saying true,
> Rails rain for Quails, for Manna Dew.
>
> (ll. 401–408)

As several readers have noted, the passage imitates the well-known
rhetoric of the Parliamentary forces during the Civil War in that it
identifies the reapers with Old Testament models of the righteous
warrior. Echoing the annihilating harvest imagery of Isaiah and Jeremiah,
Oliver Cromwell had exclaimed after the Royalist debacle at Marston
Moor, 'God made them as stubble to our swords.' In the present instance,
however, it is the poet who has likened the mowers to Israelites, and
Thestylis overhears and corrects him. She shatters the separateness of
the poet's narrative frame and arrests his effort to palliate and distance
what he observes by assimilating it to classical or Hebraic analogues.
She insists (in accordance with the prevailing pattern of the poem) on the

literal truth of his trope. The mowers are indeed Israelites because they are sustained in the wilderness with rails and meadow dew.

Of course, to interpret the mowers as Parliamentary soldiers would reverse the poet's terms. Enlistees in the New Model Army likened themselves to reapers; in the poem reapers are likened to soldiers. But the distinction soon collapses. In the next stanza, as earlier in the garden passage, war and cultivation trade places; vehicle and tenor are reversed. Marvell counsels the hapless rail, emblematic of the innocent victim who falls along with the guilty:

> Or sooner hatch or higher build:
> The Mower now commands the Field;
> In whose new Traverse seemeth wrought
> A Camp of Battail newly fought:
> Where, as the Meads with Hay, the Plain
> Lyes quilted ore with Bodies slain:
> The Women that with forks it fling,
> Do represent the Pillaging.

> (ll. 417–24)

The word 'Traverse' is wonderfully equivocal, suggesting, among other interpretations, the next crossing of the field for the purpose of building the haycocks or, in a usage borrowed from masquing, a 'curtain . . . drawn across a . . . theatre'. But the iconography of this 'new Traverse' is remarkably difficult to read. At the beginning of the stanza, harvesting only seems to be battle: in or upon the traverse 'seemeth wrought' a 'Camp of Battail'. By the end of the passage, however, it is harvesting that only 'seems'; harvesting has become a metaphor for war. What the poet invites us to visualize is not a hayfield but a plain of battle, 'quilted ore with Bodies slain'. The women's flinging of the hay 'represents' pillaging and not the other way around. War and harvest are interchanged.

The mowers celebrate the end of their labors with a harvest-home, according to the 'good old fashion' of England. Marvell's description of the festival harks back to prewar images of a countryside ringing with the joy of 'public mirth'. And like the advocates of the *Book of Sports*, he assimilates country folk into landscape: females 'fragrant as the Mead' mark out *'Fairy Circles'* as they dance the Hay, an ancient harvest dance; their festivities surround them with an aura of well-being, fertility, renewal:

> And now the careless Victors play,
> Dancing the Triumphs of the Hay;
> Where every Mowers wholesome Heat
> Smells like an *Alexanders sweat*.

Their Females fragrant as the Mead
Which they in *Fairy Circles* tread:
When at their Dances End they kiss,
Their new-made Hay not sweeter is.

(ll. 425–32)

At least some readers of Marvell's poem have found the description
innocent and delightful. But after our experience with the treacherousness
of meadow rites in the poems of Damon the Mower, and after so much
jostling and dislocation of traditional festival motifs in earlier portions of
Upon Appleton House, we are to be forgiven if we approach the passage
with wariness. There are some jarring notes. The mowers are not carefree
but 'careless', which reminds us of their earlier violence against the
innocent. The harvest-home of these sweating *'Alexanders'* is also a
celebration of martial victory. Marvell's evocation of traditional images of
festival peace and prosperity is undermined by the lingering touches of
militarism. Much has been sacrificed to allow these simple peasants their
holiday dance in the hay. In the Renaissance, war, too, had its traditional
language of ritualization: it could be called a 'daunce unto the Musicke
of the field', but a *danse macabre*, a rite of violence. The dance of the
mowers is less a smoothing over of earlier discord than a reveling in its
effects. Their holiday sports are severed from the irenic associations with
which Stuart policy had invested them, no longer a carefully orchestrated
ceremony in which the overturn of hierarchy functions to enhance
existing authority but more like a popular festival run rampant and
reinvested with the menace that the Stuarts had tried to suppress.

Marvell's interweaving of festivity and military conquest replicates a
strain of contemporary rhetoric. Roundheads who opposed the more
radical elements in the New Model Army characterized them as lawless
Lords of Misrule and some of the radicals saw themselves as restoring a
primeval 'Merry England' lost as a result of the Norman Conquest and
the imposition of an alien hierarchy – a world much like the original
Eden of Damon the Mower, in which they controlled their own land
and pastimes. They repeated in varying formulas the ancient plaint that
"Twas never merry world since the gentry folk came up.' But as usual in
Upon Appleton House, both the degree of historical precision and the poet's
attitude toward the doctrine he offers for reading are left suspended in
indefiniteness. Like the earlier hegemony of the grasshoppers, the
Mowers' triumph is ephemeral, canceled out in the scenes that follow.

As the 'Antimasque of the Meadows' proceeds, its 'acts' become
progressively briefer and more chaotic, less amenable to orderly
interpretation. The effect is rather like that of Jonson's *Bartholomew Fair*
– a descent into ever deepening anarchy – but an anarchy unlike Jonson's
in that it does not generate its own mechanisms for a return to order. The

next scene, an 'Antimasque of Haycocks', displays a group of treacherous rocks or (Marvell seems to correct his first perception) pyramids like those of the Memphian desert. Again, the vehicle of earlier domination has become a 'precipice'. The Mowers had proclaimed themselves Israelites in the wilderness, escaped from an Egyptian bondage. But the grass they have mown and triumphed over remains when they have departed, a mocking monument to the authority they had overthrown. By this 'act' we can observe that an equalization has taken place in the meadows. Top and bottom are now much closer together than they had been in the antimasque of grasshoppers. The pyramids are 'Short' by contrast with the menacing height of the unmown grass. And the leveling proceeds yet further in the following scene, an 'Antimasque of the Plain'. The haycocks have disappeared, leaving the fields an 'equal flat / That *Levellers* take pattern at' (ll. 449–50).

Marvell is quite insistent in his use of the politically charged label. In the early seventeenth century, the term *leveler* had been applied to those who demonstrated their opposition to enclosure by pulling down boundary hedges and fences. But by the Civil War period the leveling of landscape had been assimilated to a vision of political equalization like the 'leveled' countryman's paradise we observed in some of Marvell's pastoral poems. That is the social model apparently realized in the empty meadows, where an erasure of monumental landmarks is simultaneously a flattening of social hierarchy. The meadows are returned to the original 'commons' which contemporary Levelers and Diggers considered the first condition of humankind, an 'ancient community of enjoying the fruits of the earth'.[2] Marvell appears initially to countenance the radical vision by portraying the 'flat' as a plain of original innocence: 'The World when first created sure / Was such a Table rase and pure' (ll. 445–60). But immediately, he undercuts its primal perfection by reinterpreting the 'Table' as a site for festive violence: 'Or rather such is the *Toril* / Ere the Bulls enter at Madril' (ll. 417–48). In the meadows of Nun Appleton, the traditional survivalist pattern of immersion in the seasonal rhythms of growth and harvesting becomes a model for political change. Social systems have their time of flourishing, then fade and perish like all else 'under the sun'. The Levelers' vision of a peaceful Eden of 'equal' unenclosed land survives no longer than the hierarchical structures that had preceded it.

In Lovelace's 'Aramantha' the meadows were dominated by a herd of sacred cattle, an intelligible hieroglyph of the feudal aristocracy. At Nun Appleton, the herd appears only after a long series of other 'acts' and is described with such a bewildering welter of images that Marvell's purpose seems rather to frustrate than to facilitate reading of the hieroglyph. In his 'Antimasque of Cattle', the herd appears first as devourers who are driven onto the common to strip off the remnants of

stubble left by the mowers – a fairly negative image of 'leveling' as
rapacity. Then they are likened to a canvas from the 'painted World'
of Sir William Davenant, a much more positive depiction of primeval
egalitarianism. Marvell's swift and antithetical glimpses of a 'leveled'
world cancel each other out. And they are followed by other confusing
images. The cattle are, in turn, likened to a smaller reflection of the
picture as would be seen in a 'Looking-Glass', mere 'Spots' in the vastness
of the pasture like 'Spots' on 'Faces', fleas magnified through 'Multiplying
Glasses', and finally '*Constellations*' in the heavens – the effect being to
create a sense of everincreasing smallness or distance. The description of
the cattle accelerates a process long at work in the meadow section of the
poem: in the course of his 'antimasques', Marvell has gradually stepped
backwards – from the unnerving immediacy of the initial plunge into
the 'Abbyss of grass' to a wider and wider 'Landskip' that suggests
a growing physical and psychological remoteness from the scenes he
describes and also a decreasing potential for coherent interpretation.

Then comes the invasion of the tidal flood, the final unmetaphoring
that creates the last image of inversion, a return to some primal chaos.
The dominant figure of the antimasques had been of the meadows as
a sea; now that image spills over into reality, obliterating, at least
temporarily, all possibility of metaphor. Imagery and imaged coalesce
into paradox, a world intrinsically 'upside down', at odds with and
'drowning' itself:

> Then, to conclude these pleasant Acts,
> *Denton* sets ope its *Cataracts*;
> And makes the Meadow truly be
> (What it but seem'd before) a Sea.
> For, jealous of its *Lords* long stay,
> It try's t'invite him thus away.
> The River in it self is drown'd,
> And Isl's th' astonisht Cattle round.

> Let others tell the *Paradox*,
> How Eels now bellow in the Ox;
> How Horses at their Tails do kick,
> Turn'd as they hang to Leeches quick;
> How Boats can over Bridges sail;
> And Fishes do the Stables scale.
> How *Salmons* trespassing are found;
> And Pikes are taken in the Pound.

(ll. 465–80)

Marvell's notion of a world unmetaphored is comical in the extreme, a
holiday inversion that cancels out the possibility of its own operation by
welding things to their opposites. It is the ultimate 'act' of the seemingly

endless upheavals. The process has reached a stalemate and can proceed no further. But its new self-devouring stasis is scarcely more comfortable than the transformations that have gone before. Marvell chooses to retreat from his vision of ultimate topsy-turvydom.

In Stuart entertainments the antimasque figures had quite commonly warred against themselves. We may think, for example, of the self-reversing Phantasms from Jonson's *Vision of Delight*. At court, a power associated with kingship had intervened to break the deadlock by banishing, annihilating, or transforming the negative energies of the antimasque. The disorders in the meadows at Nun Appleton are not so easily tidied up. Their slippery reversals operate as though by their own inner logic, impervious to human intervention, and must be allowed to play themselves out. Marvell enjoys the spectacle of it all but also seems to fear its seemingly limitless energy for annihilation. To attempt reform would be futile; instead he retreats into a more ordered realm analogous to that of the Stuart main masque. The transition to the 'main masque' of the grove at Nun Appleton is accomplished not by mastery but through an escape. Rather like the war-weary Cavaliers, Marvell fashions for himself a separate realm apart and appears quite willing to give up on a world where change has become so intractable. But the 'sacred grove' of Marvell's main masque is provisional rather than eternal, something he unquestionably needs but only for the duration of the chaos outside.

As we have already remarked, Marvell's 'sacred grove' at Nun Appleton is very similar to Royalist analogues in the poetry of Lovelace and Vaughan. He calls it a 'yet green, yet growing Ark', which suggests the familiar Old Testament type of the church, except that his 'Ark' is flourishing at a time when the Anglican Church was not. The grove is dark from without, light within, a sacred space walled off from the world and offering intimations of the political and ecclesiastical institutions that had proved so vulnerable to upheavals like those enacted in the meadows. Marvell begins his account of the grove by noting how it is structured:

> Dark all without it knits; within
> It opens passable and thin;
> And in as loose an order grows,
> As the *Corinthean Porticoes*.
> The arching Boughs unite between
> The Columnes of the Temple green;
> And underneath the winged Quires
> Echo about their tuned Fires.

(ll. 505–512)

Marvell's natural temple is Roman rather than Gothic, its Corinthian 'Columnes' topped with genuine foliage rather than the stylized marble vegetation that adorned its antique counterparts. It closely resembles the

Roman Pantheon, which Marvell had seen in his travels, and that ancient temple to all the Gods would indeed be a suitable model for the grove in which Marvell learns to read the language of a universal religion. But at least initially, the worship practiced within the grove appears identifiably Christian rather than pagan: its 'winged Quires' sing in the antiphonal fashion of Anglican choristers, much as they do in Royalist versions of the sacred grove.

In the grove, unlike the disorienting meadows, natural hieroglyphs are legible, at least to the observing poet. The animals that populate the grove constitute a natural hierarchy of benevolent paternalism. High Oaks and Elders listen like attentive statesmen to the lowly song of the Nightingale; thorns protectively retract their 'claws'; a Heron drops one of its young as if in *'Tribute'* to its feudal *'Lord'*. Marvell chooses for his special attention – his 'Musick' – the mourning song of the Stock-doves, emblems of chaste marriage that suggest the 'equal Flames' of Alexis and Lucasta in his poetic model 'Aramantha', or perhaps more nearly, their model in the union of Charles I and his queen. There is another analogue in Herrick's poem 'To the King and Queene upon their unhappy distances', in which an oracular oak prophesies the reunion of the severed royal pair. Contemplating the hieroglyph of the doves, Marvell asks, 'O why should such a Couple mourn, / That in so equal Flames do burn!' – a riddle which could be answered (if one wished) in terms of the royal pair's sad history, bemoaned as though in advance.

Of course Marvell's 'sacred grove' differs from the Cavalier pattern in that he carefully avoids the passion of love himself, even though he admires the chaste amours of the Stockdoves. But a more significant departure is that Marvell's grove proves not to be impervious to change. Its animal and vegetable elements suggest a vision of primeval hierarchical order, but the hierarchy is undermined from within. Already in the song of the stockdoves, he had read a message of enigmatic sorrow, but his observation of the woodcutter *'Hewel'* brings death into the grove. Like the mowers of the fields triumphing over the grass, the Hewel works doom upon something which had seemed to exceed it by far, the noble Oak:

> The good he numbers up, and hacks;
> As if he mark'd them with the Ax.
> But where he, tinkling with his Beak,
> Does find the hollow Oak to speak,
> That for his building he designs,
> And through the tainted Side he mines.
> Who could have thought the *tallest Oak*
> Should fall by such a *feeble Strok'*!

(ll. 545–52)

There has been much discussion of just what this curious allegory might mean. One of the applications it would unquestionably have suggested to Marvell's contemporaries was the recent death of the king. 'Royal Oak' imagery was so pervasive in the literature of the period and so consistently linked to the monarchy that the reading would have been inescapable.

Like Charles I as portrayed in the masque, the oak is oracular – it 'speaks' – but speaks only the hollow message of its own imperfection. Marvell's oak, unlike most of the trees in the Royal Oak tradition, loses its place of authority in the 'palace' of the wood by a measured act of justice. The Hewel is a natural executioner, like the mowers, but unlike them in that he only fells what has already destroyed itself through inner taint. The oak, Marvell observes, had nurtured within itself the '*Traitorworm*' that had brought on its destruction. The political analogue is almost too obvious to require explication. Charles I, in the eyes of his critics, had countenanced dangerous favorites, 'Caterpillars upon the commonwealth', who had with their corrupting influence brought down the towering authority that had sheltered them and therefore destroyed themselves, as the worm is devoured by the offspring of the Hewel that felled the oak. And to carry the reading further, Marvell intimates that even the king himself had finally seen the wisdom of the worm's 'execution', content to die, rather like the martyr of *Eikon Basilike*, in order to restore health to the nation:

> And yet that *Worm* triumphs not long,
> But serves to feed the *Hewels young*.
> While the Oake seems to fall content,
> Viewing the Treason's Punishment.

(ll. 557–60)

The natural hierarchy of Marvell's grove includes within its mysterious 'order' a judicious, controlled mechanism for the overthrow of corrupt authority.

Like the Royalist poets he imitates, Marvell responds to the idea of a monarch destroyed by filling the void himself, becoming a power like the power that was gone. Once he has read the political hieroglyphs of the grove, he terms himself an '*easie Philosopher*' and begins to sense himself at one with it, becoming another bird or tree; he learns their ancient language and they, reciprocally, 'divine' his 'Signs.' Little by little he takes on for himself a role which Charles I had so often played in his masques – the role of divine Magus, ordering his kingdom through the mystical divination of his mind. The Hermeticism of Marvell's natural temple is unmistakable. He reads the future out of the '*Sibyls* Leaves' and the past, 'What *Rome, Greece, Palestine*, ere said', in its light '*Mosaick*' – a pattern of legible glints of sun on the leaves. In the *Mosaick* he reads even the wisdom of Moses, who according to Hermetic lore, had brought the Ancient Theology to the Jews from the Egyptians. Finally, all human time becomes 'one History'. He can claim,

> Thrice happy he who, not mistook,
> Hath read in *Natures mystick Book*.

(ll. 583–84)

He has become a hermetic Magus – thrice happy as Trismegistus was thrice great – and his reverend status is established in a 'Mask' which playfully confers on him the trappings of Anglicanized Druidism. Under his *'antick Cope'* he moves 'Like some great *Prelate of the Grove'*, a Druid divining in his oak grove, but also the bishop of his sanctuary-church, his elaborate vestments adorned with oakleaves that figure forth the sacred origin of his high 'ecclesiastical' authority:

> And see how Chance's better Wit
> Could with a Mask my studies hit!
> The Oak-Leaves me embroyder all,
> Between which Caterpillars crawl:
> And Ivy, with familiar trails,
> Me licks, and clasps, and curles, and hales.
> Under this *antick Cope* I move
> Like some great *Prelate of the Grove.*

(ll. 585–92)

Marvell's 'Mask' lacks the high seriousness of Charles I's Hermetic rituals in masques like *Albion's Triumph*, but he has assumed the same posture as high priest of a British Ur-Christianity. What remains to be seen at this point in the poem is whether his Hermetic magic will be as powerful as Charles I's in entertainments at court – whether he envisions its energies as potent enough to heal the chaotic world outside.

The final stage of Marvell's sylvan metamorphosis is the healing of his mind, the shedding of thoughts and mental chaff in a playful ecstasy upon the moss that imitates the Hermetic visionary frenzy and the 'sacred rage' of the Cavaliers. He has constructed a model of the vanished order, discovered its participation in an unbroken continuum of sacred mystery from the time of Moses and the Druids through the Civil War period and on into the future. And he has used that perception of continuity in Hermetic fashion to cure his own mind. There are psychological changes in the poet which seem to demonstrate the efficacy of his method. He is altered from a mere witness of the chaos of the meadows into a stronger and more decisive figure who can rise above it, 'gaul its Horsemen' instead of being wounded himself.

How seriously are we meant to take Marvell's Hermetic self-transformation? The poet's 'mask' in the grove is quite playful, yet

Hermeticism was often playful. Indeed, the purging of melancholy humors and restoration of a sanguine temperament was one of its goals, according to Bruno and Ficino. But we may suspect that there is something else happening here as well. Part of Marvell's playfulness was surely defensive, like the Cavalier playfulness it imitates, but for a somewhat different reason. In Lovelace and many of the other Cavaliers, we can sense that the destruction of the idealized institution of sacred absolute monarchy generated real psychic distress in addition to all the external perils. The erosion of a royal power with which the Cavaliers so strongly identified created in some of them a corresponding inner deficit, a self-doubt that had to be countered with various rituals of mastery in which they reestablished their self-worth by adopting the role which the monarch had proved too weak to sustain. There may have been elements of that in Marvell, but for him, the essential issue appears to have been rather the degree of his independence from an order toward which he was profoundly ambivalent. He was attracted to the old ideas, as we can see in his praise for the 'Candid age' of Lovelace, yet he was more forcibly aware of their inherent limitations than many who found them appealing. In the magic grove of *Upon Appleton House* he gave them at least provisional credence in order to make his peace with the past, but at the same time he distanced himself from them through his jauntiness of tone. If the Cavaliers crowned themselves monarchs in order to salvage the image of kingship, Marvell adopted the role of king and high prelate to work himself out of the residual power those images continued to exert upon him.

Having played 'monarch of the grove' for a space in his own Hermetic masque, Marvell does something utterly characteristic of him and of the topsy-turvy logic of his poem: he departs altogether from the paradigm of Lovelace's 'Aramantha' and overturns his own sacred hierarchy by transforming himself from the figure at its pinnacle to one placed at the bottom, the victim of the power that appears so attractive as it was playfully exercised from the top. According to Caesar's *Commentaries*, the Druids of Britain had practiced the amiable custom of staking down human victims within their temples. This is precisely the fate Marvell envisions for himself. If he is to remain within the sacred grove, it will be as Druidic victim rather than Druid Priest. He asks the verdant greenery that had earlier helped fashion his 'Cope' of authority to pin him down instead, impale him in thorns and brambles, 'That I may never leave this Place.' What has happened to the earlier benevolent paternalism of the grove, whereby thorns were retracted lest they injure the lowly? We are suddenly reminded of the Druids' negative side, not unknown in Marvell's day – their reputation for cruel aloofness and for human sacrifice – which tended not to surface in the Hermetic Druidism of the Court. Something approximating that realization appears to strike the poet as well, creating a sudden mental distance from the ceremonial trappings of the grove. He finds himself eager to depart from his place of mental healing, albeit reluctant to allow himself to do so. But the grove opens out as though of its own accord. His poem has said a final farewell to 'Aramantha' and its ideal of perpetual retreat.

When Marvell returns to the meadows, he finds them utterly changed. Now they are peaceful, restored to their first greenness, as though his Hermetic magic in the grove has indeed imprinted its order upon the world outside:

> For now the Waves are fal'n and dry'd,
> And now the Meadows fresher dy'd;
> Whose Grass, with moister colour dasht,
> Seems as green Silks but newly washt.

> (ll. 625–28)

He plays in his new paradise, an image of 'Contentment in the Country'. Marvell seems to encourage the discovery of likeness between his happy pastoral condition after the 'mask' of the grove and the traditional Stuart model of rural bliss. In the 1650s, thanks to the strong influence of Izaak Walton, the literary portrayal of angling tended to carry strong Royalist and Anglican implications. It was an 'innocent' pastime that evoked the prewar vision of a countryside at mirth. However, the gleeful extravagance of Marvell's 'self-portrait in the throes of lassitude' pokes fun at his slackened condition amidst the twanging lines even while he is enjoying it. It is by no means clear that his comic prelapsarian indolence in a place once so chaotic has been brought about by the Hermetic magic of the grove. Even as he imitates the traditional masquing pattern of drawing peace out of chaos through the application of ancient magic, Marvell suggests another more plausible possibility that subverts it. The rejuvenation may have been brought about instead by the fertile agency of the flood. During the 'antimasques of the meadows', the flood had appeared a final act of chaos, the final stage of an escalating series of inversions run out of control. Marvell's language of natural renewal seems to suggest, however, that the seeming catastrophe has worked the survivalist transformation traditionally attributed to holiday inversion – bringing harmony, greenness, renewed fertility, a new beginning of the natural cycle – and all of it quite independent of the poet and his ordering 'mask'.

Before these half-formed speculations have a chance to coalesce, they are swept aside by the arrival of Maria Fairfax. It is she, Marvell quickly recognizes, and not the poet with his 'royal' rites in the grove or the cataclysm of the meadows, that has made them so 'whisht and fine'. Maria's presence has likewise brought loveliness to Nun Appleton's Gardens, Woods, and River. That does not mean Hermetic magic as a means for renewal is abandoned, at least not yet. The poet has merely mistaken the locus from which it is efficacious, supposing it necessarily tied to traditional images of religious and political authority, as it had been in the Caroline masque, whereas instead it flourishes quietly and free of its Stuart associations on the Fairfax estate. Maria is herself surrounded with the images of Hermeticism. She is conversant in 'all the Languages' and seems to practice her own rituals of the grove, charming the elements and inspiring the woods to draw a 'Skreen' about her as did the Magus Orpheus of old. Mistletoe was holy to the Druids, reverently cut from the oak tree as a symbol of fertility So, Maria herself will eventually be 'harvested' and given to the world. She,

> like a *sprig of Mistleto*,
> On the *Fairfacian Oak* does grow;
> Whence, for some universal good,
> The *Priest* shall cut the sacred Bud;

(ll. 739–42)

Marvell undoubtedly intended a compliment to Lord Fairfax as well as to his daughter since Fairfax took a strong interest in Hermetic ideas during his years of retirement. But, the poet is at pains to suggest, the former general's Hermeticism is not a mere reflection of Platonic magic at court. In the companion poem to *Upon Appleton House*, 'Upon the Hill and Grove at Bill-borow', Marvell imagines the 'sacred Shades' of that oak grove as speaking the '*Oracles*' of the family's renown. But that grove, significantly, is modeled not upon court hierarchy but on a more egalitarian 'parliamentary' pattern. There are many oaks, all equal, all prudent and humble despite their eminence. Joseph Summers has wittily termed the passage a 'delightfully artificial description of landscape as Republican gentlemen.'[3] *Upon Appleton House* is a poem of decentralization, as Milton's *Comus* had been. It 'redeems' Royalist motifs by wresting them out of their Caroline context and giving them new and autonomous points of departure.

Unlike *Comus*, however, Marvell's poem allows scant place for the traditional pastimes except in the 'antimasques'. Maria is severe and reforming by temperament, more like Milton's Lady, who had seemed at least initially to shun all traditional pastimes, than like the Lady's more genial parents, who had assimilated sports into an ethos of reform. In Maria's presence Marvell the poet, even nature, must recollect themselves and give up their foolish levity:

> The *young Maria* walks to night:
> Hide trifling Youth thy Pleasures slight.
> 'Twere shame that such judicious Eyes
> Should with such Toyes a Man surprize.

(ll. 651–54)

The poet has associated Maria with Flora, crowned with the blossoms to which she has given their sweetness. But we will remember the vigilance and preparedness of the Fairfax garden – scarcely the place to encourage an idyll of country indolence. Her moral energy even in retreat is inseparable from the pervasive militarism of the estate. In the 'antimasques' of *Upon Appleton House* the old seasonal pastimes with their upending of preexisting order were played over and over again until they were played out and exhausted – they were 'rehearsed' in remarkable variety for one last time before being allowed to fall into extinction. The world Maria is about to enter and Marvell about to reenter will demand a new set of equilibrating mechanisms as yet unspecified but based on the recognition that peace is not always the highest good and that moral renewal may require the doing of violence.

In Maria's new world, Marvell implies, the Hermeticism that pervades the Fairfax estates may no longer be important. In 'Upon the Hill and Grove at Bill-borow' the oracle of the family grove bespeaks its own undoing in that it confesses its inability to do justice to the '*Garlands*' of civic achievement (ll. 69–72). As the estate at Nun Appleton had been founded upon a violation of the past – the storming of the medieval cloister – so Maria's presence erases the magnetism of earlier 'sacred groves' and gardens. Marvell offers a list of former beauty spots eclipsed by Nun Appleton and it is perhaps significant that all are either pagan or Roman Catholic: Tempe, '*Aranjuez*', the '*Bel-Retiro*', the Idalian Grove, the Elysian Fields (ll. 753–60), all of them fading into insignificance before the reforming energy of the Fairfax family estate. It is customary to regard *Upon Appleton House* as Marvell's farewell to his own life of retirement and pleasant immersion in Neoplatonic lore at Nun Appleton, with perhaps an implied message to Lord Fairfax urging him back into the political fray. Through its insistent fusion of traditional Stuart dichotomies, the poem demonstrates that there can be no such thing as permanent peaceful retreat. Even before Maria leaves her parents' house, her influence effaces the Hermetic and Laudian pattern of achieving quietude through the discovery of continuities with pagan and Roman Catholic revelation.

Marvell's long poem closes with one final fillip of playful inversion. The poet imagines the salmon fishermen with their boats as walking images of the antipodes moving tortoiselike homeward and suggests, most preposterously, that the universe at nightfall has assumed a similar aspect. It is almost as though he wanted to indulge himself with one final bout of innocuous perceptual subversion before succumbing to the more severe 'law' of Maria. But the effect is rather to suggest the continuing vitality of an 'upending', carnivalesque mode of vision. And in fact Marvell never did give up his fascination with the leveling power of popular festival forms. Later on, as a satirist under the Restoration government, he further developed his tendency to explore the spectacles of state from the viewpoint of one at the bottom.

Traditional pastimes returned to England along with the 'May Prince' Charles, who was proclaimed king on 8 May 1660, his triumphal entry into London timed to coincide with his birthday, 29 May. His return was celebrated with the erection of a maypole in the Strand and morris dancing 'not seen of twenty years before'; he was again heralded as the lord and bringer of May. In many parts of England, May Day festivities were actually shifted to 29 May and celebrated in honor of Charles II's victory over 'poor Oliver' Cromwell. And other old festival pastimes were similarly revived. Bartholomew Fair was extended to two weeks and allowed to 'license' stage plays. Jonson's *Bartholomew Fair* was more than once performed there – a fair within the fair. Poets also resurrected the earlier court Hermeticism of the masque. We find Edmund Waller, for example, praising Charles II as a Druid Magus restored to the 'oraculous shade' of his primeval 'palace' of the sacred grove to contemplate the mysteries of government and 'reconcile' the 'divided world'.[4] Marvell remained aloof from all this magic and merriment. Instead, he adopted for himself a mode of popular festivity not inscribed with the power of Stuart kings.

In *The last Instructions to a Painter*, Marvell articulates his own poetic role vis-à-vis the renewed 'public games' of government as rather like the role played by his railing Mower 'against Gardens' but without the Mower's destructive immersion in the survivalist view of life. Marvell envisions himself as keeping up the ancient custom of 'rough music' or the Skimmington through his biting satires. He calls attention to his subject like a villager with clattering stick and pan, displaying his caricatures of public figures for criticism as countryfolk might hold up effigies of their wayward neighbors in the 'Pastime, Martial and old' of processional public shaming:

> A Punishment invented first to awe
> Masculine Wives, transgressing Natures Law.
> Where when the brawny Female disobeys,
> And beats the Husband till for peace he prays:
> No concern'd *Jury* for him Damage finds,
> Nor partial *Justice* her Behaviour binds;
> But the just Street does the next House invade,
> Mounting the neighbour Couple on lean Jade.
> The Distaff knocks, the Grains from Kettle fly,
> And Boys and Girls in Troops run houting by;
> Prudent Antiquity, that knew by Shame,
> Better than Law, Domestick Crimes to tame
> And taught Youth by Spectacle Innocent!

So thou and I, dear *Painter*, represent
In quick *Effigy*, others Faults, and feign
By making them ridiculous to restrain.

(ll. 376–92)

In context, Marvell's Skimmington holds the British nation up to shame.
But the 'antique' model Marvell adopts is a popular festival form
traditionally independent of established authority and unconnected with
the holidays of the church. Marvell's role as satirist is like a 'Spectacle
Innocent' 'played' by the villagers themselves for the purpose of moral
instruction – merry, celebratory, grotesque, potentially violent, and
tending ultimately toward reform.

Notes

1. RAYMOND WILLIAMS, *The Country and the City* (New York, Oxford University Press, 1973, rpt. 1975), pp. 27–42; 55–59.
2. GERRARD WINSTANLEY, *The Works*, ed. George H. Sabine (Ithaca: Cornell University Press, 1941), pp. 15–16.
3. JOSEPH SUMMERS, 'Marvell's "Nature"', (1953), reprinted in Michael Wilding (ed.) *Marvell: Modern Judgements* (London: Macmillan, 1969), pp. 141–54.
4. EDMUND WALLER, 'On St. James's Park, as Lately Improved by His Majesty', *The Poems*, ed. G. Thorn Drury (1893, reprint New York: Greenwood Press, 1968), pp. 170–71, 173.

6 Andrew Marvell, Oliver Cromwell, and the *Horatian Ode**

BLAIR WORDEN

Literary studies have had a tendency to treat history reductively. One or two concepts are frequently used to characterise periods when the reality is a much more complex, less easily defined field. As a historian, Blair Worden is concerned to position *An Horatian Ode* precisely into the events of 1650 which gave rise to it. For Worden, this is a watershed year in Marvell's political orientation: 'he was a Royalist before that year, and a Cromwellian and then a Whig after it.' Examining contemporary pamphlets and newspapers, Worden reveals Marvell's poem echoing their language and employing many of the same arguments, if in a sharper form. This and David Norbrook's essay following show how a poem which has traditionally been praised for its 'balance' between Royalist and Commonwealth positions actually celebrates the new English Republic. An important example of the increasing interdisciplinary approach found in Marvell studies – embracing history, literature, political theory – Worden's work illustrates how poems such as *An Horatian Ode* are responsible to their occasions. But this essay does not try to attenuate the significance of Marvell's poem to a reflection on the politics of a few months in 1650. Detailed historical contextualisation is an opportunity to show how *An Horatian Ode* reflects the larger visionary possibilities of its time – notably the emerging belief of the English Republic as a new 'Rome in the West', a power which would lead a Protestant assault on Roman Catholic Europe, an enterprise imbued with messianic, millenarian, potential. This essay demonstrates how a recovery of the histories which inspire writing also enables a recognition of the powerful imaginative contexts which help generate history.

---

* Reprinted from KEVIN SHARPE and STEVEN N. ZWICKER (eds), *Politics of Discourse: The Literature and History of Seventeenth-Century England* (Berkeley, Los Angeles, London: University of California Press, 1987), pp. 150–62.

Still keep thy Sword erect:
Besides the force it has to fright
The Spirits of the shady Night,
    The same *Arts* that did *gain*
    A *Pow'r* must it *maintain*.

I

Andrew Marvell's *An Horatian Ode upon Cromwel's Return from Ireland* is
the most private of public poems. It may be a solitary meditation; it may
be written, after Horace, for a 'forward youth' whose identity is now
unknown to us; but it scarcely seems addressed to the public audience
of Marvell's tribute to Cromwell in *The First Anniversary*. We enter an
imaginative landscape beyond politics, outside the movement of history,
where the figures of the ode appear stilled as upon some ancient vase:
restless Cromwell, the bowing royal actor, the clapping soldiers, the
running architects, the confessing Irish, the hunted Pict. Yet the poem's
transcendence of events need not be taken for detachment from them,
or its privacy for retreat. I want to suggest that the celebrated poise and
urbanity of the poem have been created out of an urgent preoccupation
with current political debate. Marvell has given timelessness to a
desperate and portentous moment in his country's history, the arrival of
Oliver Cromwell in England in the summer of 1650. Language has been
immortalized too: the language of ephemeral tracts and newspapers,
which is near enough to the surface of the poem to suggest a younger
Marvell as close to the world of political journalism as the Restoration
MP and Whig pamphleteer were to be; a Marvell around whose head
there ran the phrases of the arguments that presented Englishmen with
such grave choices during that dismal year.

    In 1650, Marvell was twenty-nine. To simplify, he was a Royalist
before that year, and a Cromwellian and then a Whig after it. Marvell,
as always, resists such simplification. He is a man, as his correspondence
and pamphlets testify, who can inhabit a range of voices, each of them
authentic at the moment of delivery. His public poems are occasional
poems, responsible only to their occasions. To describe as Royalist the
political poems that survive from the late 1640s is to risk forgetting
the sympathies that traversed party lines, and to court the danger of
mistaking Cavalier nostalgia or personal loyalty for commitment to a
political cause for which Marvell, who spent the years of the first civil
war on the Continent, never fought. The hatred of the regicide that is
unmistakable in the two political poems of 1650 – the *Horatian Ode* and
'Tom May's Death' – is foreshadowed only in a poem that cannot be
attributed to Marvell with perfect confidence, the bitter elegy proposing

revenge for the death in battle of the Royalist Francis Lord Villiers in 1648. Some readers find the poems of 1649 to the Royalist poet Richard Lovelace and on the death of that forward youth of a Royalist house, Henry Lord Hastings, to be Cavalier only in a looser sense. Even so, 1650 marks a divide. After that year Marvell's public poems all support the Roundhead cause. There is the poem early in 1651 to Oliver St John, Cromwell's cousin and intimate friend. *The First Anniversary*, written in the winter of 1654–55, and the elegy on Cromwell in 1658, unambiguously favor the Cromwellian regime.

Like Horace, Marvell becomes a lesser poet once he has accepted the new order. Did he observe the resemblance? Horace, the republican soldier of Philippi, came to terms with the rule of Augustus Caesar. The political odes of Horace that are most admired, those of the first three books, convey the losses as well as the gains of that painful transition. Marvell's *Horatian Ode* does something similar. Marvell would doubtless have been glad by the mid-1650s to hear his relationship with Cromwell compared to that of Horace with Augustus. The ode of 1650 tells us about Marvell's Horatian transition. It may even have assisted it.

II

The opening lines of the *Horatian Ode*, as is well known, refer to those early passages of Lucan's *Pharsalia* which relate Julius Caesar's decision to cross the Rubicon and the chill dread of the inhabitants of Ariminum as he camped before the town. The allusion has been more often explained than felt. We need to understand why Cromwell's return across the Irish Sea could seem as critical an event in England's history as Caesar's crossing of the Rubicon had been in Rome's, and why at that moment an Englishman might feel an affinity with the people of Ariminum.

Oliver Cromwell was the leading personality of the regime that emerged after the execution of Charles I in 1649. To the surprise of his contemporaries, his preeminence received no formal recognition. He was second-in-command of the army, but the army was the servant of the purged House of Commons, the Rump, of which he was one among many equal members, and which was to hold power until he forcibly dissolved it in 1653. In the summer of 1649, aged fifty, he led an expedition to Ireland, where the alliance of Royalist and Catholic forces threatened the infant republic. The massacres of Drogheda and Wexford in the autumn added to his long and, as it seemed to his friends and foes alike, divinely appointed sequence of military triumphs. In May 1650, just before his return to England, he successfully concluded the protracted siege of Clonmel, not now one of his best-known victories but known well enough to contemporaries to earn a proud place in Marvell's elegy on Cromwell in 1649.

Before his departure for Ireland in 1649, Cromwell had somehow held the regime together, by reconciling moderate with radical MPs and by persuading Parliament and the army to suspend their many differences. In the winter of 1649–50, when the government's fortunes reached a low ebb, his guidance was sorely missed. Royalist plots and Presbyterian propaganda threatened national security. Even if the Royalist resistance could be overcome, there was the potentially still greater threat of an invasion from Scotland, led by Charles II. The republic's attempts to broaden the base of its support had backfired; taxation was soaring; and it proved difficult to raise and finance the recruits anxiously needed to revive the county militias and to strengthen the new model army both in England and in Ireland. Politicians and pamphleteers lamented the divisions within the Puritan cause. MPs alternated between panic and despair. One of them committed suicide on the first anniversary of the king's execution, 30 January 1650; another died the following month after depression about the regicide; a third found himself 'full of melancholy and apprehensions of death'; Lord General Fairfax was said to be 'melancholy mad'; and the army officers wondered whether God had turned against them. Sir Henry Vane, one of the leaders of the republic, admitted in April 1650 that his colleagues

> were now in a far worse state than ever yet they had been; that all the world was and would be their enemies; that their own army and General [Fairfax] were not to be trusted; that the whole kingdom would rise and cut their throats upon the first occasion; and that they knew not any place to go unto to be safe.[1]

Well might Marvell write of England's new rulers, in lines 69–70 of the ode,

> A bleeding Head where they begun,
> Did fright the Architects to run. . . .

Royalists derived what cheer they could from the republic's difficulties, but their morale was no higher. Bitterly divided, embarrassed by their dependence on foreign aid, they could win no more enthusiasm in England than could the government. The mood was no happier across the broad spectrum of opinion committed to neither cause. In the political literature and the private correspondence of 1650 there can be detected a pervasive sense of political and moral dislocation. Regicide seemed to have been both a divine punishment for national sins and an act of constitutional rape, so traumatic that no one before Marvell could write adequately about it. A rash of millenarian speculation in the pamphlet literature reflected a yearning for an apocalyptic solution, beyond the exhausted resources of human responsibility and choice.

Andrew Marvell

In the first five months of 1650 the absent Cromwell held the public imagination, where he had acquired an elemental force. Royalist satire paid tribute to his public stature by portraying him as a demon, a monster with a huge, copper, swathelike nose. He was feared and hated, but respected too. He seemed what Clarendon would later call him: 'a brave, bad man.' On 4 March 1650 the underground newspaper *The Royal Diurnal* acknowledged of Cromwell's Irish exploits: 'Noll yet goes on without fear of the strength or combination of enemies about him. Brave desperate rebel! And in an ill cause too! Were his cause just or honest, I profess I should love him.' Such ambivalence is worth recalling when we assess Marvell's presentation of Cromwell in the *Horatian Ode*. So may be the experience of another poet whose loyalties during the Interregnum have proved hard to chart: Abraham Cowley, a Royalist who submitted to the Protectorate in 1656 and who would remember of Cromwell that 'sometimes I was filled with horror and detestation of his actions, and sometimes I inclined a little to reverence and admiration of his courage, conduct and success.'

The Royalists of early 1650 claimed to be certain of Cromwell's intentions. He would swiftly return to England, replace Fairfax as Lord General, turn out Parliament, and either become king or install John Bradshaw, the president of the Council of State, as a puppet monarch. Yet Cromwell remained in Ireland. Why? As the months passed, the question became a mystery. On 8 January the Commons 'desired' him 'to come over and give his attendance here in Parliament.' State palaces and gardens were awarded him on 25 February, in anticipation of his arrival. On 19 March, still without an answer to its earlier request, the Commons asked 'to know your resolution, and when we may expect you.' Puzzled Royalist propagandists improvised explanations: Cromwell was ill; Cromwell was dead; Cromwell was trapped by the Irish army. Parliament dispatched a more urgent message on 27 March; there were two further letters in April, when a ship was sent to collect him; an 'express' followed on 4 May; and on 10 May the Commons resolved to inform him 'that the House still continues in its resolution of having him over; that he is therefore to have his affairs in order that he may repair hither.' It was in response to this last instruction that he finally returned at the end of May.[2]

An obvious solution to the puzzle is the politically innocent one that Cromwell believed himself to be needed in Ireland, where a winter of sickness and death had weakened the army's morale. While Parliament longed for his safe return, he waited with equal anxiety for fresh supplies of men and money with which to finish the surprisingly tenacious Irish resistance. Yet that explanation may not be complete. There may have been a political motive as well, although if so it will have lain not in Cromwell's ambition but in the lack of it. Always hesitant before major political decisions, he tended especially to delay those that would elevate him. Whatever the tone of lines 81–95 of the *Horatian Ode*, which dwell on Cromwell's subservience to Parliament, they tell the truth. He had not 'grown stiffer with Command', and he was 'still in the *Republick*'s hand'. He always liked to think of himself as a servant rather than a master in politics, and he encouraged the army to do the same. Even his enemies acknowledged, although they were unable to comprehend, his strenuous attempt in the summer of 1650 to persuade Fairfax to keep his command. Yet as the pressure for his return to England increased, he must have known that the crisis born of Fairfax's disaffection and of the Scottish threat would elevate his position. It would have been in character to postpone the grasping of the nettle.

Had Marvell sensed Cromwell's reticence? If so, he was unusually perceptive. An unambitious Cromwell accorded with few people's suppositions. When he accepted command of the Irish expedition in 1649 Cromwell felt it necessary to counter the notion that he was prompted by 'private respects'. At the beginning of February 1650, the MP Lord Lisle, noting Cromwell's failure to answer Parliament's invitation to return, had 'some doubt of his coming, his interest, I believe, being in many respects to stay there.' Bulstrode Whitelocke, another MP, noted in his memoirs for April 1650 that by his Irish successes Cromwell 'got a great interest, not only in the officers of the army, both here and there, but likewise in the Parliament and Council of State, with their whole party.' It would not have seemed cynical to suppose that by remaining at the head of his victorious forces Cromwell was biding his time before crossing his Rubicon. At the time of his subsequent reentry into England, in August 1651, when he allowed the Scots to move south and followed them with his own army, members of the Council of State 'raged and uttered sad discontents against Cromwell, and suspicions of his fidelity.'

The suspicions of his fidelity in 1650 were heightened by the publication of a disingenuous letter of 2 April in which he explained to the Speaker his continued absence. That document, with its recurrent use of the words 'obey' and 'obedience', gives an edge of irony to (and could lie behind) Marvell's observation that Cromwell 'can so well obey' (l. 84). At first, wrote Cromwell, he had learned of Parliament's resolutions only through 'private intimations'. He had awaited a formal letter, 'which was to be the rule of my *obedience* . . . it being not fit for me to prophesy whether the letter would be an absolute command, or having limitations with a liberty left by the Parliament to me, to consider in what way to yield my *obedience*.' Thinking that the Commons might have changed its mind now that the spring campaign in Ireland was under way,

> I did humbly conceive it much consisting with my duty, humbly to
> beg a positive signification what your will is; professing (as before the

Lord) that I am most ready to *obey* your commands herein with all alacrity; rejoicing only to be about that work which I am called to by those God hath set over me, which I acknowledge you to be; and fearing only in *obeying* you, to *disobey* you.[3]

Marvell's Cromwell is 'fit to sway' and 'fit for highest Trust'. Since 'So much one Man can do', what role will be left for the disordered factions of Parliament now that he has returned to England? Can we expect that the Cromwell who has crossed the Rubicon, and who in the concluding couplet of the ode is to maintain power by the military arts that have gained it, will be content to remain a submissive 'Falcon' (l. 91) throughout the Scottish and the continental campaigns which the later part of the poem foresees? The Cromwell of the ode (unlike the Cromwell of the later poems) may not seem to be a particularly Horatian (or at least not a particularly Augustan) figure. Burning through the air, rending palaces and temples, he has something of the demonic Cromwell painted by Royalist newswriters. With his 'wiser Art', 'twining subtile fears with hope', and with his 'Courage high', we might take him for the Royalists' brave bad man – until we learn in line 79 that he is 'good'. The same line calls him 'just' – even though in line 37 justice has vainly protested against the fate that has advanced him. What do we make of these seeming contradictions? Is line 79 ('How good he is, how just') an informed assessment? Is it ironical? Is it wishful thinking? Is it praise of the kind legitimized by the panegyric, which exhorts to the virtues it describes? Perhaps we should not, perhaps we could not close the door Marvell has left open. The poem's ambiguity about Cromwell's constitutional intentions is apposite to the tense uncertainty that greeted his return to England. Fear and hope, twined by Cromwell in the poem, were inseparable in the public expectation of him.

He landed at Bristol on 28 May. Volleys of gunfire saluted him, as they were often to do in the days that followed. Accompanied by 'some few gentlemen and officers of the army', he reached Windsor on 31 May, where he was met by

many persons of eminence, Members of Parliament, and of the Council of State, and chief officers of the army; after much time spent in expressing civil respects one to another, and in congratulating his welcome thither, they had some discourse on the affairs of Ireland, and of the prosperous success wherewith it hath pleased God to crown his happy undertakings.[4]

So reported the government press, which stressed the 'modesty' of Cromwell's demeanor and his desire to be spared excessive 'pomp' on his entry into the capital the following day. His reception, on 1 June, was nevertheless heroic. It was the greatest public event in London at least since Cromwell's return from the suppression of the Levellers a year earlier, and perhaps since the execution of the king. After a large gathering of MPs and officers had welcomed him on Hounslow Heath, he passed through Hyde Park to arrive at Westminster, 'accompanied by many more lords, and most of the Members of Parliament and the Council of State, the officers of the army, and many hundred well-affected gentlemen and citizens.' On 2 June he had a private conversation with Fairfax, an interview distinguished, the official press nervously asserted, by 'remarkable expressions of love and courtesy', 'sufficient to check the false tongues'. The same day brought a delegation to Cromwell from the mayor and aldermen of London, who acknowledged 'God's mercy in carrying his Excellency through so many difficulties in Ireland and bringing him victoriously hither, etc. Unto which his Lordship made a modest reply, returning the praise and glory to God alone.' On 4 June, when the Commons gave Cromwell 'the hearty thanks of this House for his great good service', the Speaker delivered 'an eloquent oration, setting forth the providence of God in those great and strange works, which God hath wrought by him, as the instrument.'

The events of the week that followed Cromwell's landing on 28 May are the occasion of the *Horatian Ode*. We cannot be certain when Marvell wrote the poem (or know whether he ever revised it), but the evidence we shall consider suggests that, at the least, the work had taken shape in his mind within a short time of Cromwell's reception in London – perhaps within a matter of days. Admittedly it was not known in early June that Cromwell would replace Fairfax and lead the military campaign that is foretold near the end of the poem, but both developments had been long and confidently predicted in the press. Both, in any case, came about quickly. Cromwell succeeded as lord general in late June and led the army into Scotland in July. The expedition was to produce the seemingly miraculous victory at Dunbar in September and to end a year later in the Scottish invasion and defeat at Worcester.

Cromwell's move across the Scottish border in July 1650 was regarded and presented by the government as the only alternative to an incursion by the barbarous Scots, whose presence in England during the civil wars had fortified the traditional hatred of them. As early as March 1649 Cromwell, wondering whether to lead the forces to Ireland, had understood that campaigns against England's neighbors might unite the country against Charles II:

> The quarrel is brought to that state, that we can hardly return unto that tyranny that formerly we were under . . . but we must at the same time be subject to the kingdom of Scottland or the kingdom of Ireland, for the bringing in of the King. Now that should awaken all

> Englishmen, who perhaps are willing enough he should have come in upon an accommodation [with his English opponents], but not that he must come from Ireland or Scotland.[5]

Cromwell's argument is vindicated by the concluding, almost messianic section of the *Horatian Ode*, a poem that appears to enjoy its mockery of both Irishmen and Scotsmen. Marvell, like Horace, is a national poet, looking to a great leader who, through foreign conquest, will rescue a land torn by civil war and restore harmony to its troubled inhabitants. During the Protectorate, when he wrote nationalist (or jingoist) war poetry against the Dutch and the Spanish, his love of Cromwell would belong to his love of country.

So a patriotic task might await the forward youth, who, at a time when the government is stepping up its recruitment drive, must lay down his pen for the sword. Some months earlier the government newspaper, *A Brief Relation*, in a rare editorial comment, had suggested that peaceable pursuits were appropriate only to peaceful times, and had urged 'such whose genius leads them to the sword, and who desire instruction in the art military' to read a forthcoming book by the London militia captain Richard Elton, *The Complete Body of the Art Military*. There Elton addressed himself to 'the apt and forward soldier' and to 'the young soldier'. The forward youth of Marvell's poem was not alone in being offered Cromwell as a model: a government publication describing Cromwell's reception at Windsor on 31 May hoped that readers would 'imitate' the 'valour' he had shown in Ireland; and on 5 July a new government newspaper, *Perfect Passages*, reported from Lancashire that

> a regiment is raising in these parts for his Excellency the Lord General [Cromwell], and many young men of quality are seeking that employment, desiring to do something worthy of their births . . . for where there is discourse of war, it is a shame for a gentleman to say that he hath read it only, [not] that he saw it.

It sounds as if Marvell's forward youth, taking down rusty armor in the hall, likewise has a birth of which to prove worthy.

III

Although Marvell's treatment of Cromwell's constitutional intentions raises a live issue of the summer of 1650, the vision of the poem is hardly a constitutional one. By 1650 the constitution was dead. It had been put to the sword in the winter of 1648–49 by Pride's Purge and the regicide. Like Hobbes, whose *Leviathan* appeared in 1651, Marvell has moved beyond arguments about legality:

Though Justice against Fate complain,
And plead the ancient Rights in vain:
    But those do hold or break
    As Men are strong or weak.

(ll. 37–40)

The lines say what page after page of government propaganda in 1650 tried to say. John Wallace is right to set the *Horatian Ode* (as Quentin Skinner sets *Leviathan*) against the controversy that convulsed the country after the government's decision, at the start of the year, to impose an 'engagement' of loyalty on the nation.[6] Opponents of the regime faced a stark problem of conscience. If they remained loyal to the defeated cause, they would lose their political and legal rights. Government apologists adopted a Hobbesian argument that obliged subjects to give allegiance to any government that afforded protection. *De facto* theories of obedience may seem vulnerable or amoral to men who study them during times of constitutional security; in periods of breakdown they can acquire a pressing logic.

The *Horatian Ode* gives poetic life to the public mood fostered by the engagement controversy. We do not know whether Marvell was required to take the engagement, but the prospect must have confronted him, and he will have been aware of the bitter divisions that the test brought to his native Hull, that contentious garrison town. No lettered Englishman could have escaped the engagement controversy. Of the pamphlets that supported the government's position, one of the most eloquent was Marchamont Nedham's *The Case of the Commonwealth of England Stated*, published in May 1650, the month of Cromwell's return from Ireland. 'The power of the sword', Nedham asserts, 'is, and ever hath been, the foundation of all titles to government.' E.E. Duncan-Jones has noted a series of striking verbal resemblances between the pamphlet and the *Horatian Ode*.[7] The careers of Nedham and Marvell, both 'particular friends' of John Milton, have suggestive parallels. Before 1650, while Marvell wrote poems about Royalists, Nedham wrote Royalist tracts. But Nedham (a year Marvell's senior) was also a poet of sorts. The volume of elegies that marked the death of Henry Lord Hastings in the summer of 1649, *Lachrymae Musarum*, 'The Tears of the Muses', carried an appendix of poems that appear to have been submitted after the book had reached the printer. The first of these poems is Marvell's. The second is by 'M.N.', almost certainly Marchamont Nedham. The possibility of collaboration is heightened if we set Marvell's lines

Therefore the *Democratick* Stars did rise,
And all that worth from hence did *Ostracise*

('Upon the Death of Lord Hastings', ll. 25–26)

beside Nedham's couplet (later appropriated by Dryden)

> It is decreed, we must be drained (I see)
> Down to the dregs of a Democracie.

To Nedham, who did not hesitate to take the engagement, the winter
of 1649–50 presented what a less acrobatic conscience might have found
a more searching test. Imprisoned for his Royalist activities, he was
offered release and employment if he would turn his nimble pen to the
government's use. Having duly produced *The Case of the Commonwealth* in
May, he became in June the first editor of the weekly republican journal,
Mercurius Politicus.

Where Nedham can alter allegiance without pain, even with relish, the
Marvell of the *Horatian Ode* is a man of troubled and divided loyalties.
Even so, we may profit from a comparison between the ode and the early
issues of Nedham's *Mercurius Politicus*. The first number, published on
13 June, although appearing too late for Cromwell's return to be news,
included a full account of it and remarked that Royalists should 'stoop
with reverence at the name of that victorious commander Cromwell',
whose

> most famous victories in Ireland, being added to the garland of his
> English victories, have crowned him in the opinion of all the world,
> for one of the wisest and most accomplished leaders, amongst the
> present and past generations. . . . It is the wonder of our neighbour
> nations, that so much should be done in so little time.

On 25 July, Nedham's readers learned that Cromwell was 'as restless
in his own sphere' (compare 'So restless *Cromwel* could not cease') 'as
the great intelligencers are in theirs' (compare 'Urged his active Star').
Cromwell would defeat the Scots 'because it is the privilege of this
General, consigned from Heaven, to conquer wherever he goes' (cf.
''Tis Madness to resist or blame / The force of angry Heavens flame').

The proximity of the ode to propaganda becomes striking in the
nationalist conclusion to the poem. That propaganda drew on literary
and mythological inheritances which likewise surface in that part of the
ode. Despite the government's difficulties at home, the might of its army
and navy had raised England's standing abroad. Lines 67–70 of the ode

> So when they did design,
> The *Capitols* first Line,
> > A bleeding head where they begun,
> > Did fright the Architects to run

point to Livy's tale of the prophecy that Rome would be 'the chief castle
of the empire and the capital place of the whole world', and so seem to
allude to the notion, which developed in the early 1650s, that republican
England would become – in Milton's words – 'another Rome in the West.'

Marvell's Cromwell will clear the path to empire by defeating the Scots and then moving into Europe to level its monarchies:

> A *Caesar* he ere long to *Gaul*,
> To *Italy* an *Hannibal*,
>   And to all States not free
>   Shall *Clymacterick* be.

(ll. 101–104)

This vision, which called on an ancient prophetic tradition, also belonged to a tradition of Protestant imperialism by which ancient prophecy had been appropriated: a tradition that had led Sir Philip Sidney (according to Fulke Greville) to believe that if only Europe's Protestants had been able to persuade their rulers to send a united force south, 'the passage . . . over the Alps would have been . . . more easy than Hannibal's was.' Sidney had urged men to remember

> the state of Italy; which excellent temper of spirits, earth and air, having long been smothered, and mowed down by the differing tyrannies of Spain and Rome, shall we not be confident they would, upon the approaching of these [Protestant] armies, both bestir up those benumbed sovereignties, which only bear the name of free princes, to affect their own manumissions, and help to chase away those . . . oppressing garrisons . . . ?[8]

In the seventeenth century the same idea was taken up both by republicans and by Puritans with apocalyptic hopes. The republicans were particularly concerned with the liberation of Florence from the tyranny of the Medici. Sir Philip Sidney's great-nephew Algernon Sidney, a member of the Rump and an active proponent of its aggressive foreign policy in the early 1650s, would write later of Tuscany and its neighbors: 'Nothing is more certain than that those miserable nations abhor the tyrannies they are under'; 'many would resist, but cannot; and if they were not mastered by a power that is much too great for them, they would soon free themselves.' Marchamont Nedham, writing in *Mercurius Politicus* for 8 January 1652, lamented the extinction of 'the Free-State of Florence' ('And to all States not free') but noted that 'after so long a time, the old freedom is still fresh in memory, and would show itself again upon a favourable occasion.' Puritan hopes of liberating Europe from the Papacy were strengthened by the epidemic of revolutions in Europe in the 1640s. Christopher Hill observes that

> John Spittlehouse in 1650 warned Rome to 'beware of Nol Cromwell's army, lest Hugh Peter [the Cromwellian chaplain] come to preach in Peter's chair.' In the same year Arise Evans had a vision in which he

107

went through France to Rome, where 'a voice came to me saying, So
far as thou art come, so far shall Cromwell come'.[9]

It was in 1650 too that the Puritan minister Ralph Josselin began to look
forward to 'our actings in France', which would usher in the destruction
of Rome and Antichrist.

Late in April 1650 Royalist newspapers began to hint at the scenario
to which the *Horatian Ode* alludes. 'Must Cromwell to France?' asked
one of them. 'Is this your way to peace, to make all nations our enemies?'
Another's sarcasm dubbed Cromwell 'the great conqueror of the world,
who when he hath conquered Ireland, must go to conquer France, and so
the world over.' In May, Nedham's *The Case of the Commonwealth Stated*
observed:

> If it be considered how the worm works in many parts of Europe to
> cast off the regal yoke, especially in France, Scotland, Ireland, and
> other places, it must needs be as much madness to strive against the
> stream for the upholding of a power cast down by the Almighty as it
> was for the old sons of earth to heap up mountains against Heaven.

Again,

> Tis Madness to resist or blame
> The force of angry Heavens flame.

(ll. 25–26)

France, which was already engaged in an unofficial piracy war with
England, was regularly portrayed by government journals as a
battleground between a tyrannous government and the freedom-loving
rebels of Bordeaux. Events in France, claimed *Mercurius Politicus* on 4
July, were symptoms of 'an age for kings to run the wild goose-chase.' If
Gaul was given warnings by the press, so was Italy. On 20 June *Mercurius
Politicus* prophesied that 'if things go on as they begin, in Great Britain,
Ireland, and France, the Pope himself may in a short time be put to live
upon shifts, as well as his faction.' In July the government published a
document that had been sent by Charles II to Pope Innocent X, and in
which the exiled king, seeking papal support, had claimed that England's
rulers were 'openly asserting . . . that they will invade France, and after
that run through Germany, Italy, and all Europe, throwing down kings
and monarchs.' Cromwell's role in this program was indicated on
3 October by *Mercurius Politicus*, which urged that 'this brave Scipio,
my Lord General Cromwell, after he hath wholly subdued Ireland
and Scotland to the Commonwealth of England, ought to do the like
elsewhere, that so our domineering and insolent neighbours may be
brought under.'

Notes

1. For this paragraph see my *The Rump Parliament 1648–1653* (Cambridge: Cambridge University Press, 1974), ch. XI, esp. pp. 224–6.
2. All extracts from Cromwell are from W.C. ABBOTT (ed.), *Writing and Speeches by Oliver Cromwell*, 4 vols (Cambridge, Mass.: Harvard University Press, 1937–47).
3. *Ibid.*, II: 231–35.
4. *Perfect Diurnal*, 27 May–3 June 1650.
5. *A Brief Relation*, 18–25 December 1649.
6. JOHN M. WALLACE, *Destiny His Choice: The Loyalism of Andrew Marvell* (Cambridge: Cambridge University Press, 1968) chs 1–2; Q. SKINNER, 'Conquest and Consent: Thomas Hobbes and the Engagement Controversy', in *The Interregnum: The Quest for Settlement*, ed. G.E. Aylmer (London: Macmillan, 1972), pp. 99–120.
7. E.E. DUNCAN-JONES, 'The Erect Sword of Marvell's Horatian Ode', *Etudes Anglaises*, XV (1962), pp. 172–74.
8. SIMON NOWELL SMITH (ed.), *Sir Fulke Greville's Life of Sir Philip Sidney* (Oxford: Oxford University Press, 1907), pp. 44–45, 104.
9. CHRISTOPHER HILL, *The World Turned Upside Down* (London: Maurice Temple Smith, 1972), pp. 77–78.

7 Marvell's *Horatian Ode* and the Politics of Genre*

DAVID NORBROOK

Citing Jerome McGann, David Norbrook proposes that 'all literary works . . . are inhabited by lost and invisibilised agencies' and 'one of the chief functions of criticism is to remember the works which have been torn and distorted by those losses.' For Norbrook, the agency inhabiting Marvell's *Horatian Ode* is the desire to establish a distinctive republican culture in England after the overthrow of the monarchy. This has been lost sight of both because of the failure of republicanism in Britain and because the traditions of public poetry and political rhetoric familiar during the Renaissance have been lost sight of by a post-Romantic criticism which came to value inner integrity over all else. Norbrook's essay builds on the precise historic contextualisation of Marvell's poem which Worden's preceding piece developed. Norbrook, though, is principally concerned to illustrate how Marvell manipulates the generic and rhetorical expectations raised by the classical precedents of *An Horatian Ode* in order to demonstrate the emergence of a new cultural dynamic: a Republican sublime. Matching detailed literary analysis with extensive cultural contextualisation, Norbrook's essay is a powerful illustration of recent Marvell criticism's alertness to how issues of genre, rhetoric, politics and history are inseparable within the poetry, and how readers need to be careful of their own ideological dispositions colouring their readings. Challenging the view that the best literature is somehow politically disengaged or 'balanced', this essay raises questions about current readers' responses to Marvell's particular politics, especially over issues such as England's relation with Ireland.

An Horatian Ode upon Cromwel's Return from Ireland has played a central part in twentieth-century discussions of the relationship between poetry

---

* Reprinted from THOMAS HEALY and JONATHAN SAWDAY (eds), *Literature and the English Civil War* (Cambridge: Cambridge University Press, 1990), pp. 147–69.

and politics. The poem has often been applauded for avoiding political partisanship, for maintaining an equal balance between Charles and Cromwell, between the arts of peace and war, between feudal and bourgeois orders, and so on. But as critics have begun to situate the poem more closely in its historical context, that 'balance' has become harder and harder to locate. The 'Ode' is grim, witty, exuberant, explosive, savage, elliptical, elegiac, apocalyptic, but not balanced and transcendent. It is a poem urgent with the pressure of a particular moment in Marvell's life and in English history, a moment when the future seemed to lie not with monarchy but with a republic. As Blair Worden has shown, this was a Machiavellian moment: the fledgling republic was in danger, and it was essential to seize the occasion of decisive action or the cause would be lost.[1]

It is because, in the end, the cause was lost that the Ode's political complexion has often been misread. Jerome McGann has argued that 'all literary works . . . are inhabited by lost and invisibilised agencies', and that 'one of the chief functions of criticism is to remember the works which have been torn and distorted by those losses'.[2] Interpretations of Marvell's Ode, and, indeed of the Revolution itself, have exemplified such losses. From the right, it has often been argued that the foundation of the republic was an aberration from a monarchism otherwise naturally ingrained in the English people – the term 'interregnum' represents the events as standing quite outside the normal temporality of British history. From the left, the revolution has been seen as installing a regime of ruthlessly competitive bourgeois individualism and the internal repression of the bourgeois subject. But the political and discursive regimes installed after 1660, with their renewed aristocratic ethos, were not quite those the Revolution had fought for, with long-standing consequences for British culture.

If that is so, then we should be wary of reading the Ode as simply poised between old and new orders, and should be alert to ways in which the failure to establish a distinctive republican culture in Britain may have distorted its reception. For reasons that will be discussed later, the Ode does not seem to have been published in 1650. After the Restoration, Marvell, like so many public figures, was anxious to minimise the degree of his involvement with the Commonwealth; it was in their interest to present themselves as motivated by a pragmatic loyalism rather than anything as doctrinaire as republicanism. For a brief moment the Ode again seemed about to become timely at the time of the exclusion crisis in the early 1680s, when Marvell's poems were posthumously printed. The publisher, Robert Boulter, allegedly 'did not question to see the monarchy reduced into a commonwealth and very speedily'; but he apparently changed his mind over whether this would happen speedily enough for it to be safe to print the Cromwell poems, and they were dropped. Thus for a century and a quarter after the poem's composition, Marvell's image as a zealous Protestant patriot was untarnished by republicanism. The Cromwell poems were not published until the auspicious republican year of 1776, when James Barry issued an engraving showing Marvell, Milton and other patriots saluting the phoenix of liberty arising across the Atlantic. But by this time the tradition of Marvell the unwavering monarchist was so strong that it could be used by a circular process to read back into the Ode itself.

And by then the tradition of public poetry and political rhetoric that went back to the early Renaissance was nearing a climacteric that was also to lead to its eclipse, in the reaction against the French Revolution. That reaction, which has moulded the idiom of modern literary studies, involved a reaction against rhetoric, against public political poetry in the name of inner integrity. The long-term result was the privileging of Marvell's lyrics over his public poetry and prose. Equally significantly for the interpretation of the Ode, the Romantic period saw also the eclipse of the idea of genre, of poetry as performing a particular kind of public action, and the emergence of the notion of the poem as a timeless artefact standing above the debased world, and expressing an individual sensibility that would be repressed by strict generic categories. Charles himself, the royal actor, becomes in this tradition an emblem of the lost autonomy of the artefact. Hazlitt, knowing the poem only by report, thought of it as an elegy for Charles, while Hartley Coleridge, initiating the tradition of balanced opposites, said that the poem could be either a satire or a eulogy of Cromwell.

In the heyday of the New Criticism such 'balanced' readings were to become the norm. There have always been dissenting voices, especially from historians; Christopher Hill long ago argued that the poem enacted a move towards Cromwell rather than contemplative neutrality.[3] Such interpretations, however, have been liable to criticism as historical readings which fail to take account of the poem's literary qualities. The terms of that antithesis need challenging: it is precisely by sharpening the analysis of the poem's formal properties beyond a narrow conception of the 'literary' that it becomes possible to return it to history. Recent scholarship, in regaining an understanding of rhetoric and genre, has become better equipped to understand the links between poetry and politics. Rather than seeing the Ode as pure literature, and Marvell as an isolated genius transcending lesser poets who wrote mere propaganda, it becomes possible to recover the role of the poem's generic acts in a far wider cultural movement. In the analysis of the poem as act, many questions remain to be answered: Marvell's own personal allegiances and the circumstances of the poem's production and reception remain obscure. I believe, however, that the hypothesis of the Ode as radically revisionary opens the way to making more sense both of the poem and of its context.

Both parts of the poem's title arouse royalist expectations. In giving the bald generic characterisation 'Horatian Ode' – as far as I know uniquely – Marvell evoked the royalist admiration of Horace, with his cult of peace under a worthy emperor. In an Ode of 1630 Sir Richard Fanshawe celebrated Charles's preservation of the peace while 'warre is all the world about'.[4] Marvell himself had written a monarchist Horatian Ode, a close imitation of the second ode of the first book which he contributed to a volume of panegyrics in 1637. In the aftermath of the Second Civil War there had been a resurgence of royalist Horatianism, and Fanshawe's Ode was one of many ceremonial poems from the 1630s which were published as a loyal gesture in the period leading up to the regicide. The other element in the title, the reference to a return, is also a strong generic signal. Renaissance rhetoric recognised a distinct kind of demonstrative or panegyrical oration, a celebration of a hero's return, a *prosphonetikon* or *epibaterion*. Horace's odes were regularly classified in Renaissance editions according to panegyrical genres: for example, the fourth ode of the fourth book, long recognised as one of Marvell's chief models for his Ode, was classed as a *prosphonetikon*. The second and third decades of the seventeenth century saw a proliferation of poems in this genre: Oxford and Cambridge were issuing more and more volumes of commendatory verse to commemorate royal births and also royal returns: Charles's return from Spain in 1623 and his returns from Scotland in 1633 and 1641. The word 'return' appeared prominently in such volumes; and it took on broader significances, as the king was hailed as returning or restoring the realm to a lost golden age.

Some critics have taken this use of royalist forms to indicate that Marvell is balancing royalist poetry against Puritan politics; or, more radically, that he is using the Horatian echoes to undermine and obliquely satirise Cromwell. It is often assumed that Marvell began as a royalist and remained sympathetic to that position down to 'Tom May's Death'; Wallace argues that he was consistent to the end in preferring government with a monarchical element. But we need to be wary about constructing an unproblematic grand narrative of Marvell's career: in a period of massive political upheaval, major discontinuities may have marked personal and poetic histories. If the Ode evokes royalist genres, it is in order to subvert them, to return English poetry to a truer course. For the 'balanced' or royalist readings tend to take at face value the claim that Renaissance culture was essentially royalist and centre on whether he is vindicating that culture against Cromwellian anarchy or saying a sad farewell to it. But it all depends what is meant by the Renaissance, and by culture.

Renaissance humanism centred on the recovery of classical texts; and deeply engrained in some of the most prestigious texts was an enthusiasm for republican liberty and a disdain for monarchy as a primitive and superstitious form of government. For the more radical humanists, then, the restoration of classical culture was not a narrowly literary matter. Roman eloquence had reached its height with Cicero the defender of the republic, and under the Empire it had become flabby and ornamental, debased by courtly flattery. In the *First Defence of the English People* Milton immodestly compared himself to Cicero and pointed out that he had the advantage of a happier theme for his eloquence: whereas Cicero's story had ended tragically, with the senate disregarding his warnings against rule by one man, the English had been able to reverse this outcome and move from monarchy to republican liberty. A *Tragedy of Cicero*, published in 1651, pitted a virtuous Cicero against a corrupt and devious Octavius. Machiavelli had linked this decline with larger social causes; the selfishness of the nobility which grabbed more and more land, leading to a polarisation between an easily manipulated propertyless multitude and an idle nobility which had bartered political liberty for a luxurious life on its country estates. As J.G.A. Pocock has shown, the Machiavellian analysis was developed in the 1650s both by Harrington and, in a very radical direction, in the newspaper *Mercurius Politicus*. It was symptomatic of the thinking in this period that Harrington, in his translation of Virgil's eclogues, should have taken for granted a rudimentary sociology of literature, pointing out that the changes in land-holding alluded to in the first eclogue were to lead directly to the establishment of the debilitating feudal order which must now be swept away.[5] Maecenas after all earned much of the enormous wealth which he consumed so conspicuously from confiscations from defeated republicans, the kind of confiscation to which Horace owed the substantial estate he liked to present as a modest country farm.

In the context of Marvell's Ode, it is particularly interesting that the politician who did most to win poets to the republic, Henry Marten, should have attempted to revise the cult of Horace. It was Marten who gave a classical cast to the iconography of the new republic, proposing that before the statues of the king were taken down their heads should be struck off in imitation of Brutus's mutilation of the images of Tarquin, and devising the aggressively final inscription 'Exit Tyrannus Regum Ultimus'. A more thoroughgoing republican than the Levellers, Marten risked their hostility in 1649 to support Cromwell as the only effective agent for getting rid of the monarchy. He remained suspicious of Cromwell's ambitions, however, and in 1653, when Cromwell dissolved the Long Parliament, Marten wrote a poem in protest. His 'Antepod[um] Horatian[um]' was a direct inversion of Horace's most celebrated epode, the second, 'Beatus ille qui procul negotiis', which had been translated by Jonson and echoed by innumerable cavalier poets. Horace praises the life of rural retirement; Marten inverts Horace's opening to attack retirement as a cowardly shunning of public business:

Ignavus ille qui sepultus ocio
    (Vt bruta gens animalium)
Materna bobus rura vexat pigrior,
    Inhians decuplo foenori
Rostris ineptus, impar et se iudice
    Civis, cliensq[ue] civium.

(Cowardly, slothful is he who buried in leisure, like the brute race of
animals, more sluggish than his oxen, vexes his mother lands, gaping
for tenfold increase, unfitted for the rostra, even in his own judgement
unequal to a citizen, and a dependent of citizens.) This poem turns
upside down the values of aristocratic Horatianism in the name of civic
humanism: Marten entitled it 'Vitae civicae laudes'.

For classical republicans, in fact, the problem with Renaissance culture
was that it had not yet happened, in the sense that there had not been a
full return to the central principles of the Roman republic; instead, there
had been various botched compromises with feudal institutions and
monarchical superstition. It was the commonwealth, not the monarchy,
that permitted a true return to the golden age, a true renaissance, a true
restoration. Marten seems to have been responsible for the inscription on
the Commonwealth's seal: 'in the first year of freedom by God's blessing
restored'. All these words overlap with the term 'revolution', which
also had the sense of returning to origins, of restoring. But there was an
important difference between restoring a recent status quo and restoring
some very distant and half-mythical era: in that sense, the word
'revolution' was already acquiring its modern connotations. There was
even talk of reforming the entire calendar, in anticipation of the French
revolutionary regime, and some books were dated according to the
years of the restoration of liberty. When taxed in parliament with
the outrageousness of presenting the abolition of the monarchy as a
'restoration', Marten cheekily replied that 'there was a text had much
troubled his spirit for severall dayes and nights of the man that was
blind from his mother's womb whose sight was restored at last'.

Marten urged the new regime to recruit writers who would
disseminate this view of a possible cultural revolution and to show
clemency for former royalist poets who might be won round. This
campaign was at its height at the moment when Marvell was probably
writing his Ode, in June 1650, when Marchamont Nedham started the
aggressively republican journal *Mercurius Politicus*. The recruitment
of prominent writers was important for the regime's national and
international prestige. It is true that the number of committed
republicans was small, but hindsight has tended to diminish the degree
of support the new regime could begin to muster. Amongst those
who rallied to the cause was the veteran Spenserian George Wither;

interestingly, in January 1651 he directly recalled Caroline *prosphonetika* in a collection of poems celebrating the regicide:

> It fareth, now with me, as on that *morning*
> Which, first, inform'd us, of his *safe returning*

– that is, Charles's return from Spain in 1623.[6] Payne Fisher wrote several volumes of pompous neo-Latin panegyrics. A far more prestigious champion for the new regime was John Milton; and his example would have been most significant for Marvell, whose early verse is full of echoes of the 1645 *Poems*. Milton had recently glorified the regicide, Cromwell, and the Irish campaign in his *Observations upon the Articles of Peace* (published in May 1649), polemically contrasting the language of republican 'fortitude and Magnanimity' with courtly flattery. Not only the political content but the form of Marvell's poem has Miltonic analogues: for Milton too was experimenting with revisions of Horatian poetic models. He ended his *Second Defence* with a quotation from the last ode of the third book, adapting Horace's claims for the immortality of his odes to his own panegyric of the republic, whose foundation in his view surpassed any of the political feats Horace had celebrated. Milton's sonnets of the 1640s and 1650s adapt the Horatian ethos to new political circumstances. And Milton seems to have seen the odes through the eyes of didactically minded critics who presented him as a *sacerdos*, a poet-priest who summons readers to civic virtue and whose own linguistic skill is a pattern of the discipline demanded of the citizen. Marvell's Ode needs to be seen in the context of these attempts at a radical rethinking of the politics of poetry and of classical culture; its tone is not that of a merely pragmatic loyalism. Marvell's title has complex associations: he both criticises royalist Horatianism as falling short of classical standards of public responsibility and to some extent criticises Horace himself and revises him in a republican direction.

To illustrate this point it will be necessary to analyse Marvell's inversion of the generic expectations raised by the title in five main areas. Generic patterns were never rigid, and a considerable degree of deviation from the norms laid down in rhetorical handbooks was expected; but the norms of the *prosphonetikon* had been made particularly prominent by the orchestrated chorus of adulatory verse in the first part of the century.

The revision begins very strikingly with the opening, the *exordium*. In an extreme literalisation of the conventional declaration of modesty, the poet presents the very writing of his own poem as a deviation from the political imperatives of the moment. In Horace's *prosphonetika*, and still more in Caroline panegyric, the hero's return is normally a signal for conflict to end and the arts of peace to revive. In direct contrast, Marvell's forward youth is urged to turn from the shadows, from 'Numbers languishing'. As A.J.N. Wilson has pointed out, Roman poets in militaristic vein often censured the shadowy 'vita umbratilis'.[7] 'Languish' was a potent term in republican vocabulary, going back to Cicero and associated with the opposition between republican activism and monarchical lethargy. John Hall, an ambitious young poet who went to Scotland in the summer of 1650 to support Cromwell's campaign, warned recalcitrant Scots monarchists that despite its superficial peace and elegance Caroline society had been rotten at the core: courtiers knew how to lull the people asleep 'with some smal continuance of peace (be it never so unjust, unsound, or dangerous) as if the body politick could not languish of an internal disease, whilst its complexion is fresh and chearful'. Before Marvell's triumphal poem has begun the youth is already setting off, so that the *prosphonetikon* turns into a *propemptikon* for Cromwell's departure to Scotland. It is only at the very end of the poem, when Cromwell is imagined as setting off, that the poet addresses him directly. This is in the first instance an *occasional* poem, responding to a particular, and very real, crisis: Charles was on his way to Scotland, and if his alliance with the presbyterians succeeded the republic would be in grave danger. Marvell is not necessarily making a general claim that war is superior to peace, but he is appealing to the Machiavellian idea of the armed citizen (Marten had raised his own force during the Second Civil War without consulting parliament). When liberty is in danger, retirement is irresponsible.

After the *exordium*, the *prosphonetikon* would be expected to continue with an analysis of the hero's birth, education and character. In his portrait of Cromwell, Marvell radically revises the kind of idealised image of authority to be found in Caroline panegyric: indeed, by inserting a portrait of Charles, Marvell heightens the contrast between monarchical man and republican man. Caroline panegyric idealised the figure of the monarch, making him a living embodiment of transcendental justice and of the unity of the body politic; Caroline odes and masques constantly identify the royal family with mythological figures. This idealisation goes with a strong sense of social as well as aesthetic decorum. Marvell presents Charles in such terms – he is comely, he fastidiously disdains the vulgar, the common, the mean. By contrast, Marvell emphasises that Cromwell climbs up from a relatively modest position – though he confutes royalist attacks on him as base-born by placing him in a gentlemanly garden. For the socially conservative, 'industrious' was a condescending term; but Blair Worden has pointed out that 'industrious Valour' might be a translation of Machiavelli's *industria* and *virtù* and the Machiavellian usage may lie behind the prominence Marvell gives in his poem to the simple word 'man': 'Much to the Man is due', 'So much one Man can do'.[8] Whereas monarchs rely on the ornamentation of high rank to beautify their actions, Cromwell is all the more impressive because he draws on elemental human qualities. This fact is heightened by a very striking absence: there is no classical mythology. Of course Cromwell is not presented in merely human terms, he fulfils a divine will, but it is made clear that he does so by opening himself to a mysterious and transcendent force rather than by occupying a traditional divinely sanctioned role: he is a bolt flung from above, the force of angry heaven's flame.

In human terms, however, Cromwell emerges as someone far from the conventional panegyrical frame of reference. Some writers have tried to fit the praise of Cromwell into the conventional encomiastic categories of the four cardinal virtues, but it takes a struggle. He is valiant in war, but in the context of Caroline panegyric, to value military courage so highly as to describe the arts of peace as 'inglorious' would have come as a shock. His prudence amounts to deviousness, 'wiser Art': Marvell accepts the claim put about by royalists that he deliberately manipulated Charles's escape. His temperance is pushed to the point of being 'reserved and austere', terms which in royalist discourse would have connotations of puritanical preciseness. And justice, the final cardinal virtue, is made to plead against Cromwell. Some critics therefore see the poem as ambivalent, or as a satire on Cromwell the Machiavel.

Such readings, however, take it too easily for granted that Marvell would reject a Machiavellian frame of reference. One royalist described Marvell as a notable English Italo-Machiavellian, and Worden has shown that it is worth taking this description seriously. While most defenders of the republic couched their argument in merely pragmatic terms, a few, recognising that the legality of the regicide was highly dubious, argued that a radical revision of conventional political categories was necessary, that an orthodox moral vocabulary was often no more than a mask for social conservatism. Marvell makes Cromwell break out of the frame of conventional panegyric, of the rhetoric of praise and blame: as Patterson emphasises, it is in the context of a panegyric that we are told that it would be madness to blame him.[9] Hall similarly revises traditional language in *The Advancement of Learning* (1649):

> For discomposition of the present frame, may not, I pray this be a Topicke for any Government, though never so ill grounded, never so irregular, or never so Tyrannicall? Should we sit still, and expect that those in whose hands it is, should quietly resigne it, or new-mould it themselves, or some fine chance should do it to our hands? or should we not out of this very reason, if our houses were all untiled and obvious to all injuries of the weather, forbeare to pull them down or mend them, because we would make no alteration, and so continue in our miserable patience, because we feare a change and some trouble . . . or should we expect that some Deity, or unthought of influence would rescue us from these inconveniences which we saw,

but would not remove? I am afraid whether any can be serious
upon this question: For as happinesse is the reward of courage and
industry; so what ever people ever yet obtained any Reformation
without sweat or wounds, and a just violence to the over-ruling
power; just I say, though it clashed with the letter of some *Positive*
Law for with the *Fundamentall* and true ends of government it could
not. But there is no need in this case to urge this so hard to you
[Parliament], who so nobly brake through this objection, and
redeemed the supreme power.[10]

Hall uses one particular significant word of the new regime: he says
that it nurtures 'men of sublime mindes'. In 1652 Hall published the first
English translation of Longinus's late-classical treatise on the sublime. In
his dedication to Bulstrode Whitelocke, a patron of Davenant's 'reformed'
drama, he reminds him that Longinus discusses the theory that rhetoric
flourishes best in conditions of political liberty. Though he concedes
that 'the corruption of time hath diseas'd most Governments into
Monarchies', Hall implies that the republican sublime may revive under
the commonwealth. Hall believed that what he called 'this turne of time'
was capable of a 'noble alteration': the 'highest spirits' were 'pregnant
with great matters . . . labouring with somewhat, the greatnesse of which
they themselves cannot tell'. This 'great and . . . restlesse Genius' of the
time would bring forth many a 'sublime and elevated spirit'.[11] Longinus
makes a central distinction between artistic effects which are merely
skilful and competent on the one hand and the magnanimous or sublime
on the other: sublimity, he declares, 'wheresoever it *seasonably* breaks
forth, bears down all before it like a whirlwind'; sublime poets *'burn* up
all before them'; Demosthenes *'thunder-strikes* and in a manner *enlightens*
the Oratours of all ages'. Marvell's portrayal of Cromwell burning
through the air aims at this kind of sublimity – a height, indeed,
somewhat above Horace himself. This notion of the English Revolution
as something sublime, something that transcends conventional modes
of expression, was widespread: in his *Second Defence of the English People*
Milton says that the establishment of the republic transcends all the
deeds of the ancients even if he is not able to find the words fit to
describe it. Learning after the Restoration that Milton had written some
'admirable panegyricks, as to sublimitie of wit', on Cromwell and Fairfax,
John Aubrey eagerly sought them out: even if they were in praise of the
devil, "tis the *hypsos* [sublime] that I looke after'.

Marvell heightens this sense of Cromwell as a force that can scarcely
be contained within conventional forms by his use of metre. Renaissance
humanists tended to regard rhyme as one of the feudal barbarisms which
they wanted to abolish, and made some vain attempts to restore the
classical metres of unrhymed quantitative verse. Rhyme became a symbol

of the courtly corruption of language under the later Empire, tinkling sound as opposed to moral sense. Milton, who denounced rhyme as a symbol of bondage in a prefatory note to *Paradise Lost*, had as a young man attempted an unrhymed translation of a Horatian ode. Marvell admits rhyme, but his metre is nonetheless exceptionally terse, particularly because the semantic level accentuates the impression of the necessary rigours imposed by the form. Cromwell is consistently seen as breaking out of closed spaces: nature must make room for him, he casts kingdoms into a new mould. At times his energy makes the syntax break down altogether: 'And with such to inclose Is more then to oppose'. Marvell keeps in reserve until line 114 the longest word in the poem, 'indefatigably', which almost fills up its line. And there is a pointed contrast with Charles, who *can* be contained within his form: Cromwell, with his net, chases him into Carisbrooke's narrow case, and Charles, in an almost languishing gesture, bows down in those short couplets that end his life, as if upon a bed. Charles may seem to be identified with the arts of peace, Cromwell with the arts of war, but in fact Cromwell, who can know as well as act, is constantly associated with artistic emulation: he blasts Caesar through his laurels, stages Charles's performance on the tragic scaffold, he is the bold architect of the new state. If Cromwell is the republican sublime, Charles is the courtly beautiful; Marvell is establishing a similar relationship between his forebears the cavalier poets and the new and more innovative genre of poetry he is now founding. In this sense, it could be argued that by giving a favourable portrait of Charles, Marvell makes his poem more rather than less radical: monarchical culture is weighed at its own highest self-valuation, as the source of grace, decorum, elegance, exclusiveness, and found beautiful but limited.

The poem thus rejects the Caroline aestheticisation of politics. But may not the celebration of Cromwell's sublimity be merely a new and potentially just as authoritarian aestheticisation, reducing the complex forms of political agency to a cult of personality? As Wilding points out, Marvell plays down the Leveller viewpoint. All the same, he goes into more considerable constitutional detail than would be expected in an encomium. Horace had left the precise relations between Augustus and the senate discreetly vague, but Marvell insists that Cromwell is concerned not with his own glory but only with the state's: he presents to the Commons not only the kingdom of Ireland but also his own fame, and his campaign is shown as a firmly republican one. The more conservative members of the Rump were indeed hesitant about using the word 'republic' and preferred the blander 'commonwealth'; Cromwell himself had long hesitated before deciding that the king must die. But Marvell insists on the way in which the traditional political order has been overturned. Machiavelli had argued (*Discourses*, I, 9) that only a single decisive individual could achieve radical constitutional change. Having arranged the decapitation of the king, the head of the body politic in the old political language, Cromwell lays a kingdom at the feet of the Commons, the 'feet' who have now abolished their monarchical 'head'. The prominently placed word *'Republick'* is reinforced by *'Publick'* eight lines later. Cromwell has left his 'private Gardens' to serve the public; but it will be necessary for the public to exercise their political responsibility, ensuring that he does not continue to pursue his private interests now that he exercises such influence, growing 'stiffer with Command'.

This context gives an unconventional edge to the old maxim:

> How fit he is to sway
> That can so well obey.

These lines can be taken as proposing that Cromwell should run for king. But the conventional maxim gains a new, paradoxical force in a republican context: the more prince-like he is, the more virtue resides in renouncing kingship and serving the republic. This idea is reinforced by the falcon analogy. Earlier in the poem Cromwell had been the hunter, Charles the hunted animal; now the republic is the hunter, Cromwell its tame falcon. Falcons are not always so easy to lure back: one could read the word 'sure' at line 96 in a number of tones. The analogy condenses the uneasy respect with which republicans viewed Cromwell at this stage.

That unease is also, perhaps, reinforced by the poem's unusual metrical tensions, which function as an analogue of the necessary tensions that maintain republican liberty. Machiavelli had argued that a certain element of disorder strengthened a state, that Rome had been greater when there was an element of popular participation and unrest and declined into lethargy when this challenge was lost. John Hall argued against the idea that monarchy was the best form of government because most unified: in a republic, 'among many joynt Causes, there may be some jarring, yet like cross wheels in an Engine, they tend to the regulation of the whole'. Even when celebrating Cromwell more unequivocally in *The First Anniversary*, Marvell was to retain this emphasis on structural tension, contrasting the republican 'resistance of opposed Minds' with the authoritarian unity aimed at by conservative monarchs, more 'slow and brittle then the *China* clay'. If Cromwell's sublime energy resists the confining forms of an older and more conservative poetry, Marvell's metrical austerity, the counter-pull of the terse six-syllable couplets, implies the need for a severe counter-discipline to resist energies that may potentially become dangerous to the state.

Such implicit reservations should not be overplayed, however. The poem is an encomium and its heroic mode prevails over the caricature of Cromwell as a monomaniacal social climber which had been propagated by royalists and was being taken up by the Levellers. The fact that Marvell nonetheless feels it necessary in the name of this new republican ethos to engage with opposing views may explain why as far as we know the poem was not published in 1650. It gives too much credit to Cromwell to please many parliamentarians and radicals, but is too Machiavellian and republican to please Cromwell. And before long Marvell was to enter the service of Fairfax, who had opposed the Scottish war, so that he would have had little incentive to publish it: the poem's moment was a very brief one.

The next section of the *prosphonetikon* would conventionally be an analysis of the deeds of the returning hero. But Marvell's narration is highly unconventional. He plunges into the narrative:

> So restless *Cromwel* could not cease
> In the inglorious Arts of peace
> > But through adventurous War
> > Urged his active star.
>
> > > (ll. 9–12)

The account of what he actually did, however, is oblique in the extreme: scholars still dispute the exact meaning of the densely metaphorical description of the lightning breaking through the clouds. The lightning metaphor is then continued to give an indirect description of the regicide at lines 23–24. The poem then turns back on itself to describe Cromwell's life before he became a soldier, but this retreat is used to point the contrast with the speed and force of his emergence, and we move again to the regicide at lines 34–36. Then we move back again to a narrative of the civil war campaigns, before turning yet again to the events leading up to the regicide; and here Marvell makes a striking concession to royalists by suggesting that Cromwell deliberately engineered Charles's escape from Carisbrooke. It is as if the regicide is a topic that keeps breaking through the muffled syntax that seems to obscure it. In rhetorical terms, however, the poem is not an equal balance between Cromwell and Charles: syntactically and structurally, the description of the regicide is a digression. The poem could certainly have glided over the event as the most desperately controversial and perhaps unpopular act of the new regime, and turned pragmatically to the Irish conquests as something that would unify a broad section of English opinion; instead, Marvell enacts a process of facing up to difficult and perhaps unpalatable truths even in an encomium. We are made to sympathise with the doomed king: the infinitely regressive pain of

> > with his keener Eye
> > The Axes edge did try
>
> > > (ll. 59–60)

is terrifying. But the poem gives the reader the impression of facing the fact of regicide coolly and unflinchingly, after earlier evasion, and this comes as a kind of emotional release, a surge of energy as the poem moves on, having been able to accommodate the tragic within the panegyrical.

The main event marked by the poem, the Irish campaign, formed a striking contrast with the triumphal returns of Charles I, particularly his return from Scotland in 1641. On that occasion rebellion had just broken out in Ireland. Many recent historians have argued that the panic over the 1641 Irish rebellion, fuelled by Pym, was the leading factor in precipitating political disputes into open war. But the university panegyrics for Charles's return blandly ignored the scale of the crisis: the poets prophesied that the king would bring peace like Venus from the Irish seas and even suggested that the rebellion was to be welcomed as a recreation which would allow Charles to keep his sword free from rust. Cromwell's situation in 1650 turned Charles's situation in 1641 upside down: where Charles was returning from an ill-managed expedition to Scotland to try to confront an Irish crisis he was accused of having fomented, Cromwell was returning from a decisive campaign in Ireland and about to take on the Scots. Where the Caroline panegyrists had lavished hyperboles on Charles's non-existent victories, Marvell's poem is strikingly subdued in what it says about Cromwell's victories, enacting a contrast between empty words and decisive actions.

It is disturbing to find a poem that celebrates national emancipation simultaneously endorsing Cromwell's brutal repression of Irish resistance, and some critics have argued that in putting praise of Cromwell in the mouths of the Irish Marvell was being ironic at his expense. It is certainly not true to say that all seventeenth-century Englishmen were indifferent to Irish interests. Cromwell had crushed at Burford a mutiny by Levellers who resisted the campaign; Marten, too, had spoken up for the Irish. But there were tactical reasons for the campaign, and Marten came round to supporting Cromwell's mission, though he gave it an ideological cast by proposing that it be funded with the sale of the regalia. Ireland had long been a source of difficulty for English governments, and now it threatened to become a base for a restoration; some republicans urged the most drastic possible measures. In an earlier moment of comparable crisis, Spenser had called for Irish traditions to be rooted up, for the entire political and social structure of the island to be transformed, and had quoted Machiavelli's *Discourses* in support of the appointment of a strong military leader; similar plans were being floated in the 1650s. On Cromwell's departure a newsletter declared that 'on the event of this they vary their conjectures whither ever there shall be a King of England again or not'. Later in the year William Hickman insisted to Cromwell that the Irish campaign must be the basis for radical political change:

'hetherto in the chandge of our Government nothinge materiall as yet hath bin done, but a takinge of the head of monarchy and placing uppon the body or trunck of it, the name or title of a Commonwealth, a name aplicable to all forms of Government, and contained under the former'. The new republic was 'not to be pattern'd by any Commonwealth auncient or moderne'.[12] In a similar vein, Marvell stresses the ideological, republican elements of the campaign. The Irish praise of Cromwell has a generic precedent in Hannibal's praise of the Romans in the fourth ode of Horace's fourth book; Marvell was to make foreign princes praise Cromwell in *The First Anniversary*. If there is a grim wit in lines 73–80, it lies in making the defeated conservatives adopt a mode of praise more conventional than the iconoclastic spirit of the rest of the poem: it is the Irish who use the language of conventional, non-Machiavellian panegyric.

If the Irish are presented, albeit ironically, as exquisitely courteous, no holds are barred in ethnic stereotyping of the Scots. Fairfax and the presbyterians doubted the legality of the Scottish campaign; its most vehement supporters used a cheekily anti-monarchical rhetoric. For example, in trying to woo the Scots from their allegiance to the young Charles II, John Hall drew on the radical tradition in Scots historiography, rushing through the chronicle of rebellions, depositions and regicides so quickly that he turned it into a grotesque black comedy, implying that only a perverse political masochism would have kept the Scots faithful to their kings. Marvell's portrayal of Cromwell hunting the Scots (lines 105–12) shares this ideologically charged aggression.

Having sketched the actions and character of the returning hero, the *prosphonetikon* would be expected to describe the celebrations marking his return. Aristotle declared (*Rhetoric*, I, 3) that epideictic rhetoric was especially concerned with the present tense, and 'now' is the key word of the *prosphonetikon*: Horace's 'nunc est bibendum' (I, 37). Here as so often Marvell departs from Caroline conventions just where he seems about to conform completely: 'now' appears in the second line, but the ode immediately looks to the future; rather than writing poetry the youth must be prepared to ward off the Scottish enemy. We do not return to the present tense until the 'now' of line 73, and any expectation that after the long narration there will be time for festivities is frustrated: the 'yet' and 'still' of lines 81–2 look to future possibilities before Cromwell's present actions have been fully described. Marvell's 'now' could perhaps be linked with a portrait of Marten by Lely which has 'now' inscribed on it: this seems to have been a Machiavellian injunction to decisive action, to seize the *occasione*, perhaps linked with the regicide. Marvell lays all the emphasis on Cromwell's humility, on his readiness to abnegate praise and honour; and nothing at all is said of the republic's response. It is in fact true that Cromwell discouraged elaborate preparations for his return.

The pamphlet describing his arrival at Windsor struck a somewhat unfestive note by remarking that Cromwell had been less seasick on the way back than on the voyage out to Dublin.

The festivities in classical poetry often included a sacrifice, and the cavalier poets adapted the pagan symbolism of sacrifice to their own panegyrics. Here Marvell's inversion of the conventions is at its most grimly witty. There is a sacrifice at the centre of the poem: the king himself. The famous lines about Charles on the scaffold have often been detached from their context. Certainly they do arouse sympathy for the king at his moment of death. But in formal terms this is a digression – Horace was celebrated for his digressions – and Marvell meshes his account of the regicide in with his narration, beginning with a 'that' taking up from Cromwell's actions and ending with a 'So' emerging as the first term in a comparison:

> So when they did design
> The *Capitols* first Line,
> A bleeding Head where they begun
> Did fright the Architects to run;
> And yet in that the *State*
> Foresaw it's happy Fate.

(ll. 67–72)

The architectural metaphor is Marvell's addition to the Roman legend; this, and the fact that the head is bleeding, enable him to tie in the regicide to the theme of sacrifice, to modulate from the tragic to the conventions of the *prosphonetikon*. Cromwell's victories in Ireland do not require any new sacrifice to be made, for they were implicit in the original sacrifice that formed the new republic.

The symbolism of founding a republic on the basis of sacrifice was widely diffused in the Renaissance, and appears in several defences of the regicide. Writing of the death of Tarquin, the last Roman king, Machiavelli argued, in a *reductio ad absurdum* of traditional monarchist imagery of the body politic, that the founders of the Roman republic were wise in cutting off the sick head when the body was healthy. It was perhaps in Machiavelli's admired Livy that Marvell found the story of the head whose discovery gave new hope to the builders of the Temple of Jupiter. His analogy of the frightened architects presents accurately enough the reaction of many members of the Rump Parliament who were backing away from the radical implications of the regicide. Cromwell, by contrast, is someone who does not fall back on a familiar model but has the boldness to push on with a new one which will be more securely founded than the elegant but brittle world of the Caroline court. If Caroline panegyric tended to gloss over violence and seek to contain political conflict within the mythological structures of the masque, the new, republican panegyric is prepared to persevere in the face of uncomfortable facts. The leading republicans took pride in the fact that, as Thomas Harrison declared on the scaffold, the regicide 'was not a thing done in a corner'. Wither boasted that whereas tyrants had often been removed secretly,

> we, with *open face*;
> By *Publick Justice*; in a *Publick place*;
> In presence, of his *friends*, and, in despight
> Of all our *foes*, and ev'ry opposite,
> Try'd, Judg'd, and Executed, without fear;
> The greatest *Tyrant*, ever reigning here.[13]

Marvell, in much more circumspect terms, makes the regime acknowledge the blood on its hands. Cromwell lays the foundation even though its line runs through the king's neck; similarly, Marvell celebrates the new state and makes his own line decapitate the king: the moment when the king's eye tries the axe is the exact mid-point. If the poem's first sixty lines embody in their form the 'memorable Hour' of the execution, the Ode moves on to a new political world: its structure is centrifugal, not symmetrical, moving out both at the beginning and end from the encomiastic present to the uncertain but urgent future. On the scaffold Charles had called on God, declaring that if he failed to make a speech he would be conceding his guilt; Marvell's silent king refuses to call on God to vindicate his right. In the context of 1650, what is most remarkable about the poem is its complete silence about the young Charles II. What royalists in the 1650s were eager to celebrate was not Cromwell's return from Ireland but the young prince's return from exile to avenge his father's death and turn the world the right way up again. But at the centre of his poem, Marvell maintains an eloquent silence: the Stuart dynasty is charming but irrelevant.

The final expected element of a *prosphonetikon* would be a conclusion often involving a prophecy. The jingoism of Marvell's finale has often disconcerted critics. And certainly it is yet another drastic revision of Caroline *prosphonetika* which regularly ended with praise of the peace enjoyed by Britain while war raged elsewhere. Up to a point it can be said that Marvell is here going back more rigorously than the Carolines to the Horatian model; for many of Horace's poems of return ended with prophesies of future campaigns, notably the poem that is Marvell's closest model, the fourth ode of the fourth book. In Sir Richard Fanshawe's translation:

> What is't but *Neros* can effect,
> Whom Heav'ns with prosperous Stars protect,
> And their own prudent care
> Clews through the Maze of War.[14]

The parallel here of divine aid and 'curae sagaces', prudent care, is very
close to Marvell's concluding antithesis between divine aid for Cromwell
and the secular arts of tactical skill that he will need on the coming
mission:

> And for the last effect
> Still keep thy Sword erect:
> Besides the force it has to fright
> The Spirits of the shady Night,
> The same *Arts* that did *gain*
> A *Pow'r* must it *maintain*.

(ll. 115–20)

Where Marvell's poem differs from Horace's is in its much more
radically ideological character. Where Horace celebrates campaigns that
will consolidate the power of Augustus's dynasty against the remaining
institutions of the Roman republic, Marvell celebrates wars that are
specifically directed by the newly-founded republic against monarchies
and in defence of republican values. As Christopher Hill has pointed out,
there had indeed been anti-monarchical risings in many parts of Europe
which lent at least some plausibility to such prophecies.[15] Italy, the
heartland first of Roman and then of Renaissance republicanism, showed
signs of throwing off the Spanish absolutist yoke.

There is a further twist in that many of Horace's poems prophesy
victories against the Britons. Patriotic translators took issue with this:
in his 1649 translation of the twenty-first ode of the first book, which
ends with a plea that plague and famine will light on the Britons, John
Smith writes, 'Avertat omen *Britannis*'. Fanshawe comments on the ninth
epode that Britain is '[u]nconquered, though twice attempted by the rude
Courtship of *Julius Caesar*'. To seventeenth-century Protestants, modern
Rome was the inheritor of the worst aspects of ancient Rome, its imperial
authoritarianism and idolatry. To the confident Counter-Reformation
culture of seventeenth-century Italy, the heretical Britons were seditious
inhabitants of a remote and backward region. Many critics have seen
the fact that Caesar is Charles at the beginning of the poem, Cromwell
at the end as a sign of ambivalence or satire against Cromwell; but such
readings miss another stroke of grim wit. The question of genre needs to
be considered: an encomium was expected near the end to have a section
of comparisons. And it was normal to compare on the basis of very
specific attributes. In fact a whole host of panegyrics directed to Cromwell
without any apparent ironic intent – including a report on his departure
to Ireland – compare him both to Caesar and to Hannibal. The point is
that each of these comparisons is qualified by restricting it to a particular
place or time: Caesar when he conquered Gaul but not when he
threatened liberty, and so on. Marvell specifies that his Cromwell is a

Caesar in relation to Gaul, but he also inverts the situation at the end of Horace's odes, making Cromwell a Caesar who attacks Gaul not from the south on his way to Britain but from the north on his way to an apocalyptic assault on Rome. The apparently peripheral culture of Protestant England which in fact is closer to the true spirit of Roman greatness and generosity will triumph over the decadent imperial centre.

This is not to say that some ambiguity does not play over the end of the poem: as before, there is always the possibility that Cromwell the defender of liberty, but also a Nimrodian *'Hunter'* (l. 110), may himself endanger it. The words 'force' and *'Pow'r'* of the last stanza recall the earlier 'forced Pow'r'; is the power here the new republic as a whole or simply Cromwell's personal authority? In 1650 these things were very hard to disentangle, for the one depended on the other. Marvell's ode is not unequivocally triumphal: it sees immense possibilities in the revolution, but is also aware of the deep-seated irony in the fact that its greatest defender and its destroyer might be one and the same man:

> The same *Arts* that did *gain*
> A *Pow'r* must it *maintain*.

(ll. 119–20)

The poem's wit is both youthfully irreverent and nightmarishly grim. All the same, there is an affirmative note: *if* the forward youths of the realm rally behind the young republic's campaigns, there is a world to win. And in writing the poem, Marvell had already gained one kind of victory for republican culture. The English revolution had turned upside down the monarchical order to return to republican origins; Marvell's out-troping poem of return turns royalist Horatianism, and Horace's own monarchism, upside down.

Notes

1. BLAIR WORDEN, 'Andrew Marvell, Oliver Cromwell, and the Horatian Ode', in Kevin Sharpe and Steven N. Zwicker (eds), *Politics of Discourse: The Literature and History of Seventeenth-Century England* (Berkeley, 1987), pp. 147–80, see pp. 96–109 above; see also Worden's 'Classical Republicanism and the Puritan Revolution', in *History and Imagination: Essays in Honour of H.R. Trevor-Roper*, ed. H. Lloyd-Jones, V. Pearl and B. Worden (London, 1981), pp. 182–200.
2. JEROME J. McGANN, *Social Values and Poetic Acts: The Historical Judgment of Literary Work* (Cambridge MA and London, 1988), p. 6.
3. Christopher Hill, 'Society and Andrew Marvell', in *Puritanism and Revolution* (corrected edition, Harmondsworth, 1986), pp. 324–50.
4. SIR RICHARD FANSHAWE, *Shorter Poems and Translations*, ed. N.W. Bawcutt (Liverpool, 1964), p. 5.
5. J.G.A. POCOCK's introduction to *The Political Works of James Harrington* (Cambridge, 1977), gives an important survey of republican thought; on Virgil, see pp. 579–81.

6. GEORGE WITHER, *The British Appeals* (London, 1651), p. 4.

7. A.J.N. WILSON, 'Andrew Marvell: "An Horatian Ode upon Cromwell's Return from Ireland": The Thread of the Poem and its Use of Classical Allusion', *Critical Quarterly* 11 (1969), pp. 325–41 (328–9).

8. Worden, 'Marvell, Cromwell, and the Horatian Ode', p. 165.

9. ANNABEL PATTERSON, *Marvell and the Civic Crown* (Princeton, 1978), p. 63. (See the following essay.)

10. JOHN HALL, *The Advancement of Learning*, ed. A.K. Croston (Liverpool, 1953), p. 20.

11. HALL, *The Advancement of Learning*, pp. 21–22.

12. JOHN NICKOLLS, JR (ed.), *Original Letters and Papers of State, Addressed to Oliver Cromwell* (London, 1743), pp. 31ff.

13. WITHER, *The British Appeals*, p. 29.

14. [Sir Richard Fanshawe], *Selected Parts of Horace, Prince of Lyricks* (London, 1652), pp. 54–55.

15. CHRISTOPHER HILL, 'The English Revolution and the Brotherhood of Man', in *Puritanism and Revolution*, pp. 126–53.

8 'So with more modesty we may be true': Marvell's poems on Cromwell*

ANNABEL PATTERSON

Annabel Patterson's *Marvell and the Civic Crown* may justly be claimed as the most influential study of Marvell during the past twenty years. Patterson's work combines a wide understanding of the different types of Civil War writing, and the cultural dynamic which produced them, with a thorough close reading of Marvell's poems. In the following piece she examines the two lengthy poems on Oliver Cromwell written in the 1650s, demonstrating how Marvell registers a belief in Cromwell as the centre of a developing godly commonwealth. For Patterson, the poems display the uniqueness of Cromwell and of England in Europe, a celebration of a new forceful culture. What she crucially distinguishes, though, is Marvell's true political poetry from mere propaganda, showing how he uses verse to project a critical, considered vision which is his own. His celebration of Cromwell reflects Marvell's maturing social thinking, pursued in both poetry and prose, which reveals him to be a political theorist and commentator who stands alongside the best and most influential of his age.

The *Horatian Ode,* . . . responds to political crisis by deft manipulation of appropriate traditions. At the same time as it alerts its audience to the difficulty of evaluating revolutionary events, especially 'if we would speak true', it reminds them that such difficulties are not unprecedented. Horace and Lucan faced them and drew their own conclusions; the modes of classical rhetoric provide norms for locating the new experience, and formal strategies for measuring it. But there is no rigid commitment to a one-to-one system of historical analogy or a slavish reproduction of rhetorical structures, either of which would protect the audience from participating in the process of choice. The mixture of classical sources,

---

* Reprinted from ANNABEL M. PATTERSON, *Marvell and the Civic Crown* (Princeton and Guildford: Princeton University Press, 1978), pp. 66–94.

the rearrangement of rhetorical expectations, provoke a lively, continuous movement between raw political fact and the possibility of categorization, between the strain of empiricism and the relaxation of system.

Recognition of this achievement allows us, in addition, to accept without further controversy both the 'affectivist' and the 'historicist' response to the *Horatian Ode* as products of Marvell's mediating stance. For all that was said by Douglas Bush,[1] it remains true that for many readers regret for Charles is stronger than the measured weighing of the 'antient Rights' against the necessary revolution, the requirement that we temper emotional responses with the generalities of historical experience. In this the poem itself gives formal recognition to what Milton had discovered earlier in *Eikonoklastes*, that even the most powerful arguments are weaker than pathos and sentiment. Like *Eikonoklastes*, the *Horatian Ode* reflects the appeal of *Eikon Basilike*, with its symbolic title page showing the king kneeling in acceptance of the crown of thorns, and treading in rejection upon his earthly crown. Although Marvell excluded any Christological language, and insisted upon his Roman decorum, no reader of *Eikon Basilike* could have read the *Ode* without recognizing what role it was the 'Royal Actor' played. Similarly, when the poem moves to the ghastly discovery on the Capitol, which nevertheless foretold the 'happy Fate' of the Roman Commonwealth, an affectivist response of shock is explicitly countered by a historicist recognition, however reluctant, that the analogy is appropriate, that it seems to work. It is this tension between different kinds of responses in which, I think, Marvell was interested, as it had been developed by earlier commentaries on the king's death. In taking a position somewhere between *Eikon Basilike* and *Eikonoklastes*, the *Horatian Ode* mediates not between two political camps but between two interdependent theories (which rhetoric has always recognized as pathos and ethos) of how language works upon the human mind.

At first sight the *First Anniversary of the Government Under O.C.* suggests a simple development from choice in progress to choice complete, from a mixed rhetorical stance supported by the classics to Christian determinism supported by biblical typology. However, any attempt to develop a straightforward reading of the poem as an alternative to the *Ode*, a 'committed' Puritan poem which knows where it stands, is quickly defeated. Cromwell may resemble Elijah or Gideon, but he is also an Amphion of classical harmony, particularly as that figure had been interpreted by Horace's *Ars Poetica*. The poem seems extraordinarily digressive and, while invoking the temporal structures both of classical *encomium* and Christian prophecy, it also seems to subvert them in ways which can scarcely be accidental. Considered as an *encomium*, we find that praise of Cromwell's achievements at home and abroad precedes mention of his parentage and birth (*genesis*) and that a lament for his

death (which turns out to be hypothetical) precedes his education
(*anatrophe*) and choice of destiny (*epitedeumata*).

Considered as Christian prophecy, the poem is even more subversive,
indeed explicitly so. The poet's hopes for a millennium in his own time
under Cromwell's leadership are presented not as a conclusion, but
toward the middle of the poem, and they are presented in the most
hypothetical terms:

> Hence oft I think, if in some happy Hour
> High Grace should meet in one with highest Pow'r,
> And then a seasonable People still
> Should bend to his, as he to Heavens will,
> What we might hope, what wonderful Effect
> From such a wish'd Conjuncture might reflect.
> Sure, the mysterious Work, where none withstand,
> Would forthwith finish under such a Hand:
> Fore-shortned Time its useless Course would stay,
> And soon precipitate the latest Day.
> But a thick Cloud about that Morning lyes,
> And intercepts the Beams of Mortal eyes,
> That 'tis the most which we determine can,
> If these the Times, then this must be the Man.
>
> (ll. 131–44)

This language is all conditional, in the grammatical sense; but as
compared to the conditional praise of the *Ode*, which was merely
dependent on Cromwell's fulfilling certain political responsibilities, the
Anniversary indicates the limitations of vision. Thinking, wishing, and
hoping are all very well, but a 'thick Cloud' comes between the would-be
prophet and his glimpses of the Apocalypse, as he considers exactly how
unseasonable the people are at present:

> Men alas, as if they nothing car'd,
> Look on, all unconcern'd, or unprepar'd;
> . . .
> Hence that blest Day still counterpoysed wastes,
> The Ill delaying, what th'Elected hastes;
>
> (ll. 149ff.)

As the poem continues, then, 'the most which we determine can' is that its
subject is indeed exceptional. Deprived of structural guidance, its readers
'hollow far behind / Angelique Cromwell', whose legendary speed of
action makes him as hard to catch as the shape of the uncertain future.

In fact, the more one investigates, the more the *First Anniversary*
reveals itself to be an exercise in how to *avoid* conventional definitions
and postures. The theoretical question with which the poem deals is

not the conflicting claims of two different types of hero, two different views of what is 'right', but how to express Cromwell's uniqueness, the unprecedented position he holds in England, in Europe, in God's providential plans and, above all, in the literary imagination. Marvell is here less concerned with what attitudes toward Cromwell were available to the writer than with the larger question of what, indeed, Cromwell was. His whole poem is a complex political version of the inexpressibility topos he had developed in the *Epitaph* for an unnamed lady; but in this context the problem of definition was one in which the whole country shared, the problem of what title could best express the nature of Cromwell's government and its sanctions. Rather than an argument that Cromwell ought to accept the crown of England, and so assimilate himself to traditional definitions of single rule by divine sanction, Marvell, I believe, decided in the *First Anniversary* that no conventional category, and certainly not that of kingship, was adequate to delimit the 'One Man' whose like had never been seen before. Every analogy we are offered for Cromwell's career proves not, on inspection, to be exact. The act of hypothesizing is underlined at every turn. Fictions proclaim themselves as fictions, and in the critical awareness which such discoveries promote Marvell distinguishes a 'true' political poetry from the automatic responses encouraged by propaganda. One might add that it is this quality particularly which distinguishes the *First Anniversary* from the poem *On the Victory obtained by Blake over the Spaniards*, a piece of unquestioning (and uninteresting) propaganda which does appear to argue for Cromwell's kingship. If Marvell was indeed responsible for this poem, which I doubt (since it was actually removed from the printed portion of the Popple manuscript), he must by 1657 have changed his mind considerably, not only on the kingship issue, but on the nature of political commentary.

The immediate occasion of Marvell's poem was not Cromwell's refusal of the crown, which had occurred in 1652 and was to be repeated in 1657. It was, rather, the first anniversary of the Instrument of Government, and also the session of the first Protectorate Parliament, which symbolized a return to some kind of constitutional government but which, between 3 September 1654 and 22 January 1655, when Cromwell dissolved it, fought to amend the terms of the Instrument and to limit Cromwell's powers, particularly with regard to control of the army. Written late in 1654, Marvell's poem was not designed to provide symbolic sanction for the kind of rule Cromwell apparently wanted, although that inference has been drawn from his magnificent musical and architectural metaphors for the 'ruling Instrument'. Rather he is concerned to investigate the historical significance, the internal paradoxes, and indeed even the disadvantages of that rule, subjecting the topoi normally associated with rulers to the scrupulous pressure of his own intelligence.

133

The central paradox of the Protectorate was, of course, implicit in the title of the Protector, a title with no constitutional precedent whose beneficent significance, some clearly felt, was merely a cover for despotism. Why, in any case, if Cromwell was only the servant of his country, did he need a title at all? In Milton's *Second Defence of the English People*, published earlier in 1654, there is an elaborate rationalization of the title in terms of a republican ethos: 'Your deeds surpass all degrees, not only of admiration, but surely of titles too. . . . But since it is, not indeed worthy, but expedient for even the greatest capacities to be bounded and confined by some sort of human dignity . . . you assumed a certain title very like that of Father of your country. You suffered and allowed yourself, not indeed to be borne aloft, but to come down so many degrees from the heights and be forced into a definite rank, so to speak, for the public good.' The name of Protector, Milton asserts, though an inadequate expression or devaluation of Cromwell's natural superiority, is nevertheless better than the title he has recently refused: 'The name of king you spurned from your greater eminence, and rightly so. For if when you became so great a figure, you were captivated by the title which as a private citizen you were able to send under the yoke and reduce to nothing, you would be doing almost the same thing as if, when you had subjugated some tribe of idolaters with the help of the true God, you were to worship the gods that you had conquered' (*CPW*, IV, i, 672).

In June of 1654 Milton had entrusted Marvell with the delivery of a complimentary copy of the *Second Defence* to John Bradshaw, and Marvell reported in a letter how the gift had been received, adding his own accolade. 'I shall now studie it,' he wrote, 'even to the getting of it by Heart: esteeming it according to my poor Judgement . . . as the most compendious Scale, for so much, to the Height of the Roman eloquence' (*Poems and Letters*, II, 306). It looks as though Marvell had so far succeeded in getting the *Second Defence* by heart that he incorporated this central paradox of the Protectorate into his own poem. Commenting, as in the *Ode*, on the great man's sacrifice of privacy to the demands of public life, he wrote:

> For all delight of Life thou then didst lose,
> When to Command, thou didst thy self Depose;
> Resigning up thy Privacy so dear,
> To turn the headstrong Peoples Charioteer;
> For to be *Cromwell* was a greater thing,
> Then ought below, or yet above a King:
> Therefore thou rather didst thy Self depress,
> Yielding to Rule, because it made thee Less.

> (ll. 221–28)

The similarity is palpable; but the differences are, if anything, more interesting. By avoiding all mention of Cromwell's actual title, Marvell's version of the paradox shifts slightly toward the idea of an indefinable selfhood. The idea of what it is 'to be Cromwell' appears for a moment on a confusing vertical scale, only to disappear as soon as one probes it. Nothing could be more unlike the propagandist tactics of George Wither, whose poem *The Protector . . . Briefly illustrating the Supereminency of that Dignity; and Rationally demonstrating, that the Title of Protector . . . is the most Honorable of all Titles* (1655) allows, to say the least, no possibility of misunderstanding. In all likelihood following the *First Anniversary*, which was advertised in *Mercurius Politicus* for the week beginning 11 January 1655, Wither reduces the constitutional paradox to bluntly expedient terms:

> Why by the name of King, should we now call him,
> Which is below the Honours, that befall him;
> And makes him to be rather less than great,
> (As in himself) and rather worse then better
> As to his People . . .
> It will deprive him ev'n of that Defence
> Which seems intended; and, will him expose
> To all the purposed Cavils of his Foes.

(p. 31)

The difference is not just that Marvell's obliqueness allows for a more high-minded interpretation of Cromwell's motives, though that may be relevant. It is rather that the problem of what it is 'to be Cromwell', in a constitutional sense, is more significant than any available verbal formulation. It recalls, in fact, the opening conceit of his anonymous *Epitaph upon—*, which proposed that the naming of an unnamed lady constituted her truest praise.

This functional indeterminacy also helps to explain those features of the *First Anniversary* which have caused Marvell's critics, taken as a group, to divide among themselves. On the one hand, it is clear that Marvell associates with Cromwell a range of images and topoi which have or had traditional associations with kingship, and which in some cases had acquired a new topicality in the poetry of Stuart panegyrists. On the other hand, Cromwell is also presented in terms of biblical types and metaphors more appropriate to a Puritan warrior saint. Not only do these two frames of reference conflict with each other, producing diametrically opposed readings of the poem, but the comparisons so invoked are themselves not simple. Neither 'royalist' nor 'biblical' types will apply to Cromwell without some adjustment, some diversion from their normal referential function; the effect is to make us look more closely, both at Cromwell's uniqueness and at the iconography itself. If the function of political symbolism is to endow sanctions on particular regimes, then it behooves the political poet to treat those symbols with a

respectful exactness, in order that what is of permanent power and
relevance may be preserved.

We can test this proposition by considering the best-known of
Marvell's allusions to Stuart panegyric, the comparison between
Cromwell, as creator of the Instrument of Government, and the harper
Amphion, by whose musical skill the city of Thebes was magically built.
It is generally accepted that in making this analogy Marvell was distinctly
echoing not only Horace's *Ars Poetica* but also Edmund Waller's poem,
Upon his Majesties repairing of Paul's. In Ruth Nevo's important study
of Stuart and Commonwealth poetry of state, this echo exemplifies a
tendency she sees in Marvell; he is reanimating, 'with a kind of poetic
justice', the language of Cavalier poets to celebrate the new regime.[2] But
Marvell's use of Waller is more specific than this suggests, and extends
over a larger area of the poem. The aim of Waller's poem was to justify
the repairs to St. Paul's Cathedral, undertaken by Charles and Laud in
the 1630s, against the attacks of the Puritans, who interpreted the project
as a consolidation of Anglican polity. Its rhetorical method was to praise
the modesty of Charles in merely improving a structure begun by James:

> Ambition rather would effect the fame
> Of some new structure; to have borne her name.
> Two distant vertues in one act we finde,
> The modesty, and greatnesse of his minde;
> Which not content to be above the rage
> And injury of all impairing age,
> In its own worth secure, doth higher clime,
> And things half swallow'd from the jaws of time
> Reduce; an earnest of his grand designe,
> To frame no new Church, but the old refine:[3]

It was these lines which inspired not only Marvell's superb version of the
Amphion passage but also his opening *comparatio* between Cromwell and
the 'heavie Monarchs' of a hereditary succession, who never complete
even a limited project in one generation:

> Their earthy Projects under ground they lay,
> More slow and brittle then the China clay:
> Well may they strive to leave them to their Son,
> For one Thing never was by one King don.

(ll. 19–22)

The point is not merely the speed and vigor of Cromwell's escape
from the slow cycles of classical time, but the difference in scale between
Charles's achievement and Cromwell's. Waller invoked the Amphion
image to describe a set of renovations to one end of an existing building.

No note struck by Cromwell as Amphion 'but *a new Story* lay'd' (with a pun on the making of history); and his 'great Work' is no mere tinkering, but a harmonious construct of military, civil, and religious order:

> Now through the Strings a Martial rage he throws,
> And joyning streight the Theban Tow'r arose;
> Then as he strokes them with a Touch more sweet,
> The flocking Marbles in a Palace meet;
> But, for he most the graver Notes did try,
> Therefore the Temples rear'd their Columns high:
>
> (ll. 59–64)

The building of the Temple was, of course, a favorite Puritan metaphor for reform of the English church, particularly during the Civil War. In 1642 Thomas Goodwin inspired his party with *Zerubbabels Encouragement to Finish the Temple*. In 1643 Edmund Calamy reproached the House of Lords for slackness in reform by comparing the situation of the Westminster divines with that of 'Nehemiah when he undertooke the great worke of rebuilding the Temple, he was opposed by great men especially.' In 1644 Milton had incorporated into the *Areopagitica* an appeal against those who resisted, by censorship, diversity of opinion: 'as if, while the Temple of the Lord was building, some cutting, some squaring the marble, others hewing the cedars, there should be a sort of irrational men who could not consider there must be many schisms and many dissections made in the quarry and in the timber, ere the house of God can be built' (*CPW*, II, 555). Marvell's reproach of kings who 'neither build the Temple in their dayes, / Nor Matter for succeeding Founders raise' (ll. 33–34) is therefore a direct response to Waller's praise of those conservative rulers who, like Charles, do not move forward the Protestant Reformation, who 'frame no new Church, but the old refine'. Politically, Marvell's adjustment is precise, locating his opinions on the Puritan side. In terms of literary theory he is equally exact for, by making his ideological correction of Waller within the same symbolic construct, he asserts the permanence and accepts the sanctions of the great architectural and musical metaphor.

One of the most interesting problems for the panegyrist, and one that had become topical in the 1640s, was the narrow boundary between symbolic sanction and actual sacrilege. It has been observed that, as the crisis of the Civil War approached, the classical tone of Caroline panegyric gave way to religious language and Christic imagery, and poets escaped from anxiety into idolatry. Even when fear was not the motive, in a period when the Divine Right of kingship was being most fully articulated the borderline was easily crossed. This problem was raised (and dismissed) by Ben Jonson, in his *Epigram to the Queene, then lying in* (1630):

> Haile Mary, full of grace, it once was said,
> And by an Angell, to the blessed'st Maid,
> The Mother of our Lord: why may not I
> (Without prophanenesse) yet a Poet, cry,
> Haile Mary, full of honours, to my Queene,
> The Mother of our Prince?

It was a matter of some importance, however, to writers on the other side of the political spectrum. In *Anti-Cavalierisme* (1642) John Goodwin maintained that those who sought to deify their mortal rulers by sacrilegious language and unquestioning obedience in effect only revealed their mortality: 'they that will devest the great God of heaven and earth, to cloath Kings and Princes, or whomsoever, with the spoils of his Name, as all those doe, who obey them with disobedience unto God, as in one sense they make them Gods, so in another . . . they make them indeed more men then they were, more obnoxious to his displeasure, who hath the command of their life and breath.' In the light of after-knowledge, the passage seems to contain a threat. Milton was later to return to the same theme in his efforts to justify the regicides: 'the People, exorbitant and excessive in all thir motions, are prone oft times not to a religious onely, but to a civil kinde of Idolatry, in idolizing their Kings' (*CPW*, III, 343). No more extreme an expression of this folly could have been found than in Robert Herrick's *To the King, to Cure the Evill*, which mixes Ben Jonson's notion that the 'Poets Evill' is poverty with the biblical story of the miracle at Bethesda:

> To find Bethesda, and an Angell there,
> Stirring the waters I am come; and here
> . . .
>
> I kneele for help; O! lay that hand on me,
> Adored Cesar! and my Faith is such,
> I shall be heal'd, if that my King but touch.
> The Evill is not Yours: my sorrow sings,
> Mine is the Evill, but the Cure, the Kings.[4]

Marvell's adaptation of this conceit for the last lines of the *First Anniversary* is a condensed refutation of all of Herrick's premises. Rejecting the identification between his subject and Christ, who alone has the power to subvert natural process, Cromwell comes merely as the Angel of the pool, whose mysterious but regular 'Troubling the Waters' manifested the workings of Providence in a less than miraculous form. The spirit of reform embodied in Cromwell, reactivating stagnant institutions, heals through their agency, not his own. But, most importantly, the power of healing is directed, through rhyme, to the good of the nation as a whole; and in the full significance of 'Commonweal' the poem finally rests. If one knew Herrick's version, Marvell's must have made terrible irony in the 1650s, when the King's Evil had been cured indeed.

It is in the context of echoes like these that we may set the description of Cromwell's coaching accident, an event which occupies the center of Marvell's poem. Like George Wither's *Vaticinium Causuale*, this passage is a response to various hostile responses to the incident, a conversion of material potentially open to satiric interpretation. The six runaway horses, which had been a gift from the Duke of Holstein, were all too convenient a metaphor for the three kingdoms Cromwell was trying to manage; and *A Jolt on Michaelmas Day*, which drew the obvious analogy with Phaeton but suggested that Cromwell had been saved for the hangman's cart, represented the direction of contemporary lampoons. Wither's response was to congratulate the Protector upon his escape, to replace Phaeton with Hippolytus, and to interpret Cromwell's lucky escape as a sign of his special relationship with Providence, which had nevertheless given him due warning of his mortality. His poem draws the obvious constructions in a tone of pompous didacticism. Marvell's response is to replace ambitious Phaeton with Elijah, 'the headstrong Peoples Charioteer' (l. 224), itself a neat inversion, and by concentrating not on the escape but the danger, he produces a radical innovation in poetic strategy.

Preservation from danger (or recovery from sickness) of a public figure was in itself a recognized subject for poetry, producing *soteria*, as in Statius's congratulation to Rutilius Gallicus (*Sylvae*, I, iv), and all too many imitations by Caroline poets. Apart from the university anthologies, Marvell would probably have been aware of Waller's *Of the danger his Majesty (being Prince) escaped in the rode at St. Andere*, or *To my Lord Admirall of his late sicknesse and Recovery*, both of which appeared in the 1645 editions. The latter, particularly, provides a close analogy for Marvell's pathetic fallacies, which have sometimes disconcerted his modern readers. The purpose of *soteria*, to define value by exploring its near loss, requires or at least justifies the use of hyperbole. Nature's lament for the death of Orpheus, which is imported from Ovid into both Waller's and Marvell's poems, is only excessive because it is not needed, because a death of equal significance has in fact been averted. It indicates the extravagance of *relief*. There is, however, a peculiar development in Marvell's poem, which goes far beyond anything similar in Waller or Jonson. The poet becomes trapped in his own fiction, and begins to describe Cromwell's death as if it had actually occurred. It only 'seem'd' that 'Earth did from the Center tear', but the effects on human institutions were less retractable:

> Justice obstructed lay, and Reason fool'd;
> Courage disheartned, and Religion cool'd.

(ll. 207–208)

In the analogy with Elijah the sense of deliverance disappears entirely
from view, to be imaginatively replaced by another kind of escape
altogether:

> But thee triumphant hence the firy Carr,
> And firy Steeds had born out of the Warr,
> From the low World, and thankless Men above,
> Unto the Kingdom blest of Peace and Love:
> We only mourn'd our selves, in thine Ascent,
> Whom thou hadst left beneath with Mantle rent.

(ll. 215–20)

Fiction has taken over, but only, paradoxically, to insist on another
kind of truth. The 'elegy' enforces dramatic recognition of Cromwell's
human status. It cuts through literary and political illusions to assert his
'Mortal cares' and 'silver Hairs', his part in the Fall, the fragility of his
regime, the problem of the succession. Its realism, Marvell tells us, is
essential to the validity of the whole poem:

> Let this one Sorrow interweave among
> The other Glories of our yearly Song.
> Like skilful Looms which through the costly thred
> Of purling Ore, a shining wave do shed:
> So shall the Tears we on past Grief employ,
> Still as they trickle, glitter in our Joy.
> *So with more Modesty we may be True,*
> *And speak as of the Dead the Praises due.*

(ll. 181–88)

The conclusion of Marvell's anonymous epitaph, that "Twere more
Significant, [S]he's Dead', is deepened in this political context. In the
Horatian Ode Marvell had perceived that 'if we would speak true' it must
be by looking to the past, to Cromwell's inarguable sacrifices and the
dead king's intelligible dignity. In the *Anniversary* he controls his praise
of Cromwell's life by imagining him dead. From that perspective, flattery
has no object, and other forms of false perspective vanish in the precise
knowledge of what we would miss.

This provocative use of 'royalist' panegyric serves both in the
particular and in general to distinguish Cromwell from previous rulers.
Without invalidating the conventions he uses, Marvell has applied them
with scrupulous attention to meaning, with an innovative seriousness
which rebukes the frivolity of less careful poets, the inadequacy of less
worthy subjects of praise. But because the materials so scrutinized have,

so to speak, been set up for him by the political opposition, it does not follow that he accepts without question the conventions of his own side. The Old Testament types and millennial images, so appropriate to a Puritan definition of the rule of the saints, do not, in Marvell's poem, attach to Cromwell as clichés. There is no exact equivalence between the new Protector and Noah, Gideon, Elijah, and the hero of the Apocalypse; and if the use of royalist topoi had had the effect of making Cromwell seem infinitely better than a king, the adjustment of biblical topoi seems, conversely, to make him seem less than perfect as patriarch, judge, prophet, or millennial hero.

To begin (where Marvell does not) with Noah, the point of connection chosen seems almost perverse. The survival of the race, the fresh start under Noah's governance, are not expressed in the Ark and the rainbow, but rather through the discreditable tale of Noah's drunkenness, which has to be twisted back to positive statements:

> Thou, and thine House, like Noah's Eight did rest,
> Left by the Wars Flood on the Mountains crest:
> And the large Vale lay subject to thy Will,
> Which thou but as an Husbandman wouldst Till:
> And only didst for others plant the Vine
> Of Liberty, not drunken with its Wine.
> That sober Liberty which men may have,
> That they enjoy, but more they vainly crave:
> And such as to their Parents Tents do press,
> May shew their own, not see his Nakedness.
>
> (ll. 283–92)

It is characteristic of Marvell's intelligence that his discussion of dictatorship should raise the question of human inadequacy even while denying it. The episode he had chosen was recognized in scriptural commentary as symbolizing the perpetually unregenerate nature of man. 'Who would look,' asked Bishop Joseph Hall, 'after all this, to have found righteous Noah, the father of the new world, lying drunk in his tent! . . . that he, who could not be tainted with the sinful examples of the former world, should begin the example of a new sin of his own!' But, as if announcing that his subject is controversial, Marvell converts the tale to an allegory of benevolent and peaceful government, which is threatened but not dishonored by the activities of Levellers and Fifth Monarchy men. It is true, of course, that the Noah passage follows, with at least some semblance of progress, Marvell's account of how Cromwell as the 'lusty mate' had seized from its incompetent steersman the tiller of the ship of state, which, during the Revolution, was often assimilated to the Ark; and it is also possible that Marvell had been attracted to the episode of Noah's drunkenness by the satirical rumor that Cromwell was a brewer's son. However, such explanations cannot account for the deliberate challenge of the passage, which in a nonpolitical poem would have been readily understood as wit. It does, in fact, quite directly recall the syntax of the inverted myths of *The Garden*: 'Apollo hunted Daphne so, / *Only* that She might Laurel grow'; Cromwell *'only* didst for others plant the Vine / Of Liberty, *not* drunken with its Wine.' And, as the impropriety of Cromwell's 'Chammish issue' may only reveal 'their own, *not* see his Nakedness', so the Pan of Marvell's metamorphosis pursues his Syrinx *'Not* as a Nymph, but for a Reed.'

Gideon and Elijah, as metaphors for other aspects of Cromwell, are no less problematic. Both sets of analogies are highly condensed and ambiguous, and their particular points of emphasis both depend on, and diverge from, contemporary interpretations of these figures. Marvell's choice of Elijah depends on a common view of the prophet as solitary and courageous proponent of reformation, opposing his moral authority to the tyranny of Ahab. The often-repeated statement that Elijah achieved more for Israel by his prayers than any military force could have done did not confine the prophet to a contemplative role. In 1643 John Lightfoot preached before the House of Commons on the theme of 'Elias Redivivus', identifying Parliament with the spirit of the prophet, for whom millennial prophecy foretold a second coming, and asserting that 'Elias is a proper and pregnant pattern for Reformers'. Milton, in the antimonarchical pamphlets, frequently identified Ahab with Charles I and, by implication, the regicides with Elijah. Elisha's ambiguous lament, 'My father, my father, the chariot of Israel, and the horsemen thereof,' was glossed by Bishop Joseph Hall as referring simultaneously to the visionary mode of Elijah's departure and, metaphorically, to his political role: 'Certainly the view of this heavenly chariot and horses, that came for Elijah, put Elisha in mind of that chariot and horsemen which Elijah was to Israel.' It is this context which explains Marvell's unstated transitions between Elijah's apotheosis, his role as the 'Peoples charioteer' and his responsibility for the rainstorm that, in 1 Kings 18, finally 'o'rtook and wet the King'. In the mood of his hypothetical elegy for Cromwell Marvell adjusts the account of Elisha's response to produce a far less positive conclusion. Elisha's grief, which causes him to tear his own clothes, should be followed by his triumphant assumption of Elijah's mantle, symbol of his inheritance of a 'double portion' of the prophet's spirit. Cromwell's survivors have no such inheritance:

> *We only mourn'd our selves*, in thine Ascent,
> Whom thou hadst left beneath *with Mantle rent.*

(ll. 219–20)

In a state where the sole ruler governs only by virtue of his unique fitness for the role, logic itself dictates that there can be no natural succession. Since Cromwell had (properly) refused the crown and its consequence, the right to found a dynasty, one hardly needed to be a prophet to foresee what would follow the Protectorate.

Like Noah's, the role of Gideon as a type was largely predetermined by a consensus of ethical and political commentary, in which he was identified as the best of the Hebrew judges, modest, moderate, without personal ambition. Arthur Jackson's *Annotations* (1646) stress his humility in threshing his own corn, and the significance of the altar building which preceded the Midian campaign: 'ere Gideon might go to fight against the Midianites the enemies of God and his people, he was enjoyned to set on foot the reformation of Religion, and the extirpation of superstition and idolatry.' The most important evidence of Gideon's character was his rejection of the crown of Israel, later to be acquired by his illegitimate descendant Abimelech, his political opposite in every way. For Bishop Hall, there was 'no greater example of modesty' than Gideon's refusal of kingship, and Jackson's commentary draws out the religious significance of the judges' rule: 'he judged Israel unto his dying day, but it was . . . the regall power, which they proffered, and he now refused . . . because the accepting of this would have been in a manner of taking of the government out of God's hand.' After the deposition of Charles I, the virtues of Gideon had taken on a new relevance for Commonwealth theorists. In Milton's *First Defence* of the regicides, Gideon exemplified the superiority of the Jewish commonwealth under the Judges to the later monarchy, and his refusal of the crown taught 'that it was not fit for any man, but for God alone, to rule over men' (*CPW*, IV, i, 370). John Cook applied the episode to his thesis that 'hereditary Kingdomes have no footstep in Scripture', and appealed to his 'miserably deluded and discontented Countrey-men' to apply to themselves the parable of Jotham: 'undoubtedly whoever shall by plots and conspiracies endeavour to introduce any of Abimelech's race or conditions to be King of England, Ireland or Scotland, or act anything against the late statute for the abolishing of kingly power shall perish by the sword of Justice. . . . The Lord grant . . . that the Parliament may give us every day more and more of the fatnes of the Olive, the peace bringing Olive quicke, cheape, and sure Justice, which can onely make peace and harmony in a Commonwealth.'[5] It is clear that Marvell accepted the general direction of this tradition in his reminder that Cromwell, like Gideon, 'would not be Lord, nor yet his Son' and, like his namesake, the 'Olive' of Jotham's parable, had refused the crown in 1652. At the same time he exploited both the ambivalence of biblical heroism and the ambiguity of fable. As with Noah, he fastened on the one episode in Gideon's career which seemed to require apology, his revenge on the elders of Succoth and Penuel for refusing his army provisions; this stands in the poem for the dissolution by force of the Long Parliament. Bishop

143

Hall, who found Gideon's revenge extremely painful to contemplate, justified it in terms which bring out its relevance to an army leader faced with a recalcitrant group of legislators: 'Well might he challenge bread, where he gave liberty and life. It is hard, if those which fight the wars of God, may not have necessary relief.' But Marvell, declining apology, presents the problem nakedly. Cromwell 'on the Peace extends a Warlike power' because that is his solution to the conflict of authority. Marvell likewise adjusts the parable of Jotham to create a more assertive Olive, one which itself puts down 'Th' ambitious Shrubs' of the Leveller party. Between the old tyranny of kingship and the new tyranny of mindless egalitarianism lies the problematic realm of Christian justice and, if the duties of the Christian magistrate include the solidification of authority, it is implicit in Marvell's allusion to Succoth and Penuel that he wished it could have been otherwise.

Perhaps the most interesting piece of scriptural rewriting, however, occurs in Marvell's treatment of the 'holy oracles' of Revelations 17 and 19, with their supporting texts from Daniel and the second Psalm. These prophecies had come in handy for Milton in *Eikonoklastes*, where with little adjustment they had authorized his attack on monarchy in general: ' "To bind thir Kings in Chaines, and thir Nobles with links of Iron," is an honour belonging to his Saints; . . . and first to overcome those European Kings, which receive thir power, not from God, but from the Beast; and are counted no better than his ten hornes. "These shall hate the great Whore," and yet "shall give their Kingdoms to the Beast that carries her." . . . Thus shall they be . . . doubtfull and ambiguous in all thir doings, untill at last, "joyning thir Armies with the Beast" . . . they shall perish with him by the "King of Kings." . . . This is thir doom writt'n, . . . and the utmost that we find concerning them in these latter days' (*CPW*, iii, 598–99). However, the small contradiction in Revelations 17:16, which Milton disposes of as 'doubtfull and ambiguous . . . doings', becomes for Marvell the basis of an appeal for reformation, the possibility that Cromwell may change the shape of the future without the necessity for force. The 'Unhappy Princes' of Europe are urged to 'Kiss the approaching, *nor yet angry Son*', and to follow Cromwell's lead toward a peaceful European Reformation. With the threats of the Apocalypse thus modified by the counsel of Psalm 2, the poet anticipates a personal role in this less destructive millennium:

> If gracious Heaven to my Life give length,
> Leisure to Time, and to my Weakness Strength,
> Then shall I once with graver Accents shake
> Your Regal sloth, and your long Slumbers wake:
>
> (ll. 119–22)

Within the temporal boundaries of the *Anniversary*, however, the ultimate
Christian epic remains a hypothesis only. Between 'the latter Dayes' and
the moment lies the cloud of human imperception, which restricts the
poet to Cromwell's actual but solitary heroism. Even the committed must
operate on trust, rather than knowledge ('And well he therefore does,
and well has *guest*, / Who in his Age has always forward prest'), but the
majority are not committed at all:

> . . . Men alas, as if they nothing car'd,
> Look on, all unconcern'd, or unprepar'd;
> And Stars still fall, and still the Dragons Tail
> Swinges the Volumes of its horrid Flail.
>
> (ll. 149–52)

The echo of Milton's *Nativity Ode* is not an accident, for it serves as a
footnote, acknowledging a strategic debt. The hypothesis of an immediate
millennium which is immediately withdrawn is central to Milton's
conception of the birth of Christ, which only initiates, not subverts, the
course of Christian history. In both poems the canceled fictions underline
the problem of wishful thinking, and serve to distinguish prophecy from
fantasy.

The 'Unhappy Princes' of seventeenth-century Europe were, in fact,
to make a final appearance in the *First Anniversary*, in a speech which
reveals how far they were from any immediate hopes of reformation.
This much expanded version of the 'praise even by enemies' provides
a hostile validation of all the poem's major themes:

> That one Man still, although but nam'd, alarms
> More then all Men, all Navies, and all Arms.
> . . .
>
> He Secrecy with Number hath inchas'd,
> Courage with Age, Maturity with Hast:
> The Valiants Terror, Riddle of the Wise;
> And still his Fauchion all our Knots unties.
> Where did he learn those Arts that cost us dear?
> Where below Earth, or where above the Sphere?
> He seems a King by long Succession born,
> And yet the same to be a King does scorn.
> Abroad a King he seems, and something more,
> At Home a Subject on the equal Floor.
> O could I once him with our Title see,
> So should I hope yet he might Dye as wee.
> But let them write his Praise that love him best,
> It grieves me sore to have thus much confest.
>
> (ll. 375–93)

145

Their recognition that Cromwell, 'although but nam'd, alarms' more
than all ordinary military threats is the enemy version of inexpressible
admiration: "Tis to commend . . . but to name.' Their half-endorsed
proposal that he possesses supernatural powers is the foreign equivalent
of idolatrous royalist panegyric. Their attempt to define the contradiction
between his domestic humility, as 'Subject on the equal Floor' and his
unquestioned superiority to themselves recalls the earlier paradox of
what it means to be 'greater . . . Then ought below, or yet above a King',
and they vainly hope to see him accept their own title which, by implying
mortality, would relieve their superstitious fears. The 'Praise . . . best/
confest' structure, which directly connects them to the conquered Irish
of the *Horatian Ode*, serves also to underline the limitations of this later
inverted praise. The Irish could, against their own interest, provide a
simple affirmation of Cromwell's goodness and justice; but the kings of
Europe can only offer inadequate standards of measurement, questions,
and paradoxes. Cromwell's enemies may have provided a more objective
evaluation of their great opponent than Cromwell's poet has been able to
achieve; but neither, finally, has succeeded in controlling the subject:

> Pardon, great Prince, if thus their Fear or Spight
> More then our Love and Duty do thee Right.
> I yield, nor further will the Prize contend;
> So that we both alike may miss our End:
> Whilst thou thy venerable Head dost raise
> As far above their Malice as my Praise.

> (ll. 395–400)

The poem can only end by reminding the audience of its title and,
therefore, that other anniversaries will present new opportunities for
evaluation.

If the first (and only) *Anniversary* for Cromwell questions its success
in defining the unique, *A Poem upon the Death of O.C.* seems to sound
a deliberate retreat. Far from adjusting or arguing with conventions,
Marvell seems to have fallen back into one of the best defined and most
luxurious, the classical *epicedion* with its well-marked topoi. A simple
chronology presents the prior circumstances and causes of Cromwell's
death (his grief for his daughter), the natural and supernatural portents,
the date (coincidentally that of the battle of Dunbar), and the response
of his survivors. To them is given the task of enumerating his cardinal
virtues (ll. 179–226) as modified by a Christian–Stoical tradition; and
giving the lament of what is 'no more' (ll. 228–46) in language imitative
both of Virgil's description of the heroic underworld and Milton's
pastoral elegy for Lycidas/King. The poem concludes with three different
but equally conventional passages of *consolatio*: Cromwell's immortality
in the imagination and 'martiall Verse' of 'th' English Souldier'; a

Christian heaven for Cromwell himself, where he can meet face to face the biblical types (Moses, Joshua, and David) he now resembles; and a political reincarnation in his successor, for 'Richard yet, where his great parent led,/Beats on the rugged track' (ll. 305–306). Our after-knowledge of Richard's inadequacies as a solution to the constitutional problem perhaps distorts our view of the last lines and makes them seem unduly fatuous; but Marvell has made no effort here to distinguish himself from conventional idiom at its most obvious.

What are we to make of this apparent collapse of critical intelligence into the swaddling bands of convention? The poem has been largely dismissed by both schools of criticism on the grounds of the same assumption, that Marvell's devotion to Cromwell had by this time become the dominant motive. The literary critic, . . . compares the *Elegy* unfavorably to the hard formalism of the *Ode*, and discovers to its credit only pathos; the political analyst is likely to grant it only a personal status, which does not justify a major evaluation. But there is no need to assume that Marvell was unable to write a public poem on Cromwell's death because a political force had become a friend, nor that feeling is incompatible with speculation. There is evidence in the *Elegy* that Marvell found Cromwell's death as *significant* as his rule, and that the conventionality of his response was a deliberate response to his understanding of it. A remarkable series of echoes link the *Horatian Ode*, the *Anniversary*, and the *Elegy* in a sequence of argument which prevents a merely sentimental reading of the latter.

In all the attention given to Marvell's use of Lucan in the *Ode*, nobody seems to have noticed that the famous passage describing Caesar as lightning is preceded by a description of Pompey as a majestic but decayed oak. In Thomas May's translation, firmly established as the source of many phrases and attitudes in the *Ode*, the passage reads:

> one in yeares was growne,
> And long accustomde to a peacefull gowne
> Had now forgot the Souldier: . . .
> . . . new strength he sought not out,
> Relying on his ancient fortunes fame,
> And stood the shadow of a glorious name.
> As an old lofty Oake, that heretofore
> Great Conquerours spoiles, and sacred Trophyes bore,
> Stands firme by his owne weight, his roote now dead,
> And through the Aire his naked boughes does spread,
> And with his trunke, not leaves, a shadow makes:
> Hee though each blast of Easterne winde him shakes,
> And round about well rooted Trees doe grow,
> Is onely honour'd;[6]

It seems clear that Marvell had this passage close at hand when, after an opening which emphasizes the peacefulness of Cromwell's last years, he describes his appearance in death:

> Yet dwelt that greatnesse in his shape decay'd,
> That still though dead, greater than death he lay'd;
> . . .
>
> Not much unlike the sacred oak, which shoots
> To Heav'n its branches, and through earth its roots:
> Whose spacious boughs are hung with trophies round,
> And honour'd wreaths have oft the victour crown'd.
> When angry Jove darts lightning through the aire,
> At mortalls sins, nor his own plant will spare;
> (It groanes, and bruises all below that stood
> So many yeares the shelter of the wood.)
>
> (ll. 257–68)

Marvell has here combined the Pompeian oak, honored but decayed, with the Caesarian lightning to give a double resonance to Cromwell's death. Once the lightning himself, blasting Caesar's head through his laurels, Cromwell has now become subject to the natural cycles of change and vulnerable to Jove's bolt. Even the phrase 'nor his own plant will spare' derives from Lucan's subsequent description of the Caesarian lightning ('Not Joves own Temple spares it'), which not only helps to substantiate the source but emphasizes the deliberate synthesis which Marvell's allusions achieve.

The *Elegy*, then, returns via Lucan to a concept of time and history essentially repetitive, a view denied by the *Anniversary* in its attempt to grapple with the man of the moment. While it corrects the perspective of the *Anniversary*, this passage also uses the fallen oak to expand and support one of the *Anniversary*'s major theoretical positions:

> The tree ere while foreshortned to our view,
> When fall'n shews taller yet than as it grew:
> So shall his praise to after times encrease,
> When truth shall be allow'd, and faction cease,
> And his own shadows with him fall; the eye
> Detracts from objects than itself more high:
> But when death takes them from that envy'd seate,
> Seeing how little, we confess how great.
>
> (ll. 269–76)

The point of the hypothetical elegy in the *Anniversary* is that epideictic cannot function properly in the view of the moment; truth and modesty of evaluation depend on the perspective of death and, by extension, the only poem which can be both occasional and a true 'praise' is the funeral

148

elegy. In the real *Elegy*, Marvell's image of the tree provides graphic expansion of this previously elliptical statement. The fallen tree and the finished career can be accurately measured; the foreshortening produced during a great man's life by irrelevant emotions of envy and political prejudice disappears when he is leveled by the common fate of humanity; and the traditional generosity of statements about the dead is revealed, paradoxically, as truly historical objectivity.

Cromwell's submission to natural law, the end of his unique trajectory, the final speed trap, allows him, in the *Elegy*, to appear as a figure no longer antipathetic to Charles. His 'last Act' recalls the 'Royal Actor' of the 'Tragick Scaffold'. Action gives way to 'gentle Passions'. His military victories are expressed as the victories of prayer. Awkward questions likely to be raised with respect to the cardinal virtues are resolved by the substitution of Friendship for Justice; while the fusion of military and spiritual values permits Cromwell to find a place, however preeminent, in the structure of Christian legend. A simple out-doing topos defines an intelligibly active/passive hero:

> Whose greater Truths obscure the Fables old,
> Whether of British Saints or Worthy's told;
> And in a valour less'ning Arthur's deeds,
> For Holyness the Confessor exceeds.

> (ll. 175–78)

None of this makes the return to convention intrinsically better, of course. The *Elegy* competes effectively neither with the strenuous mental activity of the earlier Cromwell poems nor with the voluptuous emotional activity of an elegy, like *Lycidas*, written to explore the meaning of grief. But the return to conservatism in form is at least strategic, the result of a decision to reabsorb Cromwell into the known patterns of human experience. It looks forward to the constructive conservatism of the *Rehearsal Transpros'd*, where Marvell could celebrate, as the next cycle, 'his present Majesties happy Restauration'. Nor did that later conviction that 'all things happen in their best and proper time, without any need of our officiousness' (p. 135) imply the rejection of Cromwell's phenomenal activity, since that had already been absorbed into a formal pattern of interdependent modes of experience.

Notes

1. The argument between 'affectivist' and 'historicist' readings of the *Ode* was initiated by Cleanth Brooks in 'Criticism and Literary History: Marvell's "Horatian Ode"', *Sewanee Review* 55 (1947), pp. 199–222, and continued in 'A Note on the Limits of "History" and the Limits of "Criticism"', *Sewanee Review*

61 (1953), pp. 129–35, as a rejoinder to Douglas Bush's critique of his methods in 'Marvell's "Horatian Ode"', *Sewanee Review* 60 (1952), pp. 362–76.

2. RUTH NEVO, *The Dial of Virtue: A Study of Poems on Affairs of State in the Seventeenth Century* (Princeton, 1963), pp. 20–27, 74–118.

3. EDMUND WALLER, *Works* (London, for Thomas Walkley, 1645), p. 4.

4. HERRICK, *Poetical Works*, ed. L.C. Martin (Oxford, 1956), pp. 61–62.

5. JOHN COOK, *Monarchy No creature of God's making* (Waterford, Ireland, 1651), pp. 20–21.

6. Thomas May, *Lucan's Pharsalia . . . The whole ten Bookes* (London, 1627), A3.

9 Virgins and Whores: the Politics of Sexual Misconduct in the 1660s*

STEVEN N. ZWICKER

Until recently, Marvell's Restoration satires have been accorded little
critical attention. In part, this illustrated a critical organisation which
tended to witness 1660 as a crucial dividing moment in English liter-
ature. According to the artificial period allocations which resulted,
Marvell and Milton were seen as 'belonging' to the Renaissance,
Dryden to the Restoration. Thus Marvell's later satires tended to be
overlooked by scholars of the early seventeenth century whose grasp
of Restoration issues was often insecure. Steven Zwicker's essay illus-
trates new scholarly perspectives which challenge the Renaissance/
Restoration divide. While certainly recognising differences in English
culture after 1660, the questions raised by the preceding 20 years of
civil war and republican rule are not seen as vanishing with the
return of the monarchy. In the following essay, Zwicker examines the
characteristic 'economy, neatness, and efficiency' of Marvell's longest
satire, *The Last Instructions to a Painter*. He notices how the familiar
metaphor of the body politic takes on explicit sexual perspectives in
the 1660s. While the restored monarchy tries to emphasise liberality,
generosity and fertility in rebuilding the kingdom, its critics expose
its excesses – grossness, appetite, debauchery. Zwicker's wonderfully
attentive reading of *The Last Instructions* shows Marvell developing
an increasingly coherent political vision and emerging as one of the
finest satiric poets of the Restoration.

Just past the middle of *The Last Instructions*, Marvell slackens the restless
pace of his satire; he turns from abuse and excoriation to pastoral and
panegyric. Set deep within the argument of this epic satire are two
pastoral episodes that counterpoint the poem's dominant idiom; but

---

* Reprinted from CONAL CONDREN and A.D. COUSINS (eds), *The Political Identity
of Andrew Marvell* (Aldershot, Hampshire: Scolar Press, 1990), pp. 85–110.

these vignettes do more than play country virtue to court corruption. Their position within the structure of the poem argues the vulnerability of pastoral, but, more urgently, they fix a model of physical innocence in a poem whose most fundamental corruption is sexual violence. The pastoral moment in which Marvell sets the portraits of Michael de Ruyter and Archibald Douglas suggests how powerful and pervasive is the matter of sexual corruption with which the poem opens, how crucial the attempted rape at the poem's close, and how intimate are the relations throughout this poem, and in the culture more broadly, between sexual appetite and political corruption. The Stuart court would prove vulnerable to the force of this association not only in the mid-1660s, the first moment of serious literary assault on the court, but throughout the 1670s, in Exclusion, and indeed through the final assault on James and Mary of Modena in the satires on the supposititious Old Pretender.

The body politic is a familiar literary trope; it is also a fundamental of political thought and political theory, nowhere more forcefully argued than in the 1651 frontispiece to Hobbes's *Leviathan*. It may not be a novel observation that the body politic took on an explicitly sexual life after 1660, but the power of this topic, the danger and vulnerability of its terms, the force of its polemical meaning have not been fully charted in our reading of the satiric attacks levelled steadily and brilliantly against the persons of the Stuart court or in the explication of Restoration court culture. It is, of course, difficult to read Lord Rochester's verse of the 1670s without acknowledging the brutal and relentless equation between sexual excess and corruption at court. But Rochester is not the daring exception. *The Last Instructions* gives us an occasion to chart the metaphor in the most important satiric text of the first decade of the Restoration and to map the political argument of innocence and appetite into the larger rhetorical field of the 1660s.

First, perhaps, an acknowledgement that the sensibility of our poet might make us hesitant to generalize beyond the borders of his work. But even in the delicacy, the decay and indulgence, of the lyric Marvell we can sense the larger public argument. The dating of Marvell's lyrics is vexed, but we can arrange a background for the whores and virgins of *The Last Instructions* out of the pastoral materials that marked the poet's sojourn at Lord Fairfax's estate. That background should enable us to see not only the continuity of Marvell's sensibility from lyric to satire but its larger cultural meaning. The pastoralist of 'The Garden' and 'The Nymph Complaining', and most especially the satirist and idler of *Upon Appleton House* was possessed of a peculiar and exquisite refinement; but the lyrics and lyric history suggest more than idiosyncrasy. They acknowledge the force of sexuality in imaginative exploit, in the argument of heroic venture, in the calculation of human potential, and in the luxuries of retreat. There is in the lyrics and in *Upon Appleton House* something close to an equation of sexual, ethical and civic misconduct. The indulgence of 'The Garden' is an invitation to moral disintegration; the corruption of sexual appetite in the nunnery of *Upon Appleton House* is a perversion not simply of sacred retreat but of national destiny. The ethical force of monogamous heterosexual coupling is unmistakable throughout the historical drama of *Upon Appleton House*. Destiny recognizes only one appropriate sexual model; all others are corrupt or immature. Both Maria and the angler are virgins awaiting the force of destiny; Maria is on its verge, the marital and sexual fate of the angler is unknown. But there can be little doubt about the public values the angler projects: the great vehicle of history is monogamous, reproductive union.

While the body politic is a continuous theme in renaissance political discourse, we must acknowledge as background to the satires of the 1660s not only that continuity, Marvell's own absorption in this subject, but its more immediate cultural and political resonance. The cult of Platonic love in the court of Charles I suggests the subtle and rarified ways in which the language of love relations might articulate political culture. Sexual exploit displaced Platonic love as a civic language in the 1660s, but at both Caroline courts there was a keen appreciation, at the centre and at the margins, of the ways in which the taste and exploits of the monarch defined and publicized the quality of the body politic.

Of course, the address to sexual power in the Restoration did not begin with satire; it had begun as early as the panegyrics welcoming the restoration of monarchy and pleasure. Not that the invocation of pleasure signalled sexual profligacy. The public themes of those first months argued the Restoration as a return of the person of the King and the office of kingship, and these were coupled with broader renewal: a restoration of arms and arts; a reinvigoration of science and letters; a revival of wit and eloquence; an elevation of style and manners; and for our purposes, most especially, a restoration of abundance and pleasure. At the centre of these hopes and idealizations stood the King whose words announcing return, and spoken frequently thereafter, promised forgiveness and liberality. And these were ideals not difficult to embrace. Not many in 1660 would have gainsaid forgiveness and liberality, a mythic English past of carolling and delight, or the more immediate pleasures of the alehouse. Charles's return to London on 29 May was a bacchanalian triumph, 'This day, his Majesty, Charles II came to London . . . with a triumph of above 20,000 horse and foot, brandishing their swords, and shouting with inexpressible joy; the ways strewn with flowers, the bells ringing, the streets hung with tapestry, fountains running with wine . . . the windows and balconies, all set with ladies; trumpets, music, and myriads of people flocking . . . such a restoration was never mentioned in any history, ancient or modern, since the return of the Jews from their Babylonish captivity; nor so joyful a day and so bright ever seen in this nation.'[1] But the pleasures and arts of this Court would prove rather more complex, strategic and finally more subversive than could have been reckoned in the early months of the Restoration. What seem to our eyes gestures of bucolic innocence, indeed the entire culture of pleasure, formed an important polemical position in the 1660s. Delight and abundance played a crucial role in repudiating a once much trumpeted piety and saintliness. That the 1650s were a good deal more complex hardly needs assertion; but what does need stressing is that the themes of this restoration not only projected ideals for the future and idealized images of the present, they also allowed in quite conscious and perhaps not quite so conscious ways a powerful engagement with Puritan moral regulation and reformation; in that project, abundance, liberality, and pleasure played a significant role.

It may have been chance that the person of Charles II allowed so much of this double-edged work to be done, that his history of exile and restoration offered the parallel with David in godly election as in sexual history, and that the King's personal inclinations so fully accommodated the themes of liberality and abundance that were claimed for the Restoration as a whole. But the generosity of spirit that the King announced at Breda would, in significant ways, come to characterize his reign. Nor can the King's wit and playful sense of irony be doubted; it is not difficult to believe that the restored Court provided a model for repartee in the comedy of manners, that the satires of Rochester, scurrilous and brilliant, found a forgiving audience in the king, or that he would have grasped immediately the ironies and pleasures of the opening lines of *Absalom and Achitophel*. And while abundance, generosity and pleasure took their cue from the person of the King, they had also a broader life in the literature promoting, celebrating and defending his kingship. On the abundance of the King turned the patronage system in its entirety: both the literal and figurative systems of rewards and generosity of personal attention, protection, place and pension. It was not only in the defensive and partisan gestures of *Absalom and Achitophel* that the paternalism of the King was urged as an aspect of patronage, stability and national abundance; those combined hopes were expressed in the first poems written to greet his return and frequently thereafter. And though the public assumed that sexual abundance would be harnessed by marriage and progeny, the twinning of personal and national fertility, of sexual abundance and commercial triumph, is repeatedly found in the Restoration pronouncements.

Indeed, the King's procreative promise formed the very centre of a politics of abundance. Charles's return is celebrated in the language of passion and penance, pleasure and fertility, bounty and leisure, marriage and fecundity. The explicitness of this language derived not simply from what was known or rumoured of the King's private pleasures, but from conventional assumptions about the role of those pleasures in the state. As the panegyrics and nuptial verse make clear, the royal capacity for abundance promised civic stability and continuity, qualities much prized after two decades of political turbulence. We have come to associate the Court of Charles II with bawdy and heartless licence, but there is nothing in the slightest licentious in the high-minded verse that celebrates this sexual restoration. At its centre were lineage and political continuity; from the promise of the royal line issued a series of topics that bound sexual fertility to those very qualities which the King had pronounced on his return home: liberality, generosity and forgiveness.

We cannot grasp the political issues or the complex polemical atmosphere in which the domestic politics of the early 1660s unfolded without allowing pleasure and abundance their full political meaning. Nor can we properly read the literature of the mid-1660s without contemplating how these themes might have turned in the minds of a public disappointed by the barrenness of the royal marriage and the unbridled licence of the court. But when the King returned, pleasure and fertility meant a repudiation of the immediate past and the continuity of the future. The King himself observed to his second Parliament, 'I have been often put in mind by my friends, that it was now high time to marry, and I have thought so myself ever since I came into England. But there appeared difficulties enough in the choice, though many overtures have been made to me; and if I should never marry till I could make such a choice, against which there could be no foresight of any inconveniences that may ensue, you would like to see me an old batchelor, which I think you do not desire to do. I can now tell you . . . that I am resolved to marry if God please . . . which I look upon as very wonderful, and even as some instance of the approbation of God himself.'[2] The mood of buoyant optimism and godly approbation which had greeted the Restoration and the nuptials of the King did not last very long into the 1660s.

The disappointment of returning cavaliers has been amply documented, but it was not only those trying to get back their own who were not completely gratified by the Restoration settlement. Dissenters were harried and threatened and had not of course disappeared, though some had turned to quietism under the new régime. The so-called Clarendon Code was harshly restrictive, and though the King attempted Indulgence in 1662, his Cavalier Parliament was not in a mood to grant such an indulgence to dissenters. And while the King and many in Parliament had spoken against division and recrimination, sharp words were not long in coming. The first real crises of the restoration arrived, however, with a force beyond anyone's reckoning. The middle years of this decade brought military, fiscal, natural and political disaster: the Dutch invasion of the Thames and destruction of a good part of the

English fleet; the Great Plague and Fire that decimated London's population, levelled huge tracts of the city, and left rumours of conspiracy in its wake; and the hounding from office of the Lord Chancellor in a parliamentary mood that reminded some of the destruction of Strafford. The combination of fire, plague and military defeat gave some observers the impression that the four horsemen of the apocalypse had descended on to London in rapid order; cries of divine judgment were not long in coming, nor was the apocalyptic significance of the year lost on millenarian sensibilities. To suggest that by 1667 the court was harried and beleaguered is to argue the mildest version of this crisis. Although political resentments had not yet hardened into a system of opposition politics as they would in Exclusion, they nevertheless opened a floodgate of polemical activity: sermons, broadsides, pamphlets, petitions, lampoons, and satires as well as an heroic literature of the Anglo-Dutch war, including Edmund Waller's *Instructions to a Painter* (1665) and Dryden's *Annus Mirabilis* (1667).

Waller's celebration of the English victory at Lowestoft was the opening and hopeful gesture in an heroic and highly decorative idiom, and it was quickly answered not only by the events of the Anglo-Dutch war but also by satires that engaged the premise, the topics, tropes and style of Waller's verse. In the satiric reversals of Waller's piece, the conduct of the war, the character of the Admiralty, the quality of the Court, and finally the negligence and indulgence of the King himself were put under harsh satiric scrutiny. The breadth and density of the satiric attack were such that the polemical literature itself can be said to have become part of the crisis. The Court was put on the defensive not only against defeat and disaster but also against the scurrilous charges levelled at its conduct and character, and at the suggestion that such conduct was itself responsible for the divine judgment now so clearly visited on the nation. The poems of praise and blame addressed the prosecution of the war, its heroes and heroics, and the conduct of the Ministry and Admiralty; they also undertook to manage the image of the Court and King, and rather more specifically and daringly, the King's sexual conduct.

By the mid-1660s that bacchic moment in which the King and nation first embraced had long ago disappeared; the failure of the King's legitimate sexual abundance was only too obvious, and the morals of the royal family were searched for explanations of that failure. Licence and fornication had, by the mid-1660s, an urgent moral and political significance. Who could have missed the application implied by publishing in 1667 a sermon on Hebrews 13.4 entitled 'Fornication Condemned' or the significance of the sermons preached before the King at Whitehall in 1667 on sensuality, lust and passion. In the midst of disaster, these were subjects as dangerously charged as ministerial incompetence and greed, naval mismanagement and cowardice, fire and plague. The royal

extravagance came under parliamentary scrutiny and displeasure in
1667; but the licentiousness of the Court was addressed in other forms,
no less significant for the political culture, including squibs, pamphlets,
broadsides and lampoons, and of course the series of advice poems that
culminated in *The Last Instructions*.

Waller's *Instructions to a Painter*[3] may not have been the very first
effort in politicizing pleasure for the mid-1660s, but it was a visible and
vulnerable move; in its optimistic elevation of tone it gave an opening
to satirists sceptical of its attempt to claim for this court the authority of
high culture. For example, the short, complimentary episode depicting
the Duchess of York's visit to Harwich in May of 1665 is scornfully
replayed in *The Second Advice* and *The Last Instructions*, and refurbished
in Dryden's dedicatory verse to *Annus Mirabilis*. Waller inserts the
scene between two naval battles and suggests that the resupply not only
refreshed the naval stores but renewed valor itself:

> But who can always on the billows lie?
> The wat'ry wilderness yields no supply:
> Spreading our sails, to Harwich we resort,
> And meet the beauties of the British court.
> Th' illustrious Duchess and her glorious train
> (Like Thetis with her nymphs) adorn the main.
> The gazing sea-gods, since the Paphian queen
> Sprung from among them, no such sight had seen.
> Charm'd with the graces of a troop so fair,
> Those deathless powers for us themselves declare,
> Resolv'd the aid of Neptune's court to bring
> And help the nation where such beauties spring,
> The soldier here his wasted store supplies
> And takes new valor from the ladies' eyes.
>
> (ll. 77–90)

For the moment, Waller would have us contemplate the Duchess of York
as Aphrodite and Thetis, goddess of the sea, divinity of love and fertility,
supplier of arms to Achilles. Innocent enough; but in *The Second Advice*
(1666),[4] both the subject and Waller's literary manners come under
scornful attack. Here is no Aphrodite and her train of nymphs, but
sexual caricature:

> But, Painter, now prepare, t' enrich thy piece,
> Pencil of ermines, oil of ambergris:
> See where the Duchess, with triumphant tail
> Of num'rous coaches, Harwich does assail!
> So the land crabs, at Nature's kindly call,
> Down to engender at the sea do crawl.

See then the Admiral, with navy whole,
To Harwich through the ocean caracole.
So swallows, buri'd in the sea, at spring
Return to land with summer on their wing.
One thrifty ferry-boat of mother-pearl
Suffic'd of old the Cytherean girl;
Yet navies are but properties, when here
(A small sea-masque and built to court you, dear)
Three goddesses in one: Pallas for art,
Venus for sport, and Juno in your heart.
O Duchess! if thy nuptial pomp were mean,
'Tis paid with int'rest in this naval scene.
Never did Roman Mark within the Nile
So feast the fair Egyptian Crocodile,
Nor the Venetian Duke, with such a state,
The Adriatic marry at that rate.

(ll. 53–74)

The Duchess's 'glorious train' has become a triumphant tail, Waller's elevated tone is ridiculed, his mythology exploded, his extravagance regretted. And *The Last Instructions* provides a harsher and nastier explicitness. Through the satires, in *The Second Advice*, *The Third Advice*, and in *The Last Instructions*, the elevated, heroic and complimentary materials of Waller's *Advice* and, more largely, of the literature of court compliment are inverted vividly and exactly. Rather than nymphs, gods, and goddesses, Marvell gives us anatomy and appetite, grossness and sexual license. The satirist exposes vice, extravagance and folly, but in *The Last Instructions* the particular aim, the nearly obsessive fix on enormity and appetite, is to connect sexual greed and political corruption. Marvell addresses himself to poetics, but the fundamental issue is politics. The satirist is keen to lower the tone, to debunk epic gestures and claims, to debase and embarrass; but what he angles after throughout the satire is the matter of governance. And it was clear by the mid-1660s that a deep vulnerability in the Court's armoury was the King's morals: his appetites, his personal indulgences and sexual follies.

It may seem puzzling that these attacks should have been repeatedly directed against the Duchess of York, and by implication at the Duke of York, rather than against the King himself. But the accounts of the King's sexual appetite that would come in the 1670s should not obscure the fact that direct attacks on the person of the King were quite new in the polemic of the mid-1660s. Just as it had been customary to attack a King's policies through his suppositious 'evil ministers', so was it now easier to attack Charles's morals through his relatives and mistresses. And the Duchess of York was particularly vulnerable to such attack, both

as the subject of scandalous rumours circulated at the time of her sudden
marriage to the Duke, and as the daughter of the reviled and by the
middle of 1667 discredited person of her father, Lord Chancellor Hyde,
Earl of Clarendon. One of the charges against Clarendon was his aim to
load the King with a barren wife so that he might ascend, through his
grandchildren, to the throne. It was an accusation frequently repeated
and coupled with other charges against his appetite, grandeur and
arrogance. The *Third Advice* poses the simplicity and honesty of the Duke
and Duchess of Albemarle against Clarendon. But in *The Last Instructions*
the address to luxury and vice could hardly be more sharply focused
on the Court or more centrally concerned with the relations between
sexual indulgence and political folly. What had been indirection and
innuendo becomes in *The Last Instructions* direct assault. Here the poet
is concerned with a 'race of Drunkards, Pimps, and Fools'; and steadily,
both in blame and praise, the aim of this poem is to argue sexual and
political issues as one. So the poem begins, and so the poem ends in that
daring portrait of Charles II in his bedchamber. Between lies a world of
appetite, vice and folly.

The attribution of corrupt politics and sexual profligacy to a single
court appetite begins with a portrait of Henry Jermyn, Earl of St Albans,
at the French court:

> Paint then St. Albans full of soup and gold,
> The new Courts pattern, Stallion of the old.
> Him neither Wit nor Courage did exalt,
> But Fortune chose him for her pleasure salt.
> Paint him with Drayman's Shoulders, butchers Mein,
> Member'd like Mules, with Elephantine chine.
>
> (ll. 29–34)

Although succeeding portraits are more daring and violent, the sketch
of Jermyn has a lovely economy, a neatness and efficiency that are the
signature of Marvell's satire. The conjoining of soup and gold explicates
the imbedded pun on bullion, linking not excrement and treasure but
appetite and greed; and that argument is coupled to the crucial third
term in the suggestion of Jermyn's sexual service to Henrietta Maria, 'The
new Courts pattern, Stallion of the old'. At the Restoration, Jermyn was
created Earl of St Albans and posted ambassador to the French court; the
Queen Mother was fifty-one in 1660 and dead at the beginning of 1666.
The suggestion that Jermyn, debauched in appetite, besotted with food
and drink, was stallion to Henrietta Maria is both lurid and comic. Pepys
records the rumour that St Albans was married to the Queen Mother,
but Marvell's image does not conjure nuptial propriety. Jermyn is cast
as 'pleasure salt'; the language conjoins sexual and physical appetite;
ingestion and copulation are one. 'Pleasure salt' recalls the initial figure

of Jermyn, bloated with soup and gold, and its implications are extended
in images of lechery and force: 'Paint him with Drayman's Shoulders,
butchers Mein'. Moreover the physical image is but a prelude to the
figure of Jermyn as 'instrument' of political treachery. The twinning
of lust and deceit is argued toward the close of the portrait: 'He needs
no Seal, but to St. James's lease, / Whose Breeches were the Instrument
of Peace' (ll. 41–42). John Wallace has observed of this portrait that
Marvell's political seriousness in *The Last Instructions* is shown by his
unusual concern with foreign policy, and his prescient grasp of France's
role in English diplomatic history;[5] the portrait of Jermyn also fixes this
critique in explicitly sexual terms and anticipates, in its insistent coupling
of sexual defilement and political corruption, the closing portrait of
Charles II.

More immediately, the portrait of Jermyn prepares the terms for the
figure of Anne Hyde drawn in the succeeding lines:

> Paint then again Her Highness to the life,
> Philosopher beyond Newcastle's Wife.
> She, nak'd, can Archimedes self put down,
> For an Experiment upon the Crown.
> She perfected that Engine, oft assay'd,
> How after Childbirth to renew a Maid.
> And found how Royal Heirs might be matur'd,
> In fewer months than Mothers once indur'd.
>
> Not unprovok'd she trys forbidden Arts,
> But in her soft Breast Loves hid Cancer smarts.
> While she revolves, at once, Sidney's disgrace,
> And her self scorn'd for emulous Denham's Face;
> And nightly hears the hated Guards away
> Galloping with the Duke to other Prey.

(ll. 49–56, 73–78)

Again the poet harshly and luridly mingles political, sexual and
physical appetites, a disorder suggesting not only a chaos of passions
but a violence and degradation of taste. The portrait is crowded with
particulars, with plots, treachery, ambition, hunger and enormity; it
argues a confusion of terms, it suggests that debauchery cohabits with
treason. While the portrait of Jermyn glances slanderously at the Queen
Mother, the address to Henrietta Maria's daughter-in-law is frontal and
direct: Jermyn may be the Queen Mother's stallion, but the Duchess of
York is a whore. The accusations were familiar enough by the time
Marvell drew up his indictment: her sexual career preceding marriage to
the Duke of York (rumoured to include the Earl of St Albans's nephew
and namesake Henry Jermyn), her political ambition to mount the royal

throne, her supposed murder of Lady Denham, one of the Duke of York's mistresses, the enormity of her appetite and body, and her sexual servicing by Henry Sidney, Groom to the Bedchamber of the Duke and Duchess and her Master of the Horse. The insults echo the attacks on Lord Chancellor Hyde and taint the royal family, but in their force and violence go quite beyond smearing association. Appetite and debauchery are satiric commonplaces, but the particular insults are quite this poet's own:

> Paint her with Oyster lip and breath of fame,
> Wide mouth that 'sparagus may well proclaim:
> With Chancellor's belly and so large a rump,
> There, not behind, the coach her pages jump.

(ll. 61–64)

The image is a further debasement of Waller's portrait of the Duchess, cruder than the figure in *The Third Advice*. The particulars are not only degrading, gross in every sense, they also position the rule of appetites at the centre of a realm in which governance is out of control. Slandering the Duchess of York may have been good sport in the satires of the 1660s, but in the structure of this satire, the escalating attacks bring the denunciations of raging appetite ever nearer to the body of the King. Whoring and misgovernance are the central charges laid against the King at the poem's close, and they are carefully prepared at the beginning of the satire.

Pierre Legouis has assured us that 'the more revolting charges [against Anne Hyde] may be safely rejected';[6] he means of course that they were false. But they may not be rejected if we are correctly to read their most important claim. For *The Last Instructions* attacks not simply the more revolting physical excesses of individuals, but the political deformity of the body politic, and the one is insistently metaphor of the other. Marvell's 'revolting' charges against Jermyn, Hyde and Castlemaine are intended with the utmost seriousness; they aim to disgust in their violence and particularity, and they intend our sense of disgust to be brought finally to bear against the inmost centre of the body politic. John Wallace praises the high-mindedness of *The Last Instructions*, its avoidance of debasement, its careful exemption of the King from personal abuse.[7] But it is the low-mindedness of this poem that carries its most urgent argument. For *The Last Instructions* insists on, and makes central to its political argument, the deformity, the appetites, the personal vulgarity of the Stuart Court. It may be difficult to reconcile the salacious and vulgar materials of *The Last Instructions* with the delicacy of Marvell's lyric muse, but to stress only the high-mindedness of his satire is to gloss over the vigour and particularity of his opposition poetics and politics, their connection to and incorporation of cruder forms of popular print culture, and finally to slight the matter of sexual misconduct so important to the depiction of the court and Charles II's place of pride in its articulation.

The final portrait in the opening trilogy comes yet closer to the centre of the body politic; it is a portrait of the King's then most notorious whore, the Duchess of Cleveland:

> Paint Castlemaine in Colours that will hold,
> Her, not her Picture, for she now grows old.
> She through her Lacquies Drawers as he ran,
> Discern'd Love's Cause, and a new Flame began.
> Her wonted joys thenceforth and Court she shuns,
> And still within her mind the Footman runs:
> His brazen Calves, his brawny Thighs, (the Face
> She slights) his Feet shapt for a smoother race.
>
> (ll. 79–86)

The portrait is exclusively sexual in content; the burden of Marvell's argument is that the servicing of Castlemaine by her lackey is a humiliation of the King's mistress and of the King himself. Love's cause in this scene is anatomy; but while Castlemaine discerns love's cause in her lackey's drawers, it is not in copulation that Marvell portrays the King's whore, but in a lurid 'rub down' of her groom:

> Great Love, how dost thou triumph, and how reign,
> That to a Groom couldst humble her disdain!
> Stript to her Skin, see how she stooping stands,
> Nor scorns to rub him down with those fair Hands;
> And washing (lest the scent her Crime disclose)
> His sweaty Hooves, tickles him 'twixt the Toes.
>
> (ll. 91–96)

In a blasphemous mockery of Luke 7, this woman of sin washes and anoints not the feet of her lord but the 'hooves' of her groom. The figure cuts of course against Lady Castlemaine and the quality of the entire Court; it offers a momentary and shocking juxtaposition of high and low; the scene is aligned with and inverts the Gospel. It is a fitting culmination to the initial argument of court corruption, for the actors in the scene are unaware of the travesty, but the reader is not allowed their brazen naïveté. The opening portraits fix the terms of *The Last Instructions*, and they are nothing so simple as slander and outrage. Uncontrolled appetite, lust and debauchery confounded with greed and corruption, these are the terms important not only to the satiric portraiture but as well to the discursive passages of governance and war that they frame in conjunction with the figure of the King that closes the poem. They are also terms brilliantly rewritten in the portraits of de Ruyter and Douglas that illumine the centre of *The Last Instructions*.

At line 523, Marvell takes up his description of the Dutch invasion of the Thames and destruction of the English fleet. What is shocking about the poet's handling of the narrative is not the violence of the scene but its elevation, the pastoral setting given to plunder and destruction. As de Ruyter sails from ocean to river the poem turns from heroic to pastoral scenery; the invasion is rendered as a panel, perhaps from an illustrated Ovid:

> Ruyter the while, that had our Ocean curb'd,
> Sail'd now among our Rivers undisturb'd:
> Survey'd their Crystal Streams, and Banks so green,
> And Beauties e're this never naked seen.
> Through the vain sedge the bashful Nymphs he ey'd;
> Bosomes, and all which from themselves they hide.
> The Sun much brighter, and the Skies more clear,
> He finds the Air, and all things, sweeter here.
> The sudden change, and such a tempting sight,
> Swells his old Veins with fresh Blood, fresh Delight.
> Like am'rous Victors he begins to shave,
> And his new Face looks in the English Wave.
> His sporting Navy all about him swim,
> And witness their complaisence in their trim.
> Their streaming Silks play through the weather fair,
> And with inveigling Colours Court the Air.
> While the red Flags breath on their Top-masts high
> Terror and War, but want an Enemy.
> Among the Shrowds the Seamen sit and sing,
> And wanton Boys on every Rope do cling.
> Old Neptune springs the Tydes, and Water lent:
> (The Gods themselves do help the provident.)
> And, where the deep Keel on the shallow cleaves,
> With Trident's Leaver, and great Shoulder heaves.
> Aelous their Sails inspires with Eastern Wind,
> Puffs them along, and breathes upon them kind.
> With Pearly Shell the Tritons all the while
> Sound the Sea-march, and guide to Sheppy Isle.

(ll. 523–50)

The pastoral is finally shattered by the bombardment of Sheerness (l. 560), but the long portrait of de Ruyter's invasion is rendered in a most self-conscious and heightened style. What might properly be figured as violence and plunder, rape and violation, is magically transformed into a pastoral of gallant love. And what is especially curious in its opposition to the portraits that open and close the poem is Marvell's invitation to imagine the scene as a field of modest sexual delight. The violation of

English territory by the invading Dutch is softened, rendered amorous and nearly comic. De Ruyter is transformed from an aging admiral to a gallant lover; the streams are crystal, the skies clear and the air sweet. Here amorous passion is all delicacy and courtliness; rather than coarse bodily function, love in this passage is filtered through a diaphanous pastoral. Not that the matter of desire is entirely dispersed, but it is heightened, rarified, mythologized. The banks boast shy nymphs hidden in verdant green; the Dutch sailors look longingly from ships which fly streaming silks; all is rendered innocent through song and myth. The gods smile on this scene. The distance from the harsh verisimilitude and coarse imagery of the opening portraits could hardly be more pointed. Satire, now the only literary kind fitted to render the Stuart Court, is transformed when the characters change. The mixed modes of *The Last Instructions* are made to seem determined not by the poet's will but by his subject matter. Like the commemoration of Archibald Douglas that follows, the Dutch pastoral is strikingly literary in texture and detail. The juxtaposition of pastoral and satire not only allows Marvell to play foreign virtue against native vice, it also allows the poet to remind us of the idioms and images of Stuart panegyric, of that language of abundance and pleasure so insistently invoked for our halcyon days in 1660.

The portrait of Douglas (ll. 649–96) extends both the literary and political terms and makes one further point. The nymphs and lovers of the Dutch pastoral are at once shy and gallant, an inversion of love at the English Court; but the elegy for Douglas carries a more complex argument. For in this scene, the gallant is no aging admiral but an androgynous beauty, a nymph among nymphs, a vestal virgin, yet the hero of the English fleet. The portrait of Douglas answers the figure of de Ruyter but further complicates its terms. For while de Ruyter prepares for amorous play, Douglas is a denial of sexual desire: he is innocence in a world of corruption; beauty among the deformed. It is bravery and honour that Marvell celebrates in Douglas, fortitude and constancy, virtue in all its complex senses:

> Not so brave Douglas; on whose lovely chin
> The early Down but newly did begin;
> And modest Beauty yet his Sex did Veil,
> While envious virgins hope he is a male.
> His yellow Locks curl back themselves to seek,
> Nor other Courtship knew but to his Cheek.
> Oft has he in chill Eske or Seine, by night,
> Hardn'd and cool'd his Limbs, so soft, so white,
> Among the Reeds, to be espy'd by him,
> The Nymphs would rustle; he would forward swim.

They sigh'd and said, Fond Boy, why so untame,
That fly'st Love Fires, reserv'd for other Flame?

(ll. 649–60)

In part the initial terms anticipate Douglas's immolation aboard the *Royal Oak*; but the portrait offers other displacements and claims. Heroic and steadfast, Douglas is yet hardly of age; the valiant Scot not only shames the English youth, he also rebukes the aging pimps and whores of the English Court. But more than that, he is the very denial of sexual passion. Douglas rejects the river nymphs and embraces only the flames in which the *Royal Oak* is consumed:

Like a glad Lover, the fierce Flames he meets,
And tries his first embraces in their Sheets.
His shape exact, which the bright flames infold,
Like the Sun's Statue stands of burnish'd Gold.

(ll. 676–80)

Although Douglas was married at the time of his death, in the economy of *The Last Instructions* his virginity denies not chaste marriage but the outrageous sexual appetites and deformities of the poem's opening scenes and yet more importantly anticipates the closing portrait of the King, itself prefaced by an anecdote of lust and infidelity. In death, Douglas is the 'glad Lover', for here passion is explicitly a civic duty, love is the embrace of honour, the defence of king and country. The sexual ambiguity of the figure allows Douglas to be hero and victim: the true embodiment of loyalty and honour, the innocent sacrificed to the flames created from the Court's lust and dishonour.

In an effort to rescue the seriousness of *The Last Instructions*, to differentiate it from the more libellous satires, several students of the poem suggest that the closing portrait of Charles II is neither harsh nor critical. They assume that the envoy alters the terms of the portrait of Charles (ll. 885–906), that Marvell seriously intends the device of the King's evil ministers to paper over his harsh criticism of the monarch. Such a reading would have Marvell close *The Last Instructions* by blaming others for the havoc wreaked by the King's passions and follies. But read in terms of the other figures in Marvell's gallery, the portrait of the King dreaming in his bedchamber is the most serious and most daring satire, and quite properly the culminating argument of *The Last Instructions*.

The portrait is immediately prefaced by a group of nasty lines on Speaker of the Commons, Henry Turner which close with an image of Turner being serviced by the wife of James Norfolk, Serjeant-at-Arms of the House of Commons:

At Table, jolly as a Country-Host,
And soaks his Sack with Norfolk like a Toast.

At night, than Canticleer more brisk and hot,
And Serjeants Wife serves him for Partelott.
Paint last the King, and a dead shade of Night,
Only dispers'd by a weak Tapers light.

(ll. 881–86)

Lust and infidelity anticipate the King's vision; what the weak tapers
disclose is a scene in which the King either dreams or envisions a bound
virgin, a figure whom he would press in close embrace:

Raise up a sudden Shape with Virgins Face,
Though ill agree her Posture, Hour, or Place:
Naked as born, and her round Arms behind,
With her own Tresses interwove and twin'd:
Her mouth lockt up, a blind before her Eyes,
Yet from beneath the Veil her blushes rise;
And silent tears her secret anguish speak,
Her heart throbs, and with very shame would break.
The Object strange in him no Terrour mov'd:
He wonder'd first, then pity'd, then he lov'd:
And with kind hand does the coy Vision press,
Whose Beauty greater seem'd by her distress;
But soon shrunk back, chill'd with her touch so cold,
And th' airy Picture vanisht from his hold.
In his deep thoughts the wonder did increase,
And he Divin'd 'twas England or the Peace.

(ll. 891–906)

The King's efforts to satisfy his sexual desires on the bound virgin is an
image prepared by the opening portraits and by the elegy for Archibald
Douglas. Douglas as 'the Sun's Statue of burnish'd Gold' is the counterpart
of the bound virgin illumined by candlelight. And now the argumentative
force of Douglas's virginity is brought home, for he is both an analogue
for the virgin England and a reminder of the civic uses of passion. The
slumbering monarch reaches for the captive virgin; excited by her distress,
he would satisfy his appetites on the hapless figure, and in his lust he
misreads the emblem. Luxury and sensuality at the centre of the Court
are fundamentally political in character: pleasure rather than honour or
abundance is the aim of this monarch; private passion rather than public
trust is the principle of this Court. Though not in detail as vile as the
images of the courtiers earlier offered in the poem, the implications of the
King's undifferentiating appetites are more damaging. What the scene
finally urges is the recognition that England herself is matter simply to
excite and relieve the King's desires. Perhaps because the indictment
is read so directly against the King, Marvell casts it as dream vision, a

device that allows him to soften the scene. But it also permits him to historicize the scene, to anchor it in an episode of the King's erotic history that works, with a wonderful economy, against the scene's elevation. For the allegory is a redaction of Charles's pursuit of Frances Stuart, the most protracted and least successful of the King's sexual ventures. The combination of allegory and historical narrative conjoins, as does the poem throughout, politics and whoring; and rather than disperse the criticism, the covering of the narrative by allegory concentrates the indictment and sharpens the explicitness of the case.

The shape raised up of virgin's face had appeared at Court in 1662. Painted by Lely as Diana, twice by Huysmans, and by Cooper, Frances Stuart was widely admired for her beauty, and by no one more than the King. Her sexual history was the focus of interest and gossip throughout the early 1660s, particularly in 1667, when first she sat in February, at the King's direction, for the figure of Britannia which appeared on the Peace of Breda Medal created by Roettier – hence, her certain identity in line 906 as 'England' or the 'Peace' – and subsequently and secretly eloped from Whitehall at the end of March to marry the Duke of Richmond. In so eluding the King's sexual demands and preserving her virginity, she was rumoured to have been assisted by the Lord Chancellor who, the King believed and others suggested, had arranged the secret marriage to frustrate the King's passions and correct his morals. Charles's anger and frustration help to explain the King's otherwise unaccountably vindictive attitude toward Clarendon.

The brief scene records several details of Charles's pursuit of Frances Stuart: her resistance, her virtue, her fondness for games, including, suggestively, blindman's buff – a detail that renders both poignant and ridiculous the blindfolded figure in the vision – and of course her escape from the King's hold and his surprise and frustration over her disappearance into the night. The most telling juncture of detail is provided by the puns of the portrait's final line, where the language tangles together coins, whores, medals, and politics: 'England', and the 'Peace' of l. 906 allowing the medal struck to celebrate naval victories in the Dutch wars to be collapsed with the meaning of piece as 'whore' and piece as 'money', a meaning already conjured with reference to Frances Stuart in line 761 where Marvell alludes to her appearance as Britannia on the farthing. The puns underscore, as does the whole scene, the compounding of lust with policy, and so serve as structural and argumentative cruxes linking the King's dream to the dismissal of Clarendon in the next scene. The fall of Clarendon is determined, so the structure of the poem argues, by the Lord Chancellor's role in the frustration of the King's appetite, and by the chief architects of the King's new policy, Bennet and Castlemaine (ll. 927–42) who through the summer and early fall of 1667 had been linked in their efforts to

use Frances Stuart to influence the King. In this poem, so drenched
in topicality and so insistent on its author's highmindedness, the
King's dream occupies a special position, conducting its argument
simultaneously as allegory and gossip.

The coldness of the virgin shocks the King into an awareness of the
allegory, educates him in poetics; but the King's heroic resolve proves
nothing more than fixing on a device to disperse criticism. Rather than
reform his own appetites and understanding, the King indulges the
fiction of 'evil ministers', a fiction that was, at the close of the summer
of 1667, deployed to appease the hunger of the House of Commons,
and a device savagely ridiculed earlier in *The Last Instructions* in the
parliamentary chorus that would blame all the naval disasters on
Commissioner Pett. The sacrifice of Clarendon fits the wise designs
of Castlemaine, Bennet, and Coventry, those emblems of lechery and
mistrust. While Marvell hardly means to allow sympathy for Clarendon,
the valour of the King's resolve is itself a disgrace.

The envoy (ll. 949–90) doubtless softens the closing representation
of the King; Marvell's address to the King invokes familiar literary
and political sentiments and conventions – the poet's own modesty, the
purity of his aims, the conservative constitutionalism of his politics – but
its very reliance on the trope of the King's evil ministers damages its
credibility. It is difficult indeed to reconcile the formal pieties of the
envoy with the scathing tone Marvell achieves at the close of the King's
portrait, or to assume that the device of Hyde's disgrace would effect
the restoration so affectingly glimpsed in the pastoral couplet lodged
between images of scratching courtiers, 'But Ceres Corn, and Flora is the
Spring, / Bacchus is Wine, the Country is the King' (ll. 973–74). Given
the structure of the poem, its steady accretion of images, its length, its
density and particularity, it is hard to imagine how courtly panegyric
could have been successfully wrought from satire. The pastoral figures
tucked into the envoy bear an inordinate weight if they are truly to
counterpoise the violence and corruption catalogued in the body of
the poem. I suspect that Marvell was aware not only of the failure of
resolution in the envoy but also of the aesthetic and political difficulties
of resolving this satire, and though the poem does indeed wander
toward a conclusion with images of the good subject, of 'gen'rous
Conscience and . . . Courage high', the line that finally brings the poem to
a close is anxious and dissonant, 'Give us this Court, and rule without a
Guard' (l. 990). The reference to the King's Horse and Foot Guards in the
final line of the poem conjures up the bleeding ghosts of Henry IV and
Charles I (l. 918); rather than resolution, the image offers a world closer
to the spirits of the shady night at the conclusion of *An Horatian Ode* than
to the harmonies and abundance of the pastoral state. The restoration of
Charles II in 1660 had twinned hopes of stability and abundance with the

person of the King; that his private pleasures and civic care should have proved fruitless and negligent was a conclusion to which Marvell had come by the summer of 1667, and to which he gave, in *The Last Instructions*, a brilliant, implacable and damaging form.

Notes

1. *The Diary of John Evelyn*, ed. William Bray, 2 vols (Washington and London, 1901), I, pp. 332–33.
2. *The Eloquence of the British Senate*, ed. William Hazlitt, 2 vols (London, 1808), I, p. 161.
3. Citation is to the text in *Poems on Affairs of State: Augustan Satirical Verse, 1660–1714*, ed. George de F. Lord *et al.*, 7 vols (New Haven and London: Yale University Press, 1963–75), I, pp. 21–33.
4. Citation is to the text in *Poems on Affairs of State*, I, 36–53.
5. JOHN WALLACE, *Destiny His Choice: The Loyalism of Andrew Marvell* (Cambridge: Cambridge University Press, 1968), pp. 163ff.
6. *The Poems and Letters of Andrew Marvell*, I, p. 352.
7. WALLACE, *Destiny His Choice*, p. 146.

10 Marvell's Sexuality*

PAUL HAMMOND

As Steven Zwicker, Paul Hammond notes how sexuality became a key area for satiric comment after the Restoration. What interests Hammond, though, is the contemporary innuendoes and accusations about Marvell's own sexuality. Marvell is seen as sexually ambiguous, of double or indeterminate gender. This leads Hammond to a wide-ranging consideration of the narcissistic in Marvell: a gaze involved both with the self and distinctly with the male self. Careful to avoid declaring an authentic sexual biography for Marvell, this essay is concerned with how little scope seventeenth-century culture offered for voicing male desire for men and the various ways Marvell's different types of writing may have approached this. Hammond's essay reveals how different critical directions which have developed over the last twenty years may fruitfully join. Alert to the close historical contextualisation of Marvell and the importance of his prose, this essay also recalls Jonathan Goldberg's deconstructive explorations of the Narcissus myth and its recognition that Marvell's creativity may emerge from a poetic which simultaneously both tries to write and to hide the consequences of what is missing.

Much of Marvell's poetry is prized for its enigmatic character; much of his biography is equally enigmatic. Scholars have argued about his political allegiances, and over how to interpret his public poetry, wondering whether it is possible to identify a political stance which is either coherent at any one moment or consistent across his career. I propose in this essay to explore another aspect of Marvell which raises problems about coherence and consistency – his sexuality. I must, however, immediately redefine the topic, for this is not (and because of the lack of surviving evidence cannot be) a biographical enquiry into

---

* Reprinted from *The Seventeenth Century*, vol. XI, 1 (1996), pp. 87–123.

the private sexual desires and practices of an historical individual;
rather, the Marvell of my title is a 'Marvell' who is created through two
very different groups of texts, texts whose relations to each other, and to
the historical Andrew Marvell, are difficult to interpret. I do not propose
to follow Sir William Empson[1] and speculate on Marvell's biography, nor
would I wish to claim that my account is a complete reading of the texts
involved. Rather, I wish to explore three related questions. First, I shall
discuss the uses of sexual innuendo in contemporary pamphlet attacks
on Marvell, asking what and how the allegations signify as ways of
imagining a man's sexuality which are simultaneously ways of scoring
political points. Here 'Marvell' is a set of politically-motivated caricatures.
Secondly, I shall be exploring the ways in which certain motifs which are
prominent in these pamphlets could be seen as parodic versions of sexual
interests which inform Marvell's own poetry; and though reading the
poems in the light of the pamphlets is problematic both in theory and in
practice, it may be that this approach can reveal nuances in the poetry
which critics have ignored or suppressed. And here 'Marvell' is the
variety of voices and personae which we find in his poetry, often with
characteristic erotic sensibilities which persist across the canon. Finally,
since the discussion focuses primarily on Marvell's homosexual[2] interests,
I hope that this reading of the pamphlets and the poems may illuminate
the ways in which homosexual desire could be imagined in late
seventeenth-century discourse.

I

To begin with the pamphlets. These belong to the controversy generated
by Marvell's book *The Rehearsal Transpros'd* (1672), which was an attack
on the Anglican divine Samuel Parker. Marvell had objected to Parker's
argument that the ruler should have absolute power in matters of religion,
and be able to punish dissent. He had mixed thoughtful argument with
boisterous personalized satire which included sexual innuendo: Marvell
pretended, for example, to infer that when Parker said that he had been
occupied with '*matters of a closer and more comfortable importance to himself*'
he had meant a woman (pp. 5–6). Parker, he said, had written in an
extravagant and indecent way:

> Thus it must be, and no better, when a man's Phancy is up, and his
> Breeches are down; when the Mind and the Body make contrary
> Assignations, and he hath both a Bookseller at once and a Mistris to
> satisfie: Like *Archimedes*, into the Street he runs out naked with his
> Invention. (p. 7)

Parker's admiration for Bishop Bramhall has led him to write about him
in too warm a language, 'part Play-book and part-Romance' (p. 12), and

so 'our Author speaks the language of a Lover' and has made 'a dead Bishop his Mistress' (p. 13). Marvell also presents a sketch of the young cleric consumed with self-esteem and soliciting the admiration of his female congregation:

> For being of an amorous Complexion, and finding himself (as I told you) the *Cock-Divine* and the *Cock Wit* of the Family, he took the priviledge to walk among the Hens: and thought it was not impolitick to establish his new-acquired Reputation upon the Gentlewomens side. And they that perceived he was a Rising-Man, and of pleasant Conversation, dividing his Day among them into Canonical hours, of reading now the Common-prayer, and now the Romances; were very much taken with him. The Sympathy of Silk began to stir and attract the Tippet to the Pettycoat and the Petticoat toward the Tippet. The innocent Ladies found a strange unquietness in their minds, and could not distinguish whether it were Love or Devotion. Neither was he wanting on his part to carry on the Work; but shifted himself every day with a clean Surplice, and, as oft as he had occasion to bow, he directed his Reverence towards the Gentlewomens Pew. Till, having before had enough of the Libertine, and undertaken his Calling only for Preferment; he was transported now with the Sanctity of his Office, even to extasy . . . I do not hear for all this that he had ever practised upon the Honour of the Ladies, but that he preserved alwayes the Civility of a *Platonick Knight-Errant*. For all this Courtship had no other operation than to make him stil more in love with himself . . . being thus, without Competitor or Rival, the Darling of both Sexes in the Family and his own Minion. (pp. 30–31)

Marvell never alleges any actual sexual impropriety in Parker's behaviour with these women, and the passage becomes increasingly concerned with his self-love. At this point a curious element enters Marvell's text. Into this account of Parker's relations with women there suddenly intrudes the suggestion that Parker is sexually attractive to other men, 'the Darling of both Sexes'; moreover, Parker becomes 'his own Minion', in other words not only his own favourite but also his own catamite. Marvell's flight of fancy has started with the vision of Parker as a cockerel parading in front of his admiring hens, but has arrived at an image of Parker as an object of homoerotic interest to other men, and of autoerotic interest to himself. Just why Marvell's imagination should have travelled this path is unclear, but if he had foreseen the attacks on his own sexual conduct and interests which this pamphlet provoked, he might have avoided the use of such satirical strategies.

Parker himself, in his reply called *A Reproof to the Rehearsal Transprosed* (1673), resisted the temptation to respond in kind to Marvell's sexual innuendo, and suggested that this passage bore no relation to him personally and was merely a satirical piece of character-writing recycled from Marvell's bottom drawer:

> And so we arrive at the Character of a Noble-man's Chaplain; for having heretofore (among other your juvenile Essays of Ballads, Poesies, Anagrams and Acrosticks) laid out your self upon this subject also, and your Papers lying useless by you at this time when your Muse began to tire . . . (p. 269)

Even in his posthumously published autobiography, Parker made no specific allegations about Marvell's sexual behaviour, contenting himself with the vague slur that 'he had liv'd in all manner of wickedness from his youth' and had turned into 'a vagabond, ragged, hungry Poetaster' and a 'drunken buffoon'.[3] But by the time Parker's *Reproof* appeared, other pamphleteers had already entered the fray, and in the course of their polemic had made free with Marvell's sexual interests and abilities.

The first of these rejoinders to Marvell was written by Henry Stubbe and published under the title of *Rosemary & Bayes* (1672). 'Bayes' was the name which Marvell had used for Parker, and Stubbe now applied 'Rosemary' to Marvell, referring to him in the text as 'Mr. *Rosemary*' (p. 8). Rosemary and bays were commonly linked, for they were used together as a decoration, but were also gendered in their symbolism, so that the phrase 'rosemary and bays' alludes to a proverbial contrast between masculine and feminine characteristics. The bay is the laurel, the tree of Apollo, signifying masculine strength, military conquest and poetic excellence. Rosemary is associated with women, and not only as a girl's name: Gerard says that its Latin name is 'Rosmarinus Coronaria' because 'women have been accustomed to make crownes and garlands thereof'.[4]

Rosemary was entwined in a bride's wreath. It also came to symbolize the dominance of the women, for it was said that where rosemary flourished in a garden, the women ruled the household. Marvell himself, the poet of gardens and of wreaths, would have understood this allusion well enough. Apart from this satirical renaming of Marvell, however, Stubbe's pamphlet avoids commenting on his sexuality, except for a reference to his having put on a '*perruke* and *Visor-mask*' (p. 11), the former a male fashion, the latter a female accessory which at this date was coming to be associated with prostitutes. So this phrase implies an androgynous appearance, and calls attention to some riddle which needs to be solved, some mask to be removed.

The second contribution to the controversy is less restrained. The anonymous *A Common-place-Book out of the Rehearsal Transpros'd* (1673) suggests in several ways that Marvell is a eunuch. First he is said to be 'as tough and lasting as a Stone-horse in a race; yet I have heard those who use the *Newmarket*-Course say that the *Colingwood-Gelding* would hold it out to the end as the best' (p. 22). 'Colingwood' probably puns on 'coll' meaning 'to cut close' (*OED* coll v²). So this writer who appears to have a stallion's strength and stamina may actually be a gelding. Then there is a snide reference to a fictitious bookseller operating at 'the sign of the *Counter-Tenor-Voice*' (p. 4). The pamphlet also invites us to make a comparison between Marvell and the historian Eutropius, suggesting that the parallel between the two men extends beyond their opposition to ecclesiastical power:

> Let me leave you with a passage in History, and the consideration in how many Circumstances this is, and may be your case. The short of it is thus; *Eutropius* the Eunuch was a busie Solicitor with the Civil Magistracy, to have a Law made against the Priviledges and Power of the Church, not long after it happen'd that he was utterly ruin'd by the very same contrivance, which his malice against Ecclesiastical Politie had framed. (p. 56)

With these allegations of castration and impotence so clearly established, one hears insinuations in other comments. The writer says to Marvell: 'Do you plead with the *Casuists*, that any man may dispense with his own Promise, where the *Non-performance* prejudices no one?' (p. 11; original italics). And commenting on Marvell's remark that he was on the horns of a dilemma, the writer replies: 'Now a *Dilemma* is otherwise call'd, *A two-horned Argument*; whereas most men would have believed that he could have made neither two horns nor one, since he left the Colledge' (pp. 10–11). This is to say that Marvell was incapable of making another man a cuckold (by giving him two horns), and incapable even of having an erection ('horn' = penis, especially when erect). The innuendo is given a homosexual colouring when Geneva (the home of Calvin, and thus implicitly the spiritual home of Marvell the militant Protestant) is imagined to share the same fate as Sodom (p. 10).

The third pamphlet in this series is Richard Leigh's *The Transproser Rehears'd* (1673), which is the most sustained, detailed and vituperative of all the pamphlets in the allegations which it makes about Marvell's sexuality. One passage imagines Marvell as a lover, but only to mock him with the improbability of this scenario. He is cast in the role of 'Prince *Pretty-man*' who is

> passionately in Love (you may allow him to be an *Allegorical Lover* at least) with old *Joan* (not the *Chandlers*, but Mr. *Calvins* Widow) walks discontentedly by the side of the Lake *Lemane*, sighing to the Winds and calling upon the Woods; not forgetting to report his Mistresses name so often, till he teach all the *Eccho*'s to repeat nothing but *Joan*; now entertaining himself in his Solitude, with such *little Sports*, as *loving his Love with an I*, and then *loving his Love with an O*, and the

like for the other Letters . . . To be short, after he has carv'd his
Mistresses Name with many *Love-knots* and *flourishes* in all the *Bushes*
and *Brambles*; and interwoven those sacred Characters with many an
Enigmatical Devise in *Posies* and *Garlands* of *Flowers*, lolling sometimes
upon the Bank and sunning himself, and then on a sudden (varying
his Postures with his Passion) raising himself up, and speaking all the
fine things which Lovers us'd to do. His Spirits at last exhal'd with
the heat of his Passion, swop, he falls asleep, and snores out the rest.
(pp. 137–38)

Perhaps the type of the melancholy lover is too much of a contemporary
commonplace for this passage to be making sarcastic, disbelieving
allusions to the echoing song and the complaining lover in 'To his Coy
Mistress', or to the conceit about names carved on trees in 'The Garden'.
But Leigh clearly regards Marvell as an improbable lover in any but
an allegorical context, and interprets any love-rhetoric from him as
mere imitative posturing to occupy his solitude, and leading only to
masturbation.

Once again Marvell is presented as a eunuch. In a scene set in a
coffee-house, Marvell 'the Man of Observations draws out his Table-
book ('tis his most dangerous Tool)' (pp. 36–37). Marvell the observer
makes notes on the conversation which could prove dangerous to
the participants if they were talking sedition. But clearly the notebook
is the only really dangerous weapon which Marvell has, and any
other 'tool' of his, whether sword or penis, would be ineffectual. He is
godfather to other people's children, but has no offspring of his own
(p. 8). He may bristle with ruffled pride like a turkeycock, though that
would be 'too Masculine an Emblem for a *Capon-wit*' (p. 128), a pointed
variation on Marvell's description of Parker as a '*Cock Wit*'. Slyly adapting
the mode of Marvell's own *Last Instructions to a Painter*, Leigh offers
advice to any painter who undertakes Marvell's portrait:

if ever he draws him below the Wast, to follow the example of that
Artist, who having compleated the Picture of a Woman, could at any
time, with two strokes of his Pencil upon her Face, two upon her
Breast, and two betwixt her Thighs; change her in an instant into Man:
but after our Authors Female Figure is compleated, the change of Sex
is far easier; for Nature, or *Sinister Accident* has rendered some of the
Alteration-strokes useless and unnecessary. This expression of mine
may be somewhat uncouth, and the fitter therefore (instead of
Fig-leaves, or *White Linnen*) to obscure what ought to be conceal'd
in Shadow. Neither would I trumpet the Truth too loudly in your
ears, because ('tis said) you are of a delicate Hearing, and a great
enemy to noise; insomuch that you are disturb'd with the tooting of
a Sow-gelders Horn. (pp. 134–35)

The passage continues with further play with the idea of castration, and then turns to overt allegations of sodomy:

> Some busie People there are, that would be forward enough it may be to pluck the Vizor off this *Sinister Accident*, not without an evil Eye at your Distich on *Un Accident Sinistre*, to which they imagine some officious Poet might easily frame a Repartee to the like purpose as this Tetrastich.
>
> > *O marvellous Fate. O Fate full of marvel;*
> > *That Nol's Latin Pay two Clerks should deserve ill!*
> > *Hiring a Gelding and Milton the Stallion;*
> > *His Latin was gelt, and turn'd pure Italian.*
>
> Certainly to see a *Stallion* leap a *Gelding*, (and this *leap't* fair, for he *leapt* over the *Geldings* head) was a more preposterous sight, or at least more *Italian*, then what you fancy of *Father Patrick's bestriding Doctor Patrick.* (p. 135)

Leigh is alluding to a passage in *The Rehearsal Transpros'd* where Marvell referred to an occasion when the French King Henri IV challenged his courtiers to rhyme extempore on a given subject:

> The Subject was, *Un Accident sinistre.* Straight answers, I know not whether 'twas *Bassompierre* or *Aubignè*:
>
> > *Un sinistre Accident & un Accident sinistre;*
> > *De veoir un Pere Capuchin chevaucher un Ministre.*[5]
>
> For when I said, to see Popery return here, would be a very sinister accident; I was just thinking upon that story; the Verses, to humour them in translation, being only this,
>
> > *O what a trick unlucky, and how unlucky a trick,*
> > *To see friend Doctor Patrick, bestrid by Father Patrick!*

(p. 121)

Marvell's reference is to the Anglican divine Simon Patrick and the Roman Catholic priest Father Patrick MaGinn, so that for the latter to bestride the former symbolizes the triumph of Catholicism over the Church of England. The image is primarily equestrian, fashioning the kind of emblem of inverted authority familiar from Renaissance representations of Aristotle being ridden by Phyllis; and yet the sexual implications of 'riding' cannot be excluded from Marvell's lines, which thus present sodomy as an appropriate image of political subversion. The sexual possibilities of the image are exploited by Leigh when he adapts the lines to suggest that the relationship between Marvell and Milton in their time as Cromwell's Latin secretaries was that of catamite and sodomite: Marvell the gelding played the passive role to Milton the stallion. Earlier Leigh had anticipated this slur in his play on the word 'conjunction': 'among other Calamities of late, there has happen'd a prodigious Conjunction of a *Latin Secretary* and an *English School-Master*, the appearance of which, none of our Astrologers foretold, no no Comet portended' (p. 128).

There is a further example of Leigh drawing out a sexual meaning from Marvell's own text when a remark in *The Rehearsal Transpros'd* is interpreted as revealing Marvell's own sexual interests. Marvell had written that in Parker's scheme of things, Nonconformists

> must still be subjected to the *Wand* of a *Verger*, or to the wanton lash of every *Pedant*; that they must run the *Ganteloop*, or down with their breeches as oft as he wants the prospect of a more pleasing *Nudity*. (p. 36)

To run the ganteloop (now generally called 'run the gauntlet') is a military punishment which requires an offender to be stripped to the waist, or stripped naked, and run between two lines of soldiers who rain blows on him as he passes. It is not surprising that Leigh's attention was caught by these lines, for Marvell's sentence gathers in sexual content as it moves from the Nonconformists being subject to a verger's wand of office, to them being beaten by a schoolmaster, to the homoerotic sadism of the military punishment, and finally to the bare buttocks which provide 'the prospect of a more pleasing *Nudity*'. What starts as a purely symbolic subjection to the verger's wand of office has by the end of the sentence become a literal (and explicitly visualized) physical punishment. It is not clear why such male nudity would please Parker, whom Marvell has already accused of being too interested in elegantly dressed women. Perhaps Marvell simply meant that the prospect of Nonconformists being punished would please Parker more than any sexual pleasure could. In any case, to Leigh this flight of fancy seemed evidence of Marvell's personal predilections, and he remarked that '*Nol's Latin Clerks* were somewhat *Italianiz'd* in point of Art as well as Language' (p. 136). These overt suggestions of homosexual interests may invite us to hear an innuendo in Leigh's remark that the boy who waits on the customers in the coffee-house is Marvell's 'principal Camerade . . . and no less then our Authors Library-Keeper' (p. 35). Why should Marvell prefer the boy's company to that of other adults? What might be the duties of such a library-keeper?

Other pamphlets took their cue from these earlier attacks. *S'too him Bayes* (1673) also questions Marvell's interest in removing breeches: '*Britches* again: So often *fumbling* with them? What, ar't a *Taylor*? Marry pray – He ben't *worse*' (p. 42). The eunuch topos recurs too: an argument which is too sophisticated for Marvell to grasp will have to be *'Castrated* into *Conformity* with your understanding' (p. 126). Moreover,

> thou debauchest the very *Age* too, for thou bringest *Love* it self, which should be a Divine thing, and the noblest passion of an *Heroick* mind to meer – *Boar beckons Pig-hog wilt thou be mine?* (p. 126)

Marvell is accused of having reduced the noble passion of love to the physical union of two male pigs, one a boar, the other a castrated hog. This, says the writer, is no more love's sweet variety than boiled capon would be a varied diet (p. 125).

Edmund Hickeringill's *Gregory, Father Greybeard* (1673) deploys the familiar pun in referring to Marvell as a marvel, but now he is seen as a sinister kind of marvel, a *'monstrous* beast', 'desperately disingenuous and *unnatural*' and an 'Amphibious' creature (pp. 6–7; original italics). 'Amphibious' was applied not only to a creature which lived both on land and in water (*OED* 1 and 2), but also to something which occupied two positions or combined two classes (*OED* 3); and so, for example, to a creature of indeterminate gender, or one which combined both genders. The pamphlet refers to Marvell as 'it' rather than 'he', saying that 'the thing should be female by the *Billings-gate* Oratory of scolding' which Marvell employs (p. 37). Hickeringill also refers to the 'unmanlike ... and effeminate Practices' of the Nonconformists (p. 222), remarking that their 'soft and unmanly Rules of Government and Policy, may perhaps agree with your own effeminate temper' (p. 318).[6] On the one occasion when Marvell is imagined as having a mistress, this supposition is immediately translated into something grotesque: 'this Mopsus did open so well upon the hot scent against Bayes with whoop, Holla, Holla, whoop; ten times one after another; and with so full a mouth, that sure he has been us'd to't; and has some *Thestylis* to his Mistress, whose Nephew Amyntas is out of his wits' (p. 18). This implies madness, but it also cannot be accidental that Hickeringill chooses two pastoral names out of Virgil's *Eclogue* II, a poem which had become a classic text of homoerotic love.

Sober Reflections, or, a Solid Confutation of Mr. Andrew Marvel's Works, in a Letter Ab Ignoto ad Ignotum (1673), signals in its title that Marvell presents a problem of interpretation: it is addressed *'ad ignotum'* ('to the unknown one' or 'to the unknown thing'), and in the context of the strategies deployed in these pamphlets the phrase does not simply allude to the anonymity of *The Rehearsal Transpros'd*, but implies that its author is also unknown in the sense of eluding or transgressing one's conceptual categories. *Sober Reflections* also puns on 'marvel' (p. 1) and writes of his 'Amphibious valour' (p. 5). His ambiguous state is described through an adaptation of Falstaff's innuendo-laden conversation with Mistress Quickly in *1 Henry IV* (III, 3., 119–23):

What though you are neither Flesh nor Fish, nor good Red-herring, your Adversary is not us'd to Otter-hunting, never fear him Man, let him come if he dare: Oh happy if he come not, he shall soon be taught what it is to meddle with any of the Race of *Dametus* hereafter. (p. 5)

The otter is amphibious, feeding on land and in the water, and in some respects blurs the distinction between mammal and fish. (It is also, in seventeenth-century beast lore, a symbol of those who seek a life of retirement from the world, as well as a symbol of those who dislike their rulers, but obey them out of fear.) As for Marvell being one of 'the Race of *Dametus*', at one level this simply means one of the race of poets, since Dametas is the teacher of music who passes his pipes over to the shepherd Corydon; and yet because this is another allusion of *Eclogue* II, there is the further implication that Marvell is a second Corydon nursing a sexual longing for some Alexis. The double allusion neatly associates oppositional verse with unorthodox sexual interests.

Marvell is also imagined in the unedifying position of being

set Doctor-*Cathedraticus* in a Cucking-stool, Lording it over your Female-Auditory, the Water-*Nymphs* of Wapping, Magisterially maintaining your polemical Arguments and Debates. (p. 3)

His female audience greet him with this 'chearful *Antyphon*',

Welcome Cloris *to the Shore,*
Thou shalt go to Sea no more.

(p. 6)

But although Cloris/Marvell is surrounded by women and has his head well rubbed with their shifts, he is unable to oblige them sexually: 'what think you now of a comfortable importance? I am afraid in this critical minute you would be found *minus habens*, and when once a man pleads *non solvent*, it is high time to put up his Pipes and go to sleep' (p. 6) ('*Minus habens*' means 'having too little', and '*non solvent*' means 'they are unable to fulfil their obligations'.) Moreover, his arguments are equally impotent:

Marvel of *Marvels*, for that is the *Character* given you by a certain sort of Impertinent People who love mischief; Mischief your Minion Medium, which like a rich vein runs through the heart of all your Syllogismes, to the utter impoverishing of their Consequences; for, from a vicious medium (as unfledg'd a Logician as you are) you may Cock-sure, inferr, there must necessarily follow a vile consequence.
    But, how defective soever you are in your *Syllogismes*, you make ample satisfaction; nay, you supererrogate in your *Dilemma's*. (pp. 1–2)

179

This rather intricate insult draws parallels between styles of writing and forms of sexual behaviour, and starts from the assumption that Marvell's sexual impotence is reflected in his impotence as a writer and a logician, for he is defective in his syllogisms which do not arrive at any consequence – or, we might say, come to a climax. This is because he prefers another form of writing, mischief-making, which is his 'Minion Medium', 'minion' meaning 'servant' or 'favourite' but also 'catamite'. As a logician Marvell is unfledged, so a virgin (or perhaps a *'Capon-wit'*) though he is certainly 'Cock-sure' (sure of obtaining a cock?). He knows that from a vicious medium (use of mischief / use of catamites) there must follow vile consequences (subversion / sodomy). Though inadequate in syllogisms, Marvell excels in the field of dilemmas (the state of being caught between two paths, so an ambiguous or amphibious condition), and here he can indeed give ample satisfaction. The mischief-making of his writing is therefore the appropriate public medium for one who makes mischief with his minions in private. Moreover, if a vein of mischief runs through and destabilizes his logical arguments, then implicitly a vein of homoeroticism runs through and destabilizes his heterosexual writing. We have already noted two instances in *The Rehearsal Transpros'd* where Marvell unaccountably introduces suggestions of homosexual interests into his attack on Parker, troubling the coherence of his text. I shall be arguing later that a vein of homoeroticism runs through and complicates his ostensibly heterosexual poetry.

My final example of an attack on Marvell is a manuscript satire entitled 'A Love-Letter to the Author of the Rehearsall Transpros'd'[7] This also alleges that Marvell has been castrated, echoing Leigh's jibe about the turkey-cock and the capon-wit:

> You bristle, like a Turkey-cock,
> But have not half so fine a Dock,
> 'Tis as in vain to attempt to spread
> Your tail, as it would be to tread;
> You dare not walk among ye Hens,
> Lest they find out your impotence:

(p. 45)

Later in the poem a Nonconformist conventicle is discussing how to reward Marvell for his services to their cause, and how to relieve his want, since he has apparently been left destitute and 'naked, without one Ragg on him'. One brother says:

> But let us call to mind his Crosses,
> His person's, & his purs's Losses,
> For ye first, you may conceive what pain,

What anguish, he must needs sustein,
When he, so sadly, underwent
The Barber's cutting Instrument:

(p. 46)

This reference to the 'Barber' (i.e. the surgeon) is the most explicit
indication so far that the impotence which these pamphlets allude to is
the result of surgical castration. A 'malicious Sister' opposes the proposal
for a collection, and objects to giving

money, rings, & plate
To one, who could not propagate;
To one, of wonderfull abilities,
When ye Barber hangs up his Virilities
On an old musty Pack-thread, with
Dry'd Orang-peel, & rotten pith.
What's more apparent than his lewdness?
And since where's his reformed goodness?

(pp. 47–48)

The satire goes on to recommend that Marvell hang himself, since this is
what all decent men are expecting of him, and suggests that he could
pass this off as the act of a jilted lover thrown into despair by the
unkindness of this Nonconformist sister. If he followed this advice,
Marvell would be using the tropes of a familiar kind of heterosexual
narrative to cover a very different story – which may be what happens
in some of his poems. Linked with these references to his castration
are suggestions of effeminacy, for he is renamed 'Tom Thimble' the
prick-louse tailor, and the satirist helpfully suggests that if all else fails
he could sell his services to the Turk. The Turks' disposition to sodomy
was proverbial in this period.

How did Marvell respond to these attacks? After all the printed
rejoinders had appeared, he published *The Rehearsall Transpros'd: The
Second Part*, and the chastened tone of much of *The Second Part* suggests
that he had been unprepared for the personalized abuse which he had
received. Anxiety for his reputation seems actually to have preceded the
publication of the attacks, for he relates how he had contacted Parker to
warn him that 'any unjust and personal reflections' in Parker's reply
would result in severe retaliation on him and his friends (p. 171). But
while Parker assured him that 'my private reputation nor no mans else
should ever be injur'd in publick by his consent' (p. 171), others did the
job on Parker's behalf. Some of Marvell's reflections in *The Second Part* on
his own previous handling of Parker have an apologetic tone, suggesting
that he regretted his tactics now that he saw their consequences, and
was reconsidering the ethics of such rough discourse. He recognizes that

people's reputation can be damaged not only by lies but also 'by a truth too officious' (p. 161). In his own polemic he had mixed fact and fantasy, and 'as is in that stile usual, intermixed things apparently fabulous, with others probably true, and that partly out of my uncertainty of the Author' (p. 170). But although one might expect a controversialist to mount a vigorous defence of himself, or to reply in kind, Marvell does not take issue with the pamphleteers' fabulous accounts of his own sexuality. He reflects that it had taken the extraordinary provocation of Parker's treatise to 'tempt me from that modest retiredness to which I had all my life time hitherto been addicted' (p. 169), and the sombre tone of these pages bespeaks a man who has been badly hurt by having his private life caricatured before the public. But more than his reputation was at stake: since sodomy was a capital offence, Marvell was wise not to become embroiled in arguments about what was fact and what was fiction.

If we pause to assemble these allegations about Marvell, we find that he is not so much a marvel as a monster, an amphibian of indeterminate or double gender; he is a solitary figure whose mistresses are fictitious; he is impotent, perhaps surgically castrated, but in any case incapable of performing sexually with a woman; he is effeminate, womanly, and belongs with other women; he has sexual desire for other men, and is interested in male nudity; he engages in sodomy, particularly as the partner who is penetrated. There are several ways in which we might attempt to make sense of this farrago: as a description of a particular individual; as a reading of his texts; as the fashioning of a sexual stereotype; and as a trope within the discourse of Restoration politics. Let us first consider the political dynamic which is motivating these caricatures.

It is by no means uncommon to find sexual allegations used in political controversy – contemporary satires on Charles II are an obvious example – but the question at issue here is why the abuse directed at Marvell should take this particular form. One explanation is the association between different kinds of nonconformity, religious, political and sexual, and one might seek parallels in the allegations of free love which were made about the Ranters in the 1650s, though a more precise parallel would be with the treatment of Titus Oates, who was frequently accused of sodomy in the early 1680s, once the political tide had turned against him and he could be seen as a grotesque danger to the body politic rather than the saviour of the nation. Explicitly in the pamphlets against Oates, and implicitly in the pamphlets against Marvell, sodomy is a sign of religious and political nonconformity. We should also ponder the political significance of the emphasis on sexual ambiguity, on Marvell as an amphibian. The pamphleteers seem uneasy about his political and cultural allegiance. There were good reasons for regarding him as amphibious politically: a respectable Restoration MP, but also a sometime republican; a sharp political and theological writer, but within the same text also a purveyor of personalized abuse and almost frenzied comedy; a denizen of coffee-house society, but more as an observer than a participant, the eunuch who can watch but not act. But who could know that the role of impotent observer was not just assumed for some ulterior motive, as would happen with Horner in Wycherley's *The Country Wife* (written 1672–4; performed and printed 1675)? In a society which was paranoid about spies and plots, any ambiguity, inscrutability or secrecy could be dangerous. Marvell himself told Aubrey that 'he would not play the good-fellow in any man's company in whose hands he would not trust his life'. 'He had not a generall acquaintance' comments Aubrey, and adds that he preferred to drink alone in his room.[8] Evidently he was a difficult man to know.

One can also see why readers might have doubts about whether the attitudes expressed in *The Rehearsal Transpros'd* were those in which Marvell actually believed. He was known to have served Cromwell's government and to have written in his praise, and yet in *The Rehearsal Transpros'd* he deplored Parliament's resort to arms (p. 135) and in *The Second Part* wrote that when taking office under Cromwell he had chosen an employment which seemed to him at the time to be doing the least harm to the interests of the exiled King (p. 203). An otter indeed. Moreover, Marvell was known to be a current friend and erstwhile political colleague of Milton, and yet in *The Second Part* Marvell represented Milton not as a man of principle but as one who had been passively 'toss'd' on to the wrong side by war and fortune, and whose errors were now being 'expiated' by his silence and retirement (p. 312). It is unlikely that Milton would have appreciated this account of his life. Marvell's readers might well wonder whether these rewritings of history were masking a very different story.

Another way of understanding this anxiety about Marvell's ambiguity might relate it not to political paranoia but to an increasing awareness of male homosexuality, with a consequent unsettling of commonplace assumptions about other men's probable sexual behaviour. The last years of the seventeenth century saw the emergence of the molly houses and cruising grounds in London, sites of a self-defining homosexual culture which had its own language and rituals. Within the visible cultural geography of London there were new secret places for specialized associations, and a repertoire of signs which could be read only by initiates. Outsiders might well be anxious about how to locate this culture within a culture, and how to interpret its signs. Secrecy might now betoken sodomy; a man's inscrutability or marginality in the masculine milieux of the coffee-houses and alehouses might suggest a secret sexual life. This development is generally dated roughly to the 1690s or 1700s, but some evidence from Restoration poetry and drama suggests that a recognition of an alternative male sexuality as a present social reality rather than just as a mythological or poetic fiction was already spreading in the 1670s. Some confusion about what homosexual interests entailed can be seen in the very multiplicity and incoherence of the allegations.[9] The Marvell who is being produced by these pamphlets is a figure of incoherence and excess. This is itself significant, for he is principally being thought of as the opposite of a certain kind of masculinity and male sexual behaviour which is implicitly assumed to constitute a norm: this 'norm' is supposedly single, recognizable and unproblematic, the man who has intercourse with women. The opposite to this is multiple and difficult to read, with multiplicity itself used as a sign of confusion, a sexual confusion which both threatens and symbolizes a moral and ideological confusion in society. The satirical allegations are grotesque and excessive, but excess was an element in the definition (or the aetiology) of sodomy, for it was conceptualized by theologians and moralists as the acme of wickedness, the ultimate transgression which exceeded all boundaries. As in Spenserian allegory, truth is single, error multiform. The multiple images which are generated as a series of opposites to this assumed masculine norm are not necessarily mutually compatibile, either as elements of a logically coherent conceptual category or as constituents of a plausible individual subjectivity.

So what, if any, are the implications of all this material for biographers and for readers of Marvell's poetry? We need hardly consider as a biographical possibility the suggestion that Milton sodomized Marvell in the office of the Latin Secretary, because their 'conjunction' is obviously presented as a sign of their political alliance, and the representation of Milton as a stallion reminds readers that he had been an advocate of divorce, and thus supposedly of freer sex. In Milton's case sodomy is being used simply as a marker of moral turpitude and political deviance, without any implication about his personal sexual preferences. But the caricatures of Milton the stallion and Marvell the gelding are not performing quite the same functions. In Marvell's case the story has an obvious polemical purpose in making him the junior partner politically, and so attempting to diminish his status as a spokesman for a version of 'the Good Old Cause' in the 1670s. But unlike the depiction of Milton, the presentation of Marvell is part of a series of such persistent allegations that biographers should not brush aside this material as casually as they have done. Common though it is to find politically-motivated allegations about the sexual conduct of public figures in the Restoration, the allegations are rarely totally without foundation, even though they may be grotesquely elaborated. Moreover, it is rare to find allegations of homosexual interests being made against individuals (rather than groups such as Italians or Jesuits), and I know of no case in this period where such allegations are wholly without some biographical grounds: examples would be the charges of sodomy against James I, the first Duke of Buckingham, Titus Oates, and William III, all politically inspired, but none without foundation (in so far as it is possible to know such matters at such a distance). It seems to be the case in this period that an individual's homosexual behaviour is only brought into public discourse when there is some political or social advantage in view, but this does not mean that such charges are invented out of thin air. We cannot treat these caricatures as hard evidence of Marvell's sexual behaviour or medical history, but they are certainly evidence of how some contemporaries read his behaviour, his speech, his writing, and his silences. However tendentiously, the pamphleteers were skilled and well-informed readers of his work. Their interpretations of his prose suggest that his poetry (most of which was still unpublished in the 1670s) might also bear reconsideration, and in particular that the poetic ambiguity so prized by modernist critics might be re-read in the light of these contemporary perceptions of Marvell's sexual ambiguity.

The theoretical and practical difficulties of such a reading are considerable, since the author is not readily accessible to us either biographically or textually: little is known about Marvell's sexuality beyond these caricatures by his opponents, and the personae of the poems are never uncomplicatedly autobiographical. What one can do, however, is to trace certain recurring motifs in the verse, to scrutinize its ambiguities, to examine the disturbances created by homoerotic subtexts within apparently heterosexual or homosocial narratives, and so to chart the kinds of textual spaces which Marvell created for and through his exploration of a complex – and strongly homoerotic – sexuality.

But perhaps there is one autobiographical text to be considered. In the 1681 *Miscellaneous Poems* we find this:

> *Upon an Eunuch; a Poet*
> Fragment
> *Nec sterilem te crede; licet, mulieribus exul,*
> *Falcem virginiae nequeas immitere messi,*
> *Et nostro peccare modo. Tibi Fama perennè*
> *Praegnabit; rapiesque novem de monte Sorores;*
> *Et pariet modulos* Echo *repetita Nepotes.*

> ['Don't believe yourself sterile, although, an exile from women,
> You cannot thrust a sickle at the virgin harvest,
> And sin in our fashion. Fame will be continually pregnant by you,
> And you will snatch the nine sisters from the mountain;
> Echo too, often struck, will bring forth musical offspring.'][10]

Pierre Legouis noted the connection between these verses and the allegations made by the pamphleteers, but dismissed any element of self-reflection on Marvell's part, saying that 'such aspersions were flung about in seventeenth-century controversies too readily to deserve any credit; and Marvell, if he had suffered that disability, would probably have abstained from adding one more specimen to the epigrams on that well-worn theme.'[11] But it is not common for such aspersions to be so specific, or to be repeated by so many writers. Moreover, Marvell did not print the poem, and it could have been a purely private reflection left among his papers at his death. We cannot at this distance either substantiate or refute the idea that the epigram was addressed by Marvell to himself. But in any case this poem adds an important element to the topic of the eunuch, for this eunuch-poet is promised offspring by means of Echo, an allusion to the story from Ovid's *Metamorphoses* which thus implicitly casts the poet in the role of Narcissus. And this, I suggest, is actually a principal myth – perhaps the principal myth – through which sexuality is imagined in Marvell's poetry.

II

Readers of Marvell's poetry have remarked upon his recurrent use of figures of reflection, enclosure and self-resemblance. Repeatedly Marvell imagines something seeing or seeking its own reflection, being like itself, being satisfied only with its own reflection. In part this is a philosophical issue, and Marvell seems fascinated by the epistemological problem of how we identify something, how we recognize similarity and difference, and how a recognition of the other may serve to produce self-knowledge in the observer. But this process of self-observation, self-knowledge and, ultimately, self-pursuit, also has sexual implications: such a turn of mind is potentially narcissistic.

The story of Narcissus, which Marvell would have found most readily in Book III of the *Metamorphoses*, includes the image of the boy gazing at his own reflection in the water while Echo is helplessly reduced to articulating her unrequited love through repetitions of another's voice. Narcissus stands for self-love, for autoeroticism, for one so enraptured with himself that desire travels in a circle, and is reflected back on its origin. Narcissus also, therefore, exemplifies a form of homoerotic love, since the male gaze is enraptured by a male image, heedless of the charms of the female represented by Echo. To say this is not to imply that homoerotic desire *per se* is necessarily autoerotic or misogynistic, nor to endorse Freud's delineation of a narcissistic character to homosexuality, rather it is to point out how strongly (and with what a finely Freudian condensation) the story of Narcissus and Echo brings together for

Marvell a group of profoundly resonant topics: the homoerotic gaze, self-absorption, the natural setting as the mediator of desire, and the disempowered voice. There were other interpretations of Narcissus which Marvell might well have pondered. In Neo-Platonic writers (including Plotinus and Ficino) his story was taken as an allegory of man failing to distinguish material from spiritual beauty, mistaking the transitory world for the true world and so condemning the soul to confinement in the body. Others, notably Francis Bacon in *De Sapientia Veterum*, saw Narcissus as an emblem of irresponsible retirement from public life. George Sandys in his notes to his translation of the *Metamorphoses* followed Bacon's line, writing that Narcissus signifies those 'who likely sequester themselves from publique converse and civill affaires, as subiect to neglects and disgraces, which might too much trouble and deiect them'.[12] It was a multivalent myth. So in composing 'A Dialogue between the Soul and Body', or the lines which contemplate the soul's flight in 'The Garden', Marvell is revisiting the Narcissus myth, as he is when writing of the forward youth at the beginning of *An Horatian Ode*, or Fairfax in *Upon Appleton House*, or his own solitary pleasures in 'The Garden'.

The only explicit reference to Narcissus in Marvell's poetry occurs in *Upon Appleton House* where the river snakes through the meadows:

> See in what wanton harmless folds
> It ev'ry where the Meadow holds;
> And its yet muddy back doth lick,
> Till as a *Chrystal Mirrour* slick;
> Where all things gaze themselves, and doubt
> If they be in it or without.
> And for his shade which therein shines,
> *Narcissus* like, the *Sun* too pines.
>
> (ll. 633–40)

Sexual allusions had coloured the previous stanza, for the couplet 'No *Serpent* new nor *Crocodile* / Remains behind our little *Nile*' (ll. 629–30) recalls the serpent in the Garden of Eden, and Cleopatra, that 'serpent of old Nile' (*Antony and Cleopatra* I, 5.25). By contrast with these reminders of a dangerous heterosexual world, the 'wanton . . . folds' with which the river embraces the meadows are entirely 'harmless'. The muddy riverbank becomes a shining mirror in which the sun (explicitly male here) sees his own reflection ('shade' means 'reflected image' as the Oxford editors note) and pines for it. This is overtly a moment of homoerotic and autoerotic rapture.

However, the figures of reflexivity and self-regard in Marvell's poetry do not always have a homoerotic element, even though they never quite escape from having some form of sexual implication. In the lines 'On a

Drop of Dew' the water 'round in its self encloses' (l. 6), and tries to shun the impurity which would result from its contact with the world. Towards the end of *Upon Appleton House* Mary Fairfax is said to have given the gardens and meadows their beauty, and in return the brook becomes a mirror 'Where *She* may all *her* Beautyes look' (l. 702). This image of gazing at one's own beauty in the water is a version of the Narcissus story, though its sexual element is immediately translated from autoeroticism to a Diana-like modesty when 'the Wood about *her* draws a Skreen' (l. 704). Here again, as in 'On a Drop of Dew', self-enclosure is thought of as virginal. In 'Mourning', Chlora 'courts her self in am'rous Rain; / Her self both *Danae* and the Showr' (ll. 19–20), so in this instance the self-courting narcissist is a female who turns androgynous, simultaneously both Danae and Zeus. When composing 'Mourning', Marvell had been attracted to a poem in Cowley's collection 'The Mistress' for the conceit that the woman's tears are like babies; Cowley's version of the idea had included a further twist to the comparison:

> As *stars* reflect on *waters*, so I spy
> In every drop (methinks) her *Eye*.
> The *Baby*, which lives there, and alwayes plays
> In that illustrious *sphaere*,
> Like a *Narcissus* does appear,
> Whilst in his *flood* the lovely *Boy* did gaze.[13]

Marvell has altered the tenor of this conceit, but was it the Narcissus reference in the original which caught his attention, and prompted his idea of the woman's self-courtship?

A possible version of the Narcissus motif occurs in 'The Definition of Love', where

> My Love is of a birth as rare
> As 'tis for object strange and high:
> It was begotten by despair
> Upon Impossibility.

(ll. 1–4)

The loves are 'so truly *Paralel*' that they can never meet. The lovers in this poem are not given any gender, though one might suppose that a precise parallel would require two lovers of the same gender, or, even more precisely, a lover and his own parallel reflection in the water which he can never meet without destroying. Although critics have routinely assumed that the poem describes love for a woman, perhaps one of an impossibly elevated social position, nowhere in this poem does Marvell suggest that the object of this impossible love is female, and it makes very good sense as a definition of the impossible love of one man for another, or of one man for himself. Like 'Mourning', this poem too has a curious relationship to one of its sources, which is another poem from 'The Mistress'. This one is called 'Impossibilities', and suggested some of Marvell's imagery:

> As *stars* (not powerful else) when they *conjoin*,
>   Change, as they please, the Worlds estate;
> So thy *Heart* in *Conjunction* with mine,
>   Shall our own fortunes regulate;
> And to our *Stars themselves* prescribe a *Fate*.[14]

Whereas Marvell's lovers are for ever held apart, Cowley's lovers make their own destiny, and refuse to tolerate impossibilities. But this is not the most striking contrast with Marvell's poem. Cowley explicitly makes his beloved female: she is a 'gentle maid' and is compared to Hero. Marvell, in adapting some of Cowley's conceits, has erased all trace of their heterosexual context.

In the 'Dialogue between the Resolved Soul and Created Pleasure' the Soul is presented with various sensuous temptations. When Pleasure has to select one temptation which epitomizes the seductiveness of sight, it is this:

> Every thing does seem to vie
> Which should first attract thine Eye:
> But since none deserves that grace,
> In this Crystal view *thy* face.

(ll. 31–34)

Marvell can imagine no visual pleasure more seductive than that of gazing upon one's own reflection.

The Narcissus motif may be only occasionally or potentially homoerotic, but there are several texts in which a gaze of erotic appraisal is directed at another man. The most striking and extended example is the passage on Archibald Douglas in the *Last Instructions*, reworked later for *The Loyal Scot*. Here is the opening of this passage:

> . . . brave *Douglas*; on whose lovely chin
> The early Down but newly did begin;
> And modest Beauty yet his Sex did Veil,
> While envious Virgins hope he is a Male.
> His yellow Locks curl back themselves to seek,
> Nor other Courtship knew but to his Cheek.
> Oft has he in chill *Eske* or *Seine*, by night,
> Harden'd and cool'd his Limbs, so soft, so white,
> Among the Reeds, to be espy'd by him,
> The *Nymphs* would rustle; he would forward swim.

(*Last Instructions* ll. 649–58)

Politically, the function of this episode in the *Last Instructions* is primarily to foster admiration for the heroism of the young man, and a sense of the tragic waste of potential caused by the government's incompetent management of the Dutch War. One would expect the writer of a political satire to interest himself in Douglas's youthful heroism, but instead the poem relishes his youthful sexuality, making the young man's body an object of erotic interest rather than of heroic admiration. In one respect this does have a political purpose, in that it produces an icon of pure and self-contained masculinity which contrasts with the seedy and rapacious heterosexual behaviour of the court which the poem has been presenting as a sign of the régime's political and moral degeneracy. But Marvell's image of Douglas is eroticized beyond what would be necessary for this contrast to be established. Douglas's chin is 'lovely', and is only just showing signs of a beard; this hint of a still-ambiguous gender is continued in the allusion to the modest virgins' hope (rather than certainty) that he is a male. The descriptions of his hair and cheek contribute nothing to any martial image, but present a doubly narcissistic movement as the 'yellow locks' seek themselves, and also court his own cheek. Except in order to facilitate a conceit around the tragic contrast of fire and water, there is no political reason to include the account of Douglas swimming in rivers; nor, within that digression, is there any political reason to add the detail that his soft, white limbs are hardened and cooled by his swimming. The poetry is clearly offering him to the reader as an object of erotic pleasure, as happens in the description of Leander in Marlowe's poem (*Hero and Leander* II, 153–226). Douglas swimming in the river is observed by nymphs who wish in turn to be observed by him, but he swims away from them: the poem thus inserts voyeurs into this scene, introducing observers who can act as surrogates for us, while at the same time reassuring us (the implicitly male readers) that these nymphs are not our rivals, since Douglas shuns their gaze. Characteristically Marvellian interests inform this passage: the narcissistic motif; the delight in an immature body (Douglas is twice called 'boy': ll. 659, 693); the apprehensive concern for one on the verge of sexual maturity who is liable to be hurt by the flames of passion. Moreover, Douglas is made an amphibian, first through his androgynous appearance and uncertain gender, and secondly as a creature of both land and water, prior to becoming a creature of both water and fire.

The account of Douglas's death continues this eroticism. Once again he is observed, though this time by another man. Monck's gaze is the homosocial gaze of soldier on soldier ('*Monk* looks on to see how *Douglas* dies'; l. 676), though because the poem has so strongly eroticized the way the nymphs and the reader look at Douglas it is difficult to find this new act of looking to be wholly free from a homoerotic purpose, particularly since the death which Monck observes is described as a sexual encounter:

Like a glad Lover, the fierce Flames he meets,
And tries his first embraces in their Sheets.
His shape exact, which the bright flames infold,
Like the Sun's Statue stands of burnish'd Gold.
Round the transparent Fire about him glows,
As the clear Amber on the Bee does close:
And, as on Angels Heads their Glories shine,
His burning Locks adorn his Face Divine.
But, when in his immortal Mind he felt
His alt'ring Form, and soder'd Limbs to melt;
Down on the Deck he laid himself, and dy'd,
With his dear Sword reposing by his Side.
And, on the flaming Plank, so rests his Head,
As one that's warm'd himself and gone to bed.

(ll. 677–90)

Douglas is imagined as a lover, but there is no partner provided for him, male or female: the first line implies that he encounters the flames as if they were his partner, but that idea disappears as the next line makes the flames into sheets. Marvell avoids envisaging a lover for Douglas, keeping the beautiful boy single, and concentrates instead on imagining how the beauty of Douglas's body is transfigured as he loses his virginity in a consummation which is enacted with himself alone. His shape is 'exact' (i.e. 'perfect'; *OED* 1), and he becomes like a statue of the sun; his hair as it burns is like an angel's halo around his divine face. Besides this emphasis on his beauty (rather than, say, his courage), there are several details which invite us to read Douglas with homoerotic pleasure. The allusion to the statue of the sun is implicitly to the sun-god Apollo, icon of male beauty but also lover of the boys Hyacinthus and Cyparissus; at the end of the passage (l. 695) there is a comparison with Hercules, icon of male strength but also lover of the boy Hylas. And we cannot help noticing that the description concludes with the image of Douglas in bed 'with his dear Sword reposing by his side', this quintessentially phallic symbol sharing his bed like a lover.

Marvell concludes the account of Douglas with this promise of immortality:

Fortunate Boy! if either Pencil's Fame,
Or if my Verse can propagate thy Name.

(ll. 693–94)

This is an echo of the lines in *Aeneid* IX. 446–47, where Virgil assures Nisus and Euryalus of eternal fame at the end of the episode in which he has recounted their heroic death. But it is a curious echo. Nisus and Euryalus were passionate friends, and the episode was used by

Restoration writers to exemplify devoted friendship or to mourn the loss
of a much-loved friend. For Marvell to work this echo into his text goes
beyond the deployment of a classical promise of immortality, and signals
an emotional commitment to Douglas – at least as a type of the beautiful
youth if not as an individual. It may be poignantly typical of Marvell
that the story which in other writers is used to celebrate or lament a
reciprocated love is used here to lament a lost, unattainable ideal of male
beauty and singleness.

This is not the only occasion on which Marvell introduces an erotic
element into an elegy for a soldier. The much earlier poem 'An Elegy
upon the death of my Lord *Francis Villiers*' has extended praise of the
nineteen-year-old's beauty:

> Never was any humane plant that grew
> More faire than this and acceptably new.
> 'Tis truth that beauty doth most men dispraise:
> Prudence and valour their esteeme do raise.
> But he that hath already these in store,
> Can not be poorer sure for having more.
> And his unimitable handsomenesse
> Made him indeed be more then man, not lesse.

> (ll. 39–46)

As in the case of the lines on Douglas, this discussion of Villiers's beauty
seems superfluous to the occasion: indeed, the poet has to excuse this
beauty as a trait which makes him more than manly (i.e. godlike) rather
than less (i.e. womanly). Marvell's approach contrasts interestingly with
that in another anonymous elegy on Villiers. The author of 'Obsequies
On the untimely Death, of the never to bee too much praised and pitied
Francis Lord Villiers'[15] reads Villiers's face as a sign of his valour:

> Th' indented Face
> (Though no great Volume) was the *Common-Place*,
> And *Index* of Thy Valour: everie scar
> Seeming at least som mistick *Character*;

And when he does refer to Villiers's beauty, it is to make it signal the
tragedy of a youth cut down before his time in the loyal service of his
King:

> But why do I revolv the short-writ-storie
> Of fading Youth; or recollect the Glorie
> Of thy blest Beautie (which though once the Throne
> Oth' Lillie and Rose) was blasted before blown?
> Prepo'strous Fate! t' anticipate and bring
> On Winter e're Thou did'st enjoie Thy Spring!

By contrast, Marvell's fascination with Villiers's beauty has a characteristic train of thought:

> Lovely and admirable as he was,
> Yet was his Sword or Armour all his Glasse.
> Nor in his Mistris eyes that joy he tooke,
> As in an Enemies himselfe to looke.

(ll. 51–54)

One might have expected the poem to say that Villiers took no interest in his own beauty and concentrated on martial prowess, but instead it elaborates the idea of self-observation. Villiers looks at himself not in an ordinary mirror but in the polished surface of his sword or armour – implicitly, therefore, in objects which are signs of masculinity and tokens of an all-male world. There is a narcissistic, self-enclosing movement about the gaze which is directed at himself, and which finds other masculine objects – even the eyes of an enemy soldier – to reflect it back, rather than the eyes of his mistress. Marvell's conceit labours to preserve the all-male circuit of vision.

Moreover, when describing Villiers's death, Marvell allows an erotic sensibility to colour his lines:

> Such fell young *Villiers* in the chearfull heat
> Of youth: his locks intangled all with sweat
> And those eyes which the Sentinell did keep
> Of love closed up in an eternal sleep.
> While *Venus* of *Adonis* thinks no more
> Slaine by the harsh tuske of the Savage Boare.
> Hither she runns and hath him hurried farre
> Out of the noise and blood, and killing warre:
> Where in her Gardens of Sweet myrtle laid
> Shee kisses him in the immortall shade.

(ll. 105–14)

The poem dwells upon Villiers's hair entangled with sweat, and his eyes, the guardians of love. The interest in masculine sweat anticipates the poet's emphasis on the mowers' 'wholesome heat' which 'Smells like an *Alexanders sweat*' in *Upon Appleton House* (l. 428). The dead body is read as a lover's rather than a soldier's body, and is mourned as Venus had mourned Adonis. The introduction of the story of Venus and Adonis eroticizes the poem's gaze at Villiers even more strongly, for it not only makes him an icon of male beauty, it makes him an unattainable object of sexual desire. Shakespeare's handling of the story had emphasized the attractiveness of the male body, and through his shaping of the narrative had allowed a male reader to gaze with longing on this form, and align himself with Venus and her desire rather than with Adonis and his chastity. The Venus and Adonis story is not an overtly homoerotic tale, but it does permit the male body to be appreciated as the object of another man's sexual longing.

There are also some briefer instances of a homoerotic sensibility in Marvell's poetry. In 'Young Love' the 'infant' addressed by the poet is ungendered, but in stanza 4 the objects which Love (here explicitly made masculine) is said to prize include 'the lusty Bull or Ram', two obvious emblems of masculine sexuality: this implies that the 'snowy Lamb/ Or the wanton Kid' with which the child is compared are also male, but even without that assumption the stanza clearly imagines a male god of Love delighting in symbols of male sexuality. Stanzas 7–8 also imply that the addressee is male, since the poet crowns the child with his love in order to ward off Fate just as kingdoms crown their king when he is still a child in order to avoid dissension. If Marvell had wanted us to see the child as a girl, he could easily have made the comparison refer to a queen. Critical commentary on this poem has assumed that the child is female, but there is no evidence for this, and the logic of Marvell's similes clearly points the other way. At the very least critics need to consider why Marvell was so carefully unspecific about the child's gender. Similarly, it is worth remarking that 'Beauty, aiming at the heart' in *Upon Appleton House* (l. 604) is carefully ungendered, for Marvell refers to 'its useless Dart' whereas one might have expected '*her* useless Dart'. Why such diplomatic evasion, unless 'its' conceals a wish to write 'his' instead, or at least signals a preference for androgynous beauty over the unambiguously female form?

Different kinds of ambiguity beset those notoriously enigmatic and contentious poems 'The Unfortunate Lover' and 'The Nymph Complaining for the Death of Her Fawn'. First, 'The Unfortunate Lover', while it may indeed be a political allegory, is also at one level explicitly a poem about a male lover; more specifically, it is about '*my* poor lover' (l. 11; italics added), not, for example, 'this poor lover'. (Indeed, one might expect '*our* poor lover' if this were a poem about the young Prince Charles addressed to other royalist sympathizers.) The lover is 'naked' (l. 49), and although 'naked' can simply mean 'unarmed' it primarily means 'nude'. The opening stanza laments the loss of that state of innocence in which 'Infant Love' still plays, or plays with one, in a green shade, and thus echoes other poems which contemplate innocence threatened by sexual maturity. The connection between this vision and the remainder of the poem is obscure, but this evocation of a lost pre-sexual innocence was evidently a necessary prelude to the depiction of the passionate and ill-fated lover. The poem's stress on the impossibility of the unfortunate lover's plight might be thought to recall 'The Definition of Love' and its (possibly homosexual) concerns. Finally, the lover is an 'amphibium of life and death' (l. 40), and we have already seen how important the idea of the amphibium is, not only in the pamphlet attacks on Marvell, but also in his own sexual imagination. I would not dispute that 'The Unfortunate Lover' probably carries a political significance, but I would suggest that critics have been too reluctant to ponder the sexuality of the poem before proceeding to allegorize it. And yet, even its political hinterland is not without sexual ambiguity, for it has been suggested that Marvell may be drawing upon an epigram in which the young Prince James is described as 'armata Venus', an armed Venus. Perhaps the blurring of gender in this description of the lad might have been one feature which caught Marvell's attention?

As for 'The Nymph Complaining', it is possible that Marvell adopts the female persona as a way of exploring the experience of being seduced and jilted by a male lover. I do not mean to imply that the poem is therefore a coded autobiographical statement, rather that Marvell's interest in imagining how the sexual awakening of a youngster may be brought about by an adult male, and his obsession with the dangers of innocence confronted by mature male sexuality, need more discussion than critics have been willing to accord. The speaker delights in the androgynous beauty of the fawn, which is described throughout by the ungendering pronoun 'it'. This is also one of a number of poems which, while they ostensibly describe heterosexual passion, include details which suggest a homoerotic subtext. In this case there is a possible allusion to the story of Cyparissus in Book X of the *Metamorphoses* (ll. 106–42), whose beloved stag is accidentally killed. This is one of the stories which Ovid associates with Orpheus's turn to love for boys after his final loss of Eurydice. Apart from the thematic parallel, two details suggest that this fable contributed to Marvell's poem. The nymph's fawn has a 'silver Chain and Bell' (l. 28), and Cyparissus's stag has a silver boss (*bulla argentea*) on its forehead (l. 114), which is translated by Sandys as a 'silver bell' (p. 340). Secondly, the curious allusion in line 99 to the 'brotherless *Heliades*' could have been suggested to Marvell by Ovid's reference to the Heliades in the passage preceding the story of Cyparissus (l. 91).

Finally in this collection of poems with homoerotic subtexts, there is 'The Garden'. Lovers who carve their mistresses' names in the bark of trees are rebuked because the trees are more beautiful than any woman could be; moreover, Eden was only truly paradisal before the creation of Eve:

Two Paradises 'twere in one
To live in Paradise alone.

(ll. 63–4)

This pose of suave misogyny and masculine self-sufficiency does not necessarily imply any positive homoerotic interests, but there are some lines whose sexual implications seem to have been overlooked:

> *Apollo* hunted *Daphne* so,
> Only that She might Laurel grow.
> And *Pan* did after *Syrinx* speed,
> Not as a Nymph, but for a Reed.

(ll. 29–32)

These lines are usually taken to be a version of the earlier conceit about carving women's names on trees: the gods did not pursue Daphne or Syrinx because they wanted them as women, but because they wanted them as plants. But what these women actually turn into are symbols of masculinity: the laurel of Apollo and the phallic reed of Pan. This is not to deny that the overt purpose of the lines is the witty praise of trees and plants, but we ought to register that Marvell's choice of examples and phrasing has metamorphosed the gods' objects of desire from feminine into masculine.

In the lyrics discussed so far, occasional homoerotic motifs have complicated the poems' apparent presentation of heterosexual desire. But in the case of 'Damon the Mower' there is so much material which Marvell has taken from a classic poem of homosexual love that we need to reconsider the ostensible subject matter of his poem. The editors of the Oxford edition of Marvell have noted that 'Damon the Mower' has echoes of Virgil's *Eclogue* II, but without exploring the implications of this. *Eclogue* II is the poem in which Corydon expresses his unrequited love for Alexis, and it had become a *locus classicus* of homosexual love in the Renaissance. It is also a poem which was thought in antiquity to have an autobiographical element, so Marvell could have found his own homosexual desires reflected in Virgil's, and written his poem as a conscious reflection on Virgil's text. 'Damon the Mower' relates how Damon is overcome by his love for Juliana. The weather is unbearably hot, as in *Eclogue* II. 8–9, 12–13; he proposes to bring various rustic gifts to his loved one, as in *Eclogue* II. 36–51; he boasts of his rural wealth, as in *Eclogue* II. 20–22; he denies that he is ugly, as in *Eclogue* II. 25–27. All these parallels are noted in the Oxford edition. One might add a further parallel between Marvell's green frog and grasshoppers (ll. 13–14) and Virgil's green lizards and cicada (*virides lacertos* (l. 9) and *cicadis* (l. 13)). But what needs to be stressed is that to provide himself with suitable material for this poem about the devastating power of sexual desire, Marvell turned to one of the few great poems of homosexual passion, instead of one of the myriad poems of heterosexual passion. Nor is this the only homosexual aspect of 'Damon the Mower'. The 'gelid Fountain'

(l. 28) is a literal translation (only transposed into the singular) of Virgil's *gellidi fontes*, a phrase which occurs in *Eclogue* X. 42. In that poem Virgil is writing about his beloved Gallus, and Gallus's unrequited love for the girl Lychoris, and so a structural parallel suggests itself between Virgil/Gallus/Lychoris and Marvell/Damon/Juliana.

Besides these intertextual references there are also other homoerotic touches. 'The Sun himself licks off my Sweat', says Damon (l. 46), and the personification, together with the explicit reminder in 'himself' that the sun is traditionally male, makes this an obviously homoerotic gesture. Later Damon uses his scythe as a mirror (l. 58). This is a narcissistic moment in which Damon gazes at his own reflection, but it also has a strongly homoerotic overtone since the scythe was a phallic symbol. There is an echo here of the poem on Villiers. When in line 80 Damon is mown by his own scythe, the accident could be seen as the consequence of an autoerotic or homoerotic passion. But what of Juliana, who ostensibly inspired Damon's desire? Empson, who thinks that Marvell fell in love with the mower at Appleton House, comments:

> Damon keeps saying he is in despair for love of a woman, and this allows love to be talked about, but he would not have accepted the situation so passively. It is the poet who is in love with Damon; Freud calls the device 'displacement', when interpreting dreams.[16]

Without necessarily accepting the biographical speculation, I would agree with Empson that some form of displacement is at work here. Juliana may be no more than a name suggested by Herrick's Julia, or by the month of July (which was named after the homosexual Julius Caesar), and thus an elegant way of permitting Marvell to write about the 'unusual Heats' (l. 9) of homosexual desire.

But, rather surprisingly, the poem in which Marvell's imagination turned aside most insistently to seek help from homoerotic pre-texts was 'To his Coy Mistress'. The pre-text which lies behind this poem is, once again, the passage from the *Metamorphoses* recounting the story of Narcissus and Echo. It has been suggested by Robert H. Ray[17] that certain phrases in Marvell's poem were influenced by Sandys's translation of this episode. I would like to propose another source, in Arthur Golding's translation. Several striking verbal echoes, stronger than those from Sandys, suggest that Marvell had been reading this version of the story attentively when composing 'To his Coy Mistress'. First, in Golding's translation we find the phrases 'morning dew' and 'lively hue' in close proximity (ll. 614, 617).[18] This may be of particular interest to textual editors, in that these phrases lend support to the emendations derived from Bodleian MS Eng. Poet. d. 49:

> Now therefore, while the youthful hew
> Sits on thy skin like morning dew . . .

(ll. 33–34)

Other words which might have caught Marvell's attention in Golding's
passage include 'marble' (l. 523; cp. 'marble Vault' in l. 26); 'gazing'
(l. 524; cp. 'gaze' in l. 14); 'embrace' as a rhyme word (l. 523; cp.
'embrace' as an emphatic rhyme word in l. 32); the rhyme of 'rest' and
'brest' (ll. 548–9; cp. the same rhyme in ll. 15–16); and the rhyme of
'sound' and 'found' (ll. 637–8; cp. the same rhyme in ll. 25–26). The
fate of the coy mistress, reduced to a body in a vault, could have been
suggested by the fate of Echo, whose 'body pines to skin and bone'
(l. 494). Cumulatively these verbal echoes point to Golding's translation
as a source for this poem.

But as a classically trained poet, Marvell would hardly have been
content with translations, and the Latin text, together with the
commentary found in Renaissance editions, also lodged in his memory.[19]
Details which might have contributed to Marvell's poem include Ovid's
marmore ('marble'; l. 419); *amor crescit* ('love grows'; l. 395; cp. 'Love
should grow' in l. 11); and *non tamen invenio* ('however I do not find';
l. 447; which, aided by the repetition of *inveniunt* in l. 510, may have
suggested the unusual verb in 'Thy Beauty shall no more be found' in
l. 25). The lines quoted above about the mistress's 'youthful hew' being
like 'morning dew' may have taken a hint from Ovid's account of the
delicate glow on Narcissus's bare chest as he pines with love just as hoar
frost melts away (ll. 481–9). Some phrases from the editorial commentaries
may have played their part too: *scelestam* ('criminal'; l. 463n; cp. 'crime'
in l. 2); *quandocunque igitur* ('whenever therefore'; l. 503n; cp. 'Now
therefore' in l. 33); *currum* ('chariot'; l. 504n; cp. 'Charriot' in l. 22); *vastae
. . . tenebrae* and *aeternam . . . noctem* ('vast darknesses' and 'eternal night';
both together in l. 503n; cp. 'vast Eternity' in l. 24). Finally, perhaps
Marvell's attention was also caught by two bizarre coincidences: Ovid on
three occasions uses the Latin for 'marvel' (*miratur . . . mirabilis . . . mirantia*;
ll. 424, 503); and the notes three times refer to Terence's play called the
Eunuch (ll. 395n, 447n, 463n).

Some of these parallels are stronger than others, and some may be
thought insignificant coincidences, but there are sufficient traces of the
Narcissus story in Marvell's text to suggest that when he composed this
poem about desire for a woman, Marvell's imagination was dwelling
on other forms of desire. Moreover, there is a homosocial pre-text for
this poem which has been identified by Nigel Smith.[20] Here is Marvell's
concluding invitation to the mistress:

> Let us roll all our Strength, and all
> Our sweetness, up into one Ball:

And tear our Pleasures with rough strife,
Thorough the Iron gates of Life.
Thus, though we cannot make our Sun
Stand still, yet we will make him run.

(ll. 41–46)

And here are lines from John Hall's poem, 'To his Tutor, Master Pawson. An Ode':

Come, let us run
And give the world a girdle with the sun;
 For so we shall
Take a full view of this enamelled ball . . .

 O let us tear
 A passage through
That fleeting vault above;

(ll. 13–16, 50–52)[21]

It is remarkable that the very lines in which Marvell is imagining vigorous intercourse with a woman should carry echoes of a poem – addressed by one man to another – which evokes ecstatic intellectual and social pleasure between men. There are different ways in which we might read this intertextual connexion. At one level it illustrates the degree to which the language of love and friendship overlaps in this period, making it possible for a man to write to a male friend in passionate language without sexual suggestiveness. It also reminds us how Marvell's contemporaries were often ravished with excitement as they contemplated the expansion of their knowledge of the natural world. But at the level of the workings of Marvell's imagination, if we are tracing his characteristic habits of thought and the kinds of connexions which he repeatedly made between texts, it unsettles the ostensibly confident, bravura conclusion to this poem of heterosexual seduction. Why, at the very climax of his poem to the coy mistress, did Marvell's imagination turn aside to the well-known, secure, excitements of the all-male world?

There are further echoes from other texts which raise questions about the process of composition. The Oxford editors note a precedent for this poem in verses by Thomas Randolph called 'A Complaint against Cupid that he never made him in love!'. Is it significant that a poem with this title came into his mind when composing 'To his Coy Mistress'? Cowley's poem 'My Diet' also contributed hints, as did some anonymous lines discovered by Arthur Marotti.[22] Perhaps Marvell had also been studying his Herrick. If he had turned to Herrick's poem 'To the Virgins, to make much of Time', he might have noted some useful ideas: the *carpe diem* motif, the allusion to virginity, the idea of time flying, the rhyme of 'sun' and 'run', the word 'coy', and the phrase 'while we may'.[23] Leafing on through his copy of Herrick, Marvell might have noted the comparison of Julia's nipples with rubies ('Upon the Nipples of *Julia's* Breast'), and decided that although he was not capable of writing convincingly about a woman's nipples, he could find a use for rubies (in 'To his Coy Mistress', l. 6). Perhaps even Herrick's innuendo 'the rest' in the same poem suggested Marvell's identical euphemism and rhyme. The suspicion that Marvell turned for help to a clutch of heterosexual love poems because his imagination was more deeply engaged elsewhere can only be speculation, but if we compare Donne's excited blazon of the woman in 'To his Mistress Going to Bed', or Herrick's sensual delight in Julia's nipples, with Marvell's attempt to blazon the attractions of the coy mistress, there does seem to be in Marvell's poem a lack of passionate and focused sensuality.

It might be appropriate to think of this as essentially a homosocial poem, an exercise which Marvell wrote to impress a male audience, possibly in an attempt to demonstrate his heterosexual credentials. It relies heavily on other poems; it is set out as a logical argument whose structure would appeal to an educated audience; and its style invites declamation in front of a company. J.B. Leishman called attention to the poem's 'essentially dramatic tone . . . the way it makes us feel that we are overhearing one of the speakers in a dialogue',[24] but what we overhear is surely not one lover speaking to another, but a wit performing in front of an audience who are connoisseurs of such poetry. The poem is aimed at a male readership, in spite of being formally addressed to this (nameless) woman, since it hardly has the tone and rhetoric appropriate to courtship. There is evidence that 'To his Coy Mistress' was known in court circles around 1672, for that is when it was copied by Sir William Haward into the manuscript anthology which is now Bodleian MS Don.b.8, where it keeps company with poems by Rochester and Dryden. The year 1672 is exactly the time at which Marvell's heterosexual masculinity was being questioned in the satirical pamphlets. Moreover, in Haward's manuscript it has been given a more blatantly raunchy tone:

> Two hundred to adore your eyes,
> But thirty thousand to your Thighes.[25]

And in the manuscript line 'Your beauty will stand need of salt' we hear the coarse tone of the coffee-house wits. Whoever was responsible for the readings in this manuscript text, it seems that 'To his Coy Mistress' was being made more salacious in order to suit the fashionable masculine taste of the 1670s.

I would like to return to the implications of the intertextual relationship between this poem and the story of Echo and Narcissus, the story which one might even call Marvell's private myth. Here Marvell is

casting himself as Echo in pursuit of Narcissus, the poet in pursuit of
the unresponsive and unattainable boy. One implication of this is that
Marvell could only write about courting a woman if he imagined himself
courting a boy. Another is that Marvell thought of his own song as
'echoing', not simply in the sense that it reverberates in the vault, but
because, like Echo's cries, it can only imitate the fragments of other men's
speech. Marvell's song, and this poem in particular, echoes intertextually,
and the pre-texts which it echoes are frequently homoerotic.

III

In this essay I have described how Marvell's opponents called him
effeminate, impotent and a sodomite, and how his own poetry
repeatedly figures unrequited homoerotic desire and the self-sufficient,
even self-loving, observer. Perhaps the pamphlets reflect in a grotesquely
distorting mirror that sensibility which was given finer form in the
poems; and whereas the satires on Marvell present a threateningly
paradoxical and illegible amphibian, his own poetry is teaching us
how to live ambiguities, and is thinking through the strangenesses of
self-understanding.

For a poet with homosexual inclinations there were in this period
few possible ways of writing a poetry which voiced his own desires.
Renaissance verse had permitted an eroticism to colour versions of the
classics and the modern poetries of friendship, of relationships between
master and pupil, patron and poet, or soldier and soldier. There were
more explicit precedents, but highly problematic ones. Richard Barnfield's
homoerotic pastorals had created an exotic imaginary space in which a
beautiful boy could be courted with extravagant gifts, such as a golden
tennis racket or a fan of phoenix feathers: the natural world was turned
into the material of courtship, and courtship itself figured consummation
– figured rather than prefigured, for there was no prospect of narrative
development and closure (consummation in a homosexual narrative
being almost impossibly dangerous to represent), and instead only the
repeated present of looking and longing. Shakespeare's *Sonnets* had
charted the narrative of an obsession in which the very selfhood of the
poet was cast into doubt, so overpowering was his need to see himself
only through his relationship to that erring boy. Like Shakespeare,
Marvell may have found that his sexuality (or at least the sexuality and
emotional sensibilities which he wished to explore poetically) prevented
him from locating himself easily in traditional narratives of desire, and
set him at a tangent to contemporary idioms. He is typically an observer.
He writes a poetry not of relationship but of self-relationship. His verse
is enamoured of masculine prowess – admired in Villiers, in Douglas, in

the heroic nude unfortunate lover, in the Mower with his scythe, even Cromwell with his erect sword – but is also fascinated particularly by liminal states: innocence caught at play just before the fires of sexual desire begin to make themselves felt; mature manhood dying when still virginal; the male whose beauty invites us to read him as a female; the forward youth just before he decides whether the time has come to leave his books; the amphibian poised between two worlds. Marvell's characters are still unravished, whether by Time or anyone else.

The spaces which Marvell's poetry creates are singularities, places of solitude and self-reflection. And yet his textual spaces echo with other men's voices. Virgil's second *Eclogue* and Ovid's tale of Narcissus insinuate themselves into those poems where Marvell says that he is writing about heterosexual love. So how do we read such texts? Not as homoerotic poems deliberately dressed up and passed off as something else; nor as if they were a patient's dreams where repressed desires break through and leave disruptive traces. Rather, as poems which acknowledge that homoerotic desire cannot at this period inhabit a coherent textual space – even one as contrived as Barnfield's or as dislocated as Shakespeare's. Because his poems have teasing gaps, ambiguities of gender, and suggestive traces of classic homosexual texts, their textual fabric allows the reader to enter this imagined world and adjust it. Marvell wrote that the mind is

> that ocean where each kind
> Does streight its own resemblance find;

('The Garden', ll. 43–44)

and the same might be said of Marvell's poetry in which readers may find their own resemblance. Critics who have seen the poems as uniformly heterosexual have simplified them to suit their own interests. I would suggest that we attend more closely to the poems' complexities which invite us to imagine a more complex sexuality, and in particular that we recognize their fashioning of textual spaces in which homosexual desire can find its own resemblance, albeit only intermittently.

What 'kind' was Marvell? His enemies might laugh at him as an amphibian, but it is precisely its amphibious quality which gives his poetry its exceptional power. The poems seem to exist in some liminal state themselves, always on the edge of turning into something else, the tone elusive, the text teasingly suggesting subtexts and remaking pre-texts, fashioning worlds which we almost recognize but whose intensity we cannot quite account for, and whose boundaries and conjunctions we cannot quite trace. And crucial to this was Marvell's sexuality, for whatever may, or may not, have happened in his own private life, he took English poetry into new territory by finding a language for the ambiguities of sexuality – including homoerotic desire, but including also the desire to be rid of desire and its complexities and to retreat to the green shade of impossible innocence. That amphibious understanding was the real marvel.

Notes

1. WILLIAM EMPSON's essays 'Natural Magic and Populism in Marvell's Poetry' and 'The Marriage of Marvell' both appear in his *Using Biography* (London, 1984).

2. 'Homosexual' is, of course, an anachronistic term, since it entered the language only in the late nineteenth century, and carried with it psychological, medical and moral connotations which are quite different from those which obtained in the late seventeenth century. There is, however, no simple seventeenth-century vocabulary which could be used instead, and one of the aims of this essay is to illustrate the conceptual complexity of this subject in Marvell's period. While it would be a serious distortion to use 'homosexual' as a noun in this context, I see no alternative to 'homosexual' and 'homoerotic' as adjectives, if cumbersome periphrases are to be avoided. The distinction between those two words is not exact, but I would tend to use 'homoerotic' to describe feelings of sexual desire for, or erotic pleasure in the contemplation of, other men (and hence to describe texts which articulate or invite such feelings); and to reserve 'homosexual' for physical sexual contact between men. The two terms would thus distinguish between longing and looking on the one hand, and possessing and acting on the other. However, this is not offered as a definitive distinction, merely as a convenience for the present discussion. 'Sodomy' was a Restoration word, but its signification was at once too limited (to one particular act) and too vague (as a marker of moral and social deviance) to be usable in modern critical prose.

3. *Bishop Parker's History of his own Time*, translated by Thomas Newlin (London, 1727), pp. 332, 348.

4. JOHN GERARDE, *The Herball or Generall Historie of Plantes . . .* very much enlarged and amended by Thomas Johnson (London, 1633), p. 1293.

5. The French may be translated thus: 'A terrible accident and a sinister occurrence, to see a Capuchin Father bestride a Minister'.

6. In this period the word 'effeminate' slides between meaning 'too fond of the company of women and so neglecting masculine responsibilities' (applied, for example, to Charles II preferring his mistresses to state business) and 'too womanly in manner and interests (including sexual interests) to be a real man'.

7. Royal Society MS 32 (the commonplace book of George Ent), reproduced by kind permission of the President and Council of the Royal Society.

8. *Aubrey's Brief Lives*, ed. Oliver Lawson Dick (Harmondsworth, 1972), p. 356.

9. One might cite here the aptly named character Sir Jolly Jumble in Otway's play *The Soldier's Fortune* (1681), who takes a strong sexual interest in men. See PAUL HAMMOND, *Love between Men* (Basingstoke, 1996), pp. 101–2.

10. The translation of this epigram is quoted from ANDREW MARVELL, *The Complete Poems*, ed. Elizabeth Story Donno (Harmondsworth, 1972), p. 137.

11. MARVELL, *Poems and Letters*, I, 274. There is also a reference to a eunuch in 'The Mower against Gardens', ll. 27–30.

12. G.S., *Ovid's Metamorphosis Englished, Mythologiz'd, and Represented in Figures* (Oxford, 1632), p. 106.
13. ABRAHAM COWLEY, *Poems*, ed. A.R. Waller (Cambridge, 1905), p. 136.
14. COWLEY, *Poems*, p. 130.
15. In *Vaticinium Votivum: or, Palaemon's Prophetick Prayer* ('Anno Caroli Martyris Primo' [i.e. 1649]), pp. 63–67; quotations are from pp. 65–66.
16. EMPSON, p. 15.
17. ROBERT H. RAY, 'Marvell's "To his Coy Mistress" and Sandys's Translation of Ovid's *Metamorphoses*', *Review of English Studies*, 44 (1993), pp. 386–88.
18. *Shakespeare's Ovid, Being Arthur Golding's Translation of the Metamorphoses*, ed. W.H.D. Rouse (London, 1904), pp. 72–75.
19. Quotations from Ovid and his commentators are taken from the edition by Cnipping *Pub. Ovidii Nasonis Operum Tom. 2. Metamorphoseon Libri XV. Cum notis selectis. Varior: studio B. Cnippingii* (Leiden, 1670).
20. This will be included in the annotation to Nigel Smith's forthcoming Longman Annotated English Poets edition of Marvell.
21. *Minor Poets of the Caroline Period*, ed. George Saintsbury, 3 vols (Oxford, 1905–21), II, pp. 208–09.
22. For the anonymous lines see Arthur F. Marotti, *Manuscript, Print, and the English Renaissance Lyric* (Ithaca, NY, 1995) p. 81.
23. Herrick is quoted from *The Poems of Robert Herrick*, ed. L.C. Martin (Oxford, 1956).
24. J.B. Leishman, *The Art of Marvell's Poetry*, 2nd edn (London, 1968), p. 70.
25. See HILTON KELLIHER, *Andrew Marvell: Poet and Politician* (London, 1978), p. 53.

Notes on Authors

Francis Barker is Professor of English at the University of Essex. His most recent book is *The Culture of Violence: Essays on Tragedy and History* (1993).

Warren L. Chernaik retired as Professor of English at Queen Mary College and Director of the University of London Centre for English Studies in 1997. His most recent book is *Sexual Freedom in Restoration Literature* (1995).

Jonathan Crewe is Professor of English at Dartmouth College. Among his recent books are *Hidden Designs: The Critical Profession and Renaissance Literature* (1986) and *Trials of Authorship: Anterior Forms and Poetic Reconstruction from Wyatt to Shakespeare* (1990).

Jonathan Goldberg is Sir William Osler Professor of English Literature at The Johns Hopkins University. Among his books are *Endlesse Worke: Spenser and the Structures of Discourse* (1981); *James I and the Politics of Literature: Jonson, Shakespeare, Donne, and their Contemporaries* (1986); and *Sodometries: Renaissance Texts, Modern Sexualities* (1992).

Paul Hammond is Professor of English at the University of Leeds. His recent publications include the first two volumes of a major new edition of Dryden and *Love between Men in English Literature* (1996).

Leah S. Marcus is Blumberg Centennial Professor in English at the University of Texas, Austin. Her recent books include *Puzzling Shakespeare: Local Reading and its Discontents* (1988) and *Unediting the Renaissance: Shakespeare, Marlowe, Milton* (1996).

David Norbrook is Fellow of Magdalen College, Oxford. He is the author of *Poetry and Politics in the English Renaissance* (1984) and co-editor, with Henry Woudhuysen, of *The Penguin Book of Renaissance Verse* (1992).

ANNABEL PATTERSON is Professor of English at the University of Yale. Her many books include: *Censorship and Interpretation* (1984); *Pastoral and Ideology* (1988); *Shakespeare and the Popular Voice* (1989); *Reading between the Lines* (1993); *Reading Holinshed's Chronicles* (1994) and *Early Modern Liberalism* (1997).

BLAIR WORDEN is Professor of History at the University of Sussex. His most recent book is *The Sound of Virtue: Philip Sidney's* Arcadia *and Elizabethan Politics* (1996).

STEVEN N. ZWICKER is Professor of English at Washington University, St Louis. He is the author of two books on Dryden and the co-editor, with Kevin Sharpe, of *The Politics of Discourse: The Literature and History of Seventeenth-Century England* (1987). His most recent book is *Lines of Authority: Politics and English Literary Culture* (1993).

Further Reading

Editions

The standard edition of Marvell's poetry is *The Poems and Letters of Andrew Marvell*, 3rd edn, ed. H.M. Margoliouth, revised Pierre Legouis with the collaboration of E.E. Duncan-Jones, 2 vols (Oxford: Clarendon Press, 1971). There is a helpful commentary.

Good student editions include:

Complete Poems, edited Elizabeth Story Donno (Harmondsworth: Penguin Books, 1972).
Andrew Marvell, ed. Frank Kermode and Keith Walker (Oxford: Oxford University Press, 1990). The text is based on the Margoliouth edition. Some prose is also included.

General critical studies which contain useful criticism on Marvell:

THOMAS N. CORNS, *Uncloistered Virtue: English Political Literature 1640–1660* (Oxford: Clarendon Press, 1992). Has a chapter which surveys Marvell's Civil War Poetry.
THOMAS HEALY and JONATHAN SAWDAY (eds), *Literature and the English Civil War* (Cambridge: Cambridge University Press, 1990). There is a good essay on *Upon Appleton House* by Thomas Healy.
NIGEL SMITH, *Literature and Revolution in England* (New Haven and London: Yale University Press, 1994). The best general account of literature in the period 1640–1660, and Marvell's relation to it.
JAMES TURNER, *The Politics of Landscape: Rural Scenery and Society in English Poetry 1630–1660* (Cambridge, Mass.: Harvard University Press, 1979). A learned and exciting study which constantly illuminates Marvell's employment of landscape.
MICHAEL WILDING, *Dragons Teeth: Literature in the English Revolution* (Oxford: Clarendon Press, 1987). Has forceful Marxist-influenced accounts of *An Horatian Ode* and *Upon Appleton House*.

STEVEN N. ZWICKER, *Lines of Authority: Politics and English Literary Culture, 1649–1689* (Ithaca and London: Cornell University Press, 1993). Acute readings of a number of the major poems.

Critical Studies of Marvell

LYNDY ABRAHAM, *Marvell and Alchemy* (Aldershot, Hampshire: Scolar Press, 1990). Persuaded this very sceptical reader that there is much of value in this topic.

JOHN CAREY (ed.), *Andrew Marvell*, Penguin Critical Anthologies (Harmondsworth: Penguin Books, 1969). Useful survey of earlier critical views with good introduction.

ROSALIE L. COLIE, *'My Echoing Song': Marvell's Poetry of Criticism* (Princeton and London: Princeton University Press, 1970). Erudite and demanding but repays the effort.

CONAL CONDREN and A.D. COUSINS (eds), *The Political Identity of Andrew Marvell* (Aldershot, Hampshire: Scolar Press, 1990). This has excellent accounts of Marvell's letters by N.H. Keeble and the 1681 edition of the *Poems* by Annabel Patterson.

DONALD FRIEDMAN, *Marvell's Pastoral Art* (London: Routledge & Kegan Paul, 1970). A sensitive and well-written consideration of pastoralism in Marvell.

C.A. PATRIDES (ed.), *Approaches to Marvell: The York Tercentenary Lectures* (London, Henley and Boston: Routledge & Kegan Paul, 1979). Although much of the criticism uses rather dated formulations, a number of the essays remain valuable.

ANNABEL PATTERSON, *Andrew Marvell*, Writers and their Work (Plymouth: Northcote House, 1994). Patterson's most recent book on Marvell gives prominence to the prose and Restoration politics.

MARGARITA STOCKER, *Apocalyptic Marvell: the Second Coming in Seventeenth Century Poetry* (Brighton: Harvester, 1986). Makes a powerful case for millenarian aspects to Marvell's poetry.

ELIZABETH STORY DONNO, *Andrew Marvell: The Critical Heritage* (London, Henley and Boston: Routledge & Kegan Paul, 1978). Excellent survey of responses to Marvell from his death until T.S. Eliot.

CLAUDE J. SUMMERS and TED-LARRY PEBWORTH (eds), *'On the Celebrated and Neglected Poems of Andrew Marvell'* (Columbia, Missouri and London: University of Missouri Press, 1992). See particularly Douglas Chambers's fine essay on Marvell and the gothic.

Index